W9-AEK-211

# EFFECTIVE
# VIRTUAL
# CONVERSATIONS

## Engaging Digital Dialogue for Better
## Learning, Relationships, and Results

# JENNIFER J. BRITTON

Potentials Realized
Media

EFFECTIVE VIRTUAL CONVERSATIONS
Copyright ©2017 Jennifer J. Britton
All rights reserved.

Published by:
Potentials Realized Media
PO Box 93305
Newmarket, Ontario
L3X 1A3
Canada

No part of this book may be reproduced in any manner whatsoever without written permission, except in the case of brief quotations embodied in critical articles and reviews. Requests to the Publisher for permission should be addressed to Permissions Department, Potentials Realized, PO Box 93305 Newmarket, Ontario, Canada L3X 1A3.

Limit of Liability/Disclaimer of Warranty: While the publisher and author have used their best efforts in preparing this book, they make no representations or warranties with respect to the accuracy or completeness of the contents of this book and specifically disclaim any implied warranties of merchantability or fitness for a particular purpose. No warranty may be created or extended by sales representatives or written sales materials. The advice and strategies contained herein may not be suitable for your situation. You should consult with a professional where appropriate. Neither the publisher nor author shall be liable for any loss of profit or any other commercial damages, including but not limited to special, incidental, consequential, or other damages.

Cover design and Interior layout: Yvonne Parks, www.PearCreative.ca
Copyeditor: Lisa Canfield, www.copycoachlisa.com
Proofreader: Clarisa Marcee, www.avenuecmedia.com
Index: Elena Gwynne, www.quillandinkindexing.com

Publisher's Cataloging-In-Publication Data
(Prepared by The Donohue Group, Inc.)

Names: Britton, Jennifer J.
Title: Effective virtual conversations : engaging digital dialogue for better learning, relationships and
    results / Jennifer J. Britton.
Description: Ontario, Canada : Potentials Realized Media, [2017] | Includes bibliographical
    references and index.
Identifiers: ISBN 978-0-9937915-0-5 (paperback) | ISBN 978-0-9937915-1-2 (Kindle) | ISBN 978-
    0-9937915-2-9 (ePub)
Subjects: LCSH: Business communication. | Digital communications. | Interpersonal communication.
    | Teleconferencing. | Virtual work teams.
Classification: LCC HD30.37 .B75 2017 (print) | LCC HD30.37 (ebook) | DDC 651.7--dc23

Quantity discounts are available on bulk purchases of this book. Special books or book excerpts can also be created to fit specific needs. For information, please contact Potentials Realized, PO Box 93305 Newmarket, Ontario, Canada L3X 1A3 or email info@potentialsrealized.com.

# DEDICATION

This book is dedicated to leaders and team members aiming to have a more engaging virtual experience. Also dedicated to Matthew and his generation, who no doubt will further iterate our current virtual practices.

# TABLE OF CONTENTS

# FOREWORD

This book is about how to **have more Effective Virtual Conversations.** Its message is timely in today's era of rapid digitization. The only constant in this world seems to be constant change. Clients demand that more should be done with less, faster, and with higher quality. We are all looking for approaches in how to meet these challenges successfully.

Jennifer's book will boost your virtual outcomes as a leader, coach, or professional. You will learn how to make your virtual conversations more effective, easy, and professional. It offers a wide range of practical approaches and know-how for preparing, leading, and following up on a range of virtual events – from meetings, to hosting webinars, facilitating, consulting, and coaching.

The book is written with the practitioner in mind. It transforms **theory** to **practice** so that you can achieve excellent **results** in the virtual field.

Globally, there is a push for new ways of working. From blended meetings where virtual attendees participate with those in the room, to hybridizing approaches to support complex challenges, the demand for virtual ways of working is on the rise.

In order to take advantage of this push, it is, as always, best to apply a pull strategy. In other words, to learn how to create meaningful virtual events from the client's point of view. I am absolutely convinced that more professionals should learn how to do this effectively, proficiently, and productively.

If you want to avoid the biggest pitfalls when you lead virtual meetings, facilitate webinars as well as lead virtual team development, then you should read this book.

This book covers the essentials for *how* to create enhanced *outcomes* in your virtual events, and **what** to do to lead more engaging virtual conversations. It gives you a blueprint for many different virtual approaches and techniques to support you in creating more value and impact in your work. In that respect, Jennifer's book "*walks its talk*." I have also benefited from the contents of the book and Jennifer's training in virtual facilitation and coaching myself. I have recently used this roadmap successfully in my work with top management and leaders in Sweden, Serbia, and other countries. As a result, we have seen:

- More inspired, engaged team members from the virtual component of work which I undertook with Statistics Serbia.
- Deepened relationships across stakeholders including top management and leaders.
- The addition of virtual program components, pre- and post-project, helped to facilitate the transfer of skills and capacity development within their organization in a way that was faster and stickier than if I had only done in-person work. The virtual component expedited and boosted the transition of skills.
- The combination of evidence-based approaches in consulting, coaching, facilitation and change management, along with the virtual approach, was a prerequisite for these outcomes.

You will find a treasure trove of practical, actionable tips in this book. Whether you are looking for tips on how to host exceptional virtual meetings via conference call, or create a new cohort of virtual leaders, you will be sure to take away some new ideas. Benefit from the many decades of Jennifer's experience as a global virtual leader, and the thousands of hours of her hands-on experience as a masterful virtual facilitator.

Enjoy the journey!

MARTIN LAGERSTROM
Executive Coach, Consultant and Advisor, **Statistics Sweden**

# ACKNOWLEDGMENTS

It is said that it takes a village to raise a child. It also takes a community to birth a book. *Effective Virtual Conversations* has been borne out of many decades of dialogue, work, and discussion. I look at my evolution as a virtual conversationalist—from my days of virtual team leadership across the Caribbean and the Americas throughout the 1990s, to the tens of thousands of hours I have spent on the phone and in virtual rooms with learning groups, to coaching teams and groups virtually around the world since 2004.

I would also like to thank the national/global training and coaching teams I have worked with over the last decade-plus supporting their development of virtual facilitation skills and confidence in leading in the virtual space. A special thank you to the thousands of coaches, trainers and facilitators I have been able to work with since 2006 in my ICF approved CCE programs – Advanced Group and Team Coaching, and Group Coaching Essentials. In recent years, many of you have also joined me live for our Facilitation Skills Training or the Virtual Facilitation Skills Intensive.

I have many people to thank for assistance throughout the creative process of this book:

To Janica Smith, thank you for your talented eye and focus on detail, as well as your ability to keep things moving along, making the shift to controlling the creative process as an author a smooth one.

To Lisa Canfield, thank you for your for grit and polish as an editor.

To Denise Wakeman, thank you for your ongoing support and mentorship around visibility on the web.

To Yvonne Parks of PearCreative.ca, for your phenomenal design eye and the beautiful cover and layout.

I've also met a number of wonderful illustrators and designers virtually throughout the years and want to acknowledge their creative works which originally graced my Teams365 blog at PotentialsRealized.com. Since 2014 I have enjoyed the daily practice of blogging on team and leadership issues at the Teams365 blog. What started as a one year experiment has now stretched into its third year. For many more tips and ideas around virtual and remote team leadership, as well as coaching, I hope that you will check it out. There you'll find these illustration—Ricky Castello's Death by Conference call cartoon, SoyaSouya's Jo cartoons, Deviant Art's Jane cartoons, and B Dev Prakash's Teamwork cartoon.

As I've done with my other books, *Effective Group Coaching* (Wiley, 2009) and *From One to Many: Best Practices for Team and Group Coaching* (Jossey-Bass, 2013), I want to make supplementary materials available for book purchasers. You'll find many resources throughout a couple of sites including *EffectiveVirtualConversations.com* and *PotentialsRealized. com*. Use code 2424 to access PDF copies of the different templates and resources at *EffectiveVirtualConversations.com*.

As always, if you have any questions, or spot any typos needing a change, please reach out to me with comments and questions at info@ potentialsrealized.com. You'll find my other contact details under the Author page. Enjoy the book!

# CHAPTER 1

# THE CONTEXT OF VIRTUAL CONVERSATIONS TODAY

*"Learning and innovation go hand in hand. The arrogance of success is to think that what you did yesterday will be sufficient for tomorrow."* [1]

*– William Pollard*

We live in an increasingly virtual and digital world. Two decades ago, work was largely constrained to one geographic location. It was also mostly relegated to one space—the face-to-face context. I remember the day the Internet arrived while I was working in South America. In the early days, an email from my office in Georgetown, Guyana would first sit on servers in Port of Spain, Trinidad before being "sent out" overnight to Toronto. This seemed fast compared to the multi-week pace of traditional mail, or the luxury of a fax slowly making its way out of the machine.

Flash forward 20 years. Today I may start my day in dialogue with someone from Hong Kong at 6:00 a.m. my time/6:00 p.m. theirs, moving westward through Europe's afternoon and then on to an 8:00 a.m. call with someone in New York. It is customary for me to host five or six small group calls a day with participants from six or seven countries and just as many time zones. We can connect from the office, from the park, by phone or via a mobile device. Conversations are no longer just voice based, they are also video and text based.

Technology has made the world a smaller place, yet some organizational contexts are still facilitating conversations, learning, and team development events using old methodology. It leads to new challenges such as "Death by Conference Call," where employees find themselves dialing from one call to another, often being "talked at" rather than conversed with. Many see this as an opportunity to multitask, placing one meeting on mute, while catching up on the to-dos assigned from another, as overwhelmed employees juggle a load of competing priorities that all need to be done immediately, in workplaces which may not have a physical core.

As I wrote recently at the Teams365 Blog, a daily blog supporting team members and team leaders in the area of exceptional team work, "As more and more professionals start to operate in the virtual domain it is important to develop not only *skills* but also *confidence* in building connection with remote staff, facilitating meetings, and transitioning most activities to the virtual realm."[2] This change is happening quickly.

From meetings to learning events to a simple "How's it going?" virtual conversations happen all the time.

In January 2015, WhatsApp surpassed the number of texts a day[3]—30 billion texts from 750 million users. It was estimated that the average North American sends five times more texts in comparison to the number of phone conversations they have a day. Our communication modes are changing rapidly, but are they as effective? What impact are they having on learning, relationships, and results?

Conversations in both the professional and virtual realms take place across a myriad of channels—phone, text, webinar—as well as through on-demand and asynchronous channels. This book is geared to get to the essentials of what makes an effective and engaging virtual conversation. We are going to explore the best practices for design and facilitation, as well as what makes a virtual conversation great. Many teams today are virtual, never physically meeting each other. Several chapters are dedicated to more effective virtual team work.

Written with the virtual practitioner in mind, this book is designed for the person responsible for designing or leading the virtual event. You may be a **team leader, project manager, coach** or **trainer**. I hope that you will find the book **practical, grounded in experience,** and **immediately applicable**. You may not read it from cover to cover in one sitting, because it is designed to be chock full of different things you may use in different contexts—from team meetings to webinars, from virtual team development to conference calls. As such, you may find yourself earmarking some sections and flipping around. I hope that the book will provide you with many examples and tools you can use. These represent the diversity that this work embodies. I also hope that it will serve as a reference that you can use time and time again.

Given the diverse contexts in which virtual conversations take place, you are encouraged to approach this book through the lens of what makes sense for you, your learners/participants, and the context in which you lead. There are many differences in the types of virtual conversations we have based on the technology platforms used—from phone-based conference calls to video streaming via Skype, from interactive video streaming plus screen sharing with Zoom to corporate favorites like WebEx, GoToMeeting, GoToWebinar, and Adobe Connect. Each platform has its advantages, and drawbacks.

The book focuses on *principles* for creating engaging virtual conversations so that it will remain evergreen and relevant, even if the technologies and platforms change down the road—which they likely will!

Throughout the book, we'll be looking at virtual conversations through two main lenses—*leadership* and *learning*—two areas that are changing rapidly. On the leadership level, today many of us lead in complex, global environments, with diversity being the norm. On the learning front, we have moved very quickly from keeping learning events formal and in the classroom, to a world where Udemy and Teachable are creating bite-sized, on-demand learning experiences. In the new world of learning where micro-learning abounds, 15-minute video-based modules are created by experts and anyone with a message to share with the world. We'll look at what it takes to make a range of different conversational environments more effective—from virtual team meetings, to learning events, to coaching and mentoring sessions undertaken by phone.

## WHAT DO WE MEAN BY **EFFECTIVE** OR **ENGAGING**?

The words effective and engaging are commonplace in the working world today, sometimes to the point of overuse. You are likely to be very familiar with terms such as employee engagement, which research continues to point out is currently tremendously low across the globe. Gallup has found that in most workplaces today across North America, employee engagement numbers haven't changed much since 2000, with only approximately one-third being engaged in today's workplace.[4]

So what do we mean by engaging virtual conversations? Engaging means **impactful, interesting, interactive, important,** and **meaningful**. Engaging conversations invite us to be present and participate in dialogue, shaping with others the conversations we have. As we will see throughout the book, there is a range of engagement levels for different types of virtual conversations. Chapter 4 explores the range from formal virtual education to interactive virtual conversations co-created in the group and team coaching space. We will explore a variety of different ways to engage team members and learners in the virtual space.

Effective means **relevant, practical, implementable**, and **valuable**— qualities which are often missing from virtual conversations. Competing demands, multitasking, sensory overload (or deprivation) and the frenetic pace of business combine to create a scenario we refer to as **Death by Conference Call,** illustrated here in the Teams365 cartoon by Ricky Costello. It is not uncommon for leaders to be on a series of these calls all day long, leaving each one scratching their head wondering what was discussed. *What did we accomplish?* Some organizations today are calling for meeting-free days with mixed results.

Effectiveness in business requires both a focus on **results** and **relationships**. One without the other is not enough. Throughout the book, I will be sharing different tools to make your virtual conversations more focused and effective.

## WHY VIRTUAL LEARNING SPACES ARE IMPORTANT— THE CONTEXT TODAY

**DEATH**
BY
**CONFERENCE CALL**

In September 2015, it was reported that 45% of US-based employees worked from home.[5]

The workforce is distributed, remote and virtual in many organizations. In March 2016, *Forbes* reported that the majority of employees in 125 companies now work remotely or virtually given the growth of cloud technology, up from 25 companies in 2014.[6] Two-thirds of employers note increased productivity in their telecommuters.[7]

A 2015 poll by Gallup found that 37% of employees had telecommuted, much higher than the 9% who did in 1995.[8]

34% of CEOs believe that more than half of their workforce will be working remotely by 2020.[9]

Many teams ranging from startups to project teams to established businesses are now virtual. A 2014 Ferrazzi Greenlight study found that 79% of those surveyed worked frequently or always as part of at least one distributed or virtual team.[10] IBM recently switched back to a preference for co-located teams working physically together. Today's global talent pool warrants virtual teaming.

## ON THE LEARNING FRONT

The Research Institute of America indicates that e-learning has the power to increase information retention rates by up to 60% by reducing cognitive overload.[11]

In 2011, $35.6 billion dollars was spent on self-paced eLearning around the globe. By 2014 it was a $56.2 billion industry, set to double by 2016. While there have been declines in self-paced e-learning, blended learning approaches that incorporate live and digital e-learning have become increasingly popular.[12]

Globally, it is estimated that $39 billion is spent on meetings every year. In July 2012, it was estimated by CNBC that every adult in the US spent 388 minutes, or almost 6.5 hours, each month on social media.[13]

With so much time spent in meetings, in teamwork, and in conversation in the virtual space, isn't it important to take time to make our virtual conversations more effective and engaging? Here's where this book comes in—as a conversation starter and as a reference and go-to primer.

To many, the virtual world can be seen as a time-sucker—but it has become an important channel for communication. The world has become a smaller place in the last decade and that is not going to change. Even with a push to greater nationalism across Europe and parts of North America, many organizations remain global in scope and excel due to the sharing of ideas, and conversations, across geography. If physical movement of talent becomes hindered, virtual conversations will fill the void.

## WHY IS THIS IMPORTANT?

There are many reasons why it is important to take a look at virtual conversations, teamwork, and learning, namely:

> **The Move to Just-in-Time or Real-Time Processes** – We live in an era of immediate gratification. Recent research points to the "Uber effect," which is the ability to acquire anything real-time or just-in-time. This is changing the landscape of what is seen as "effective" in the learning space by professionals. Learners and other professionals are asking, "If I need it now, why shouldn't I be able to get it or access it right away?" On-demand and mobile platforms offer this real-time learning. Internet-based work allows for us to connect and work real-time, no longer necessitating long travel or delays in our collaborative spaces.

> **Time Efficiency** – Virtual approaches provide many benefits in terms of time and budget. They provide a reduction in the amount of time people need to spend away from the office to engage in learning. Why travel if you don't have to?

> **Reduction of the Carbon Footprint (Eco-Friendliness)** – Britain's Open University found that e-learning consumes 90% less energy than traditional courses. They found that the amount of $CO_2$ emissions (per student) is also reduced by up to 85%.[14]

**Bringing Expertise Together** – Virtual conversations and learning allow you to collaborate and learn from the best across time differences. These peer partnerships span geographic boundaries, changing the way we see the world, how we share information, and what we create.

**Bringing Peers Together from a Wider Cross-Section** – The virtual space allows us to connect people from around the world with similar passions. With Zoom and other video-streaming meeting services, virtual meetings sometimes feel as if we are across the table from each other in terms of our ability to see each other and engage in real-time conversation.

**Bringing Peers Together from a Wider Cross-Section** – With the advent of mobile technologies, smart devices bring conversations and learning to us immediately—from the office to commuting, our phones have created a new window to the conversation and learning ecosystem.

## WHY VIRTUAL LEARNING?

Many companies are leveraging virtual learning for a number of reasons including:

- Reducing travel and associated costs
- Supplementing learning experiences for global teams
- Fostering cross-sectoral and cross-functional learning across the organization, or locations
- Reducing the cost of meetings
- Saving time from travel
- Reducing their carbon footprint

## THE DOWNSIDE OF VIRTUAL LEARNING AND CONVERSATIONS

There is always a positive and a negative to any learning process. The downside to virtual learning and conversation can be a lack of connection participants feel with others, leading to multitasking and disengagement. This book aims to provide you with **practical** and **actionable** activities for you to incorporate to boost the **connection**, **trust,** and **engagement** of your virtual events. Part of this involves *setting everyone up for success* in the virtual space.

Trying to transplant an in-person meeting or teaching approach to the virtual world may fall flat. Lack of visual cues, competing priorities, and a diverse list of focus areas require some tweaks to the process and structure of meetings and other virtual conversations. Trust and connection are essential for people to engage, therefore, leaders and other virtual conversation hosts or facilitators benefit from having a variety of strategies on how to build trust and connection in the virtual space.

Many organizations today are undergoing transformational culture change, often at the team level. Virtual learning and meetings can create pockets or bubbles in an organization. Just like in the in-person environment, if only some people participate, silos may emerge, leading to new ideas taking root in disparate parts of the organization. As such, the process of change in the virtual realm may take longer than in-person environments.

## WHY THIS BOOK?

This book is intended to be a practical, quick, and concise collection of tools and resources you can use in your own work. It is not intended as an A to Z roadmap. Leading conversations in the virtual realm is not about complexity, it's about simplifying. In fact, the main complexity in virtual groups is the group itself.

# THE DRIVING FORCE

This book has been honed through decades of experience in virtual leadership and tens of thousands of hours of virtual conversations spanning leadership to learning. Since the 1990s, I have been involved in global and virtual leadership development, and since the early 2000s involved in supporting the development of coaches, trainers, and facilitators around the world, while working with them virtually. From leading sit-reps (situation reports) via short-range radio across South America to spending the majority of the day in dialogue with people all across the world, the book is grounded in practical, implementable tools for leaders and facilitators.

I am writing this in the post-Brexit era, when walls are being constructed—both literally and figuratively—across the global space. Disruption has become the new norm for many industries. From health care, where surgeries can be performed virtually from thousands of miles away, to financial services, where our phones have become our wallets, change is happening dramatically. The priority of the organizations I work with recognize that silos need to be softened in order to do better work, generate more profit, and also harness the best talent that exists. An important part of this silo softening and enhanced collaboration is to have better conversations in the virtual space. There is a tremendous cost—both fiscal and human—from ineffective meetings and one-way virtual events. There is also a cost in terms of health and well-being from excessive commuting, which can be minimized with the adoption of more flexible working arrangements. With the rapid changes we are seeing in technology, productivity gains are also possible, often requiring different ways of working. Flatter organizational structures, team-based work, and agile methodologies are all transforming how we work.

In creating foundations for more effective and impactful virtual work, we are building intentional, effective connections which honor the differences that exist and create a shared experience and common ground for us to learn from and move from.

## OVERVIEW OF THE BOOK

As we move through this book, we are going to be exploring a range of topics, starting with this chapter's focus on the business case and context, and setting the stage.

## CHAPTER 2

### The Foundations of Effective and Engaging Virtual Conversations

This chapter explores the foundations of creating engaging and effective virtual conversations. It explores some of the key philosophical components which underpin this work including:

- Adult learning and experiential principles
- The stages of group and team development—what groupings need throughout the conversational cycle to maximize results
- The importance of intercultural understanding
- The generational mix in today's workforce
- The Triad of virtual learning—Safety, Connection, and Trust—as well as defining what effective and engaging mean in the context of virtual conversations.

## CHAPTER 3

### What Every Conversation Needs: Essential Elements and Core Skills

Regardless of the type of conversation (webinar, group or team coaching, team meeting), virtual conversations have similar characteristics. This chapter explores:

- What it means to have an effective virtual conversation
- The role of the facilitator
- Core skills of masterful virtual facilitators

## CHAPTER 4

### The Ecosystem of Virtual Conversations: The Range of Different Approaches

This chapter explores the range of virtual learning options—the ecosystem—as well as some of the different platforms available for this work. We will start the chapter by looking at the current context and then explore the range of different approaches that make up the ecosystem of learning and dialogue.

We will examine the range of different approaches we can leverage in virtual learning including:

- E-learning synchronous or asynchronous training
- Virtual educational events—instructor/facilitator led through webinars, e-learning, webcasts
- Video-based learning
- Virtual meetings of all stripes—conference calls
- Goal-setting via strategic planning sessions and virtual retreats
- Mentoring
- Coaching
- Virtual team development
- Peer-to-peer learning—masterminds, breakouts

This chapter also looks at core platforms that are available for virtual conversations.

## CHAPTER 5

### Creating the Container: Designing for Powerful and Engaging Virtual Conversations (Core Elements and Best Practices)

This chapter explores the process of design from start to finish, as well as several tools program planners and facilitators can use to "shape the container" for engaging and effective virtual calls. The mnemonic of PEBBLLES ETC is shared to capture broad best practices for designing and implementing virtual programming.

We will look at design on two levels – the macro level from program idea to implementation, and the process of a virtual session from start to finish.

## CHAPTER 6
### Preparing for Blast Off: Focus Areas for New and Experienced Facilitators

This chapter explores the topic areas of:

- Characteristics of engaging virtual facilitators
- Setting yourself and your group up for success, and avoiding common pitfalls
- 10 key activities that will help you prepare and launch a virtual program
- Habits of exceptional virtual facilitators

## CHAPTER 7
### Activities and Engagement in the Virtual Space: The Facilitator's Toolkit

The tools of the trade are a facilitator's greatest resource. In this chapter, we explore:

- Considerations for selecting or creating activities
- Twenty-four different tools for working in the virtual space
- Tools to create engagement and dialogue, while focusing on enhanced relationships and results

## CHAPTER 8
### Pitfalls, Tricky Issues, and Resilience
### (or When Things Go Wrong)

The road to a great conversation isn't always smooth. This chapter explores:

- Pitfalls for virtual learning
- Tricky issues
- Difficult participants
- Dealing with conflict
- Recovery

## CHAPTER 9
### In Focus: Virtual Meetings

11 million meetings take place every day, with one-third of them noted as being ineffective. $37 billion is wasted every year on ineffective meetings.[15]

In this chapter, we will explore:

- Virtual meeting basics
- Setting people up for success with virtual meetings
- Keeping things on track
- Virtual meeting faux-pas/mistakes
- Preparing for a virtual meeting
- Meeting tools: pre- and post-meeting checklists, agenda

## CHAPTER 10
### In Focus: Virtual Team Leadership Development

The area of virtual team leadership continues to grow. From leaders supporting remote teams across a region to global leaders working with teams across the world, virtual team leadership development continues to expand. This chapter explores core foundations of virtual team leadership development, the nuances and differences, including:

- Global business leader attributes
- Core skills for virtual team leaders
- Key characteristics of virtual team leaders
- Matrix management

## CHAPTER 11
### In Focus: Virtual Team Development

This chapter focuses on the virtual team development space. As the Telework Research Network notes, there has been a 61% increase in the number of full-time virtual workers since 2005.[16] Even with this increase, many times virtual and remote workers do not benefit from any team development initiatives.

This chapter explores:

- The foundations of virtual teams
- What we know about High Performing Teams (HPT) and making teams excel
- Opportunities for virtual team development
- Activities you may want to use in virtual team development

## CHAPTER 12
### Partnering, Co-Facilitation, Collaboration, and Creating a Culture of Effective Virtual Conversation

Finally, we will turn our attention on one critical element: We don't do this work alone. Our clients, fellow facilitators, and the next generation of virtual conversationalists are always a click away.

We look at three important aspects of partnering and collaboration in this chapter:

- Partnering with your group members
- Collaborating with co-facilitators
- Building a culture of virtual facilitators

Virtual work is grounded in collaboration. In designing powerful programs, we want to ensure that we are creating the richest collaborative spaces, as well as expanding skills to others.

## NOTES ON THE LAYOUT AND RESOURCES FOR YOU

Each chapter includes a series of End of Chapter Questions for you to reflect on. You are encouraged to take note of these as you go.

Given the topic of this book, it is likely that you will want to refer back to certain chapters and use some information as a template for your work. Most chapters include a worksheet or template for you to use. These can be found at www.effectivevirtualconversations.com.

Throughout the book you will also be invited to join the Adventures of Jane and Jo. Jane is a virtual facilitator and Jo is a virtual team leader. Their stories will bring to life and synthesize many of the topics we are exploring.

## END OF CHAPTER QUESTIONS

What are the reasons you are looking to create more effective and engaging virtual conversations?

What approaches might you be leveraging?

What do you see as the benefits of virtual conversations in your work? What might be the drawbacks?

What chapters do you want to start with?

Make a note of any action steps from this chapter in your Action Plan Tracker (found at the end of the book).

CHAPTER 2

# THE FOUNDATIONS OF EFFECTIVE AND ENGAGING VIRTUAL CONVERSATIONS

*"The power of dialogue emerges in the cultivation, in ourselves, as well as in others, of questions for which we do not have answers."[17]*

*– William Isaacs*

This chapter explores the fundamentals of effective virtual conversations, including what every person working with groups or teams in the virtual space needs to know. This includes exploring the foundations of:

- The ecosystem of virtual conversations
- Adult learning and experiential principles
- Group and team development
- The importance of intercultural understanding
- The generational mix in today's workforce
- The Triad of virtual conversations—Safety, Connection, and Trust

As we wrap up the chapter I will explore some common enablers and derailers, as well as assumptions and myths important to debunk in undertaking this work.

## CONSIDER THIS—SINCE 2006:

We've moved from flying people across the country, to in-person meetings and trade shows held in Second Life, to an era when video conferencing is available to everyone at no cost through services like Skype and Zoom.

The largest and most popular smart phone maker no longer makes smart phones. From the days of Blackberry RIM's hold on the mobile market to today's diverse marketplace of smart devices, it can be difficult to believe that the iPhone was only unveiled in January 2007, and that the Blackberry is now hard to find.

The iPad was only introduced on January 27, 2010. Here's what their press release read:[18]

**Magical & Revolutionary Device at an Unbelievable Price**

SAN FRANCISCO—January 27, 2010—Apple® today introduced iPad, a revolutionary device for browsing the web, reading and sending email, enjoying photos, watching videos, listening to music, playing games, reading e-books and much more. iPad's responsive high-resolution Multi-Touch™ display lets users physically interact with applications and content."

Consider how the iPad, and related mobile devices such as tablets, have revolutionized your world of work and conversations since 2010.

## THE ECOSYSTEM OF VIRTUAL CONVERSATIONS

Every day, dozens of different types of virtual conversations are taking place—virtual meetings, coaching conversations, training sessions, virtual team sprints, and mentoring conversations. Throughout this book, we will be referring to the *ecosystem* of virtual conversations to represent the tremendously diverse range of approaches and platforms for virtual conversations today. From learning, to collaboration, to performance management, there are a myriad of reasons we meet and converse in the virtual realm.

As a graduate student, I studied in the Faculty of Environmental Studies, where I was blessed to be part of a multi-disciplinary learning environment—something people are now calling for more of in today's multi-faceted environment. Back then, it was a radical change from the siloed world of my undergraduate studies in Science, where distinctions were always made between Chemistry, Biology, and Physics. That experience in a multi-disciplinary graduate program shaped the approaches I've developed as a practitioner and leader over the past twenty-five years. I've learned to weave together learning from many different disciplines—from coaching, to neuroscience, to performance improvement, to conflict management.

As an environmentalist by training, I have learned to navigate the greys of the world and be comfortable with the **dichotomies,** the **tensions,** the **gradients** (grey zones) as well as the **lack of comfort** (which to me is usually a reminder that learning is taking place). All of these are present in our work in the virtual space.

In any ecosystem, we have a variety of relationships. Those that are **symbiotic** (which Merriam-Webster describes as "the living together in more or less intimate association or close union of two dissimilar organisms (as in parasitism or commensalism);" or **cooperative** (as between two persons or groups), as well as those that are **predatory**—like the so-called "Internet Trolls" who have become famous for their scathing comments and cyber-bullying on social media. We also have relationships that are **co-existing**, including virtual masterminds which bring small groups of business owners together on a regular basis to help each other learn and get inspired, and connecting virtual teams around the world allowing them to do better work.

The following graphic represents some of the major approaches to learning and conversation—coaching, facilitation, training, and mentoring. I call this the Continuum of Learning. Note the core skills integrated in each approach:

| Coaching | Facilitation | Training | Mentoring |
|---|---|---|---|
| Coaching competencies | Core facilitation competencies | Acquisition of KSAs | Not direct line management |
| Powerful Questions | Questions | Content | Mentor is expert |
| Client, not coach is expert | Focus on the process | Training objectives are drivers | Mentor's own stories |
| Goal setting | Helps client move from A to B | Trainer is expert | Experience |
| Awareness, Action, and Accountability | May, or may not, be content expert | Trainer measured on learning | Internal workings |
| Integration and application of learning | | Focused timelines | Practical past experience |
| Clients and their agenda are drivers | | | KSAs may be a focus |
| Curiosity and unattachment | | | |

Throughout the book, we will be exploring the different modalities that exist across the learning ecosystem including:

**Coaching** – The coaching industry is now a $20 billion a year industry. From executive coaching to team coaching, many coaches have been creating engaging and effective conversation spaces with their clients virtually for more than a decade. Key contributions from the coaching profession to the virtual world include the skillful use of questions to spark new insights, expand thinking and perspectives, or gain clarity. Goal setting is usually the starting point for many coaching processes, and we know that a focus on goals—individually and collectively—is a critical focus area for virtual teams. In coaching, the client's focus and their goals shapes the process and theme areas. Trust and connection is paramount for people to drop into the deeper conversation space, which requires higher levels of vulnerability and trust.

**Facilitation** – Coming from the Latin word *facilis* or "to make easy," facilitation is a core skill set for those working in the virtual domain. Facilitation is deeply focused on **process**, and on helping groups move from A to B by drawing out the knowledge of the group. The virtual facilitator's realm has also exploded with the help of input from experts from related disciplines including *visual facilitators* and *graphic facilitators*, who graphically represent the conversation.

**Training** – The learning and development field has gone through tremendous change in the last few decades. Who would have envisioned ten years ago how pervasive mobile learning would become? Today we can learn from almost anywhere we have a connection. I've led training programs where people have been logging in and learning from docks, hotels and even parked cars. The virtual realm has enabled us to make learning more real-time and impactful, as well as more bite-sized, as we are seeing in today's shift to more micro-learning. In contrast to one-hour to one-day learning sessions, micro-learning bursts are often only 3-7 minutes in length, mirroring the shortened attention span and availability of today's employees.

**Mentoring** – Mentoring is experiencing a resurgence in an increasingly VUCA—Volatile, Uncertain, Complex, and Ambiguous—world. Increasingly mentoring is also taking place in the virtual realm, pairing peers or staff together to share expertise and best practices. The focus of mentoring in both the "real" and virtual worlds is usually the support of the person being mentored, called the mentee or protégé, through the mentor sharing their own experiences. This advisory role can be invaluable in helping professionals navigate the political currents of an organization or industry.

**Meetings** – With upwards of 40% of a manager's time each week being spent in meetings, often in the virtual space of conference calls and webinars, we'll spend some time focusing on ways to make virtual meetings more effective.

# AT THE HEART OF VIRTUAL CONVERSATION IS THE ART OF DIALOGUE

Writing this book took me back to some of my roots as a graduate student, when I studied process facilitation, critical education, and organizational behavior issues. As a community worker in the early 1990s in Central and South America, part of my role was to spark conversation around vision and possibilities at the community level. One of the practical issues I would face was the need to move between fostering dialogue, to facilitating a conversation, to leading a planning session. It led me to appreciate the multi-lens of conversations today. This is reflected in the variety of different types of conversations taking place across the virtual realm, from real-time learning events, to virtual meetings bringing teams together at all times of day and night, to one-way webcasts. What we know is that the more engaging virtual events are those that are grounded in dialogue.

This past fall, at a community book sale, I found a book written in 1998 by William Isaacs called *Dialogue and the Art of Thinking Together*. In it, he makes the distinction between dialogue and discussion. He reminds us that the word dialogue comes from two Latin words: dial, meaning "through," and logos, meaning "word or meaning." So, the word could be translated as "through meaning." Isaacs also reminds us that the original root of the word logos was actually "relationship," which enables us to interpret the word dialogue to mean "through relationships." I would assert that in fact the most engaging and effective virtual conversations are through relationships. It is when we have the safety, connection, and trust present that we are able to move into the most important conversations for the moment—whether those conversations are categorized as discussion, dialogue, mentoring, or coaching.

Isaacs makes some important distinctions in this landscape of conversation, particularly in the difference between dialogue and discussion.

He writes:

"A dialogue helps to survey the alternatives and lay them side by side, so that they can all be seen in context."[19]

"Dialogue seeks to harness the 'collective intelligence' (think of this as the collective intelligence quotient, or CQ) of the people around you; together we are more aware and smarter than we are on our own. And together we can perceive new directions and new opportunities more clearly than we can on our own."[20]

He goes on to say, "Discussion is about making a decision. Unlike dialogue, which seeks to open possibilities, and see new options, discussion seeks closure and completion."[21] He continues, "Dialogue is about evoking insight, which is a way of recoding our knowledge, particularly the taken for granted assumptions people bring to the table."[22]

He also makes the distinction between "generative dialogue," which I would define as "creating meaning through the art of conversation," and "reflective dialogue," which I would call "creating meaning through the art of reflection."

*So, what are you having—dialogue or discussion? How are you, and those you are working with, creating meaning—through new conversations or through reflection?*

## SIMILARITIES AND DIFFERENCES BETWEEN VIRTUAL AND IN-PERSON CONVERSATION SPACE

There is often an assumption that leading virtual conversations and learning will be the same as in-person work. It is important to recognize some of the subtle but important differences with virtual conversations that influence everything from energy levels to engagement.

**Similarities include:**

- Conversations don't have to be one way. We can use breakouts, and small group dialogue.

- The facilitator can adopt many stances—from coaching, to training, to facilitation.

- Learners who participate bring a diverse mix of experiences, preferences, and learning styles, necessitating a robust a series of tools and approaches. In some respects, virtual conversations can require facilitation skills on steroids. Later in this book I include a mini-compendium on approaches and processes you can use in the virtual domain. Effective and engaging virtual events leverage a variety of strategies, tools, techniques, and approaches. Refer to Chapter 7 for an overview of some of the tools for engaging and impactful virtual facilitation and conversations.

- Learning doesn't just happen at the learning event. Masterful educators and facilitators consider pre-program and post-program supports and how they work. As in the in-person realm, pre-work undertaken before people come to the conversation can be of tremendous benefit, sometimes even more so within the virtual domain. Consider what types of supports and touchpoints will create an enabling environment for learning and dialogue.

**Differences include:**

- The lack of visual cues on phone-only platforms can create a challenge in terms of engagement and two-way conversation. Moving to video-streaming technologies from phone-only can address this issue. More regular check-ins and smaller group sizes can provide more feedback loops to ensure that the conversation is going as intended. With a lack of body signals, many virtual conversationalists develop deeper skills in listening and noticing the subtle cues of pace, pitch, and pauses.

- A different energy is required on the part of the facilitator. Because of the lack of immediate visual information, sometimes a virtual conversation can feel like more of a one-way conversation. Virtual facilitators often fall into the trap of thinking their facilitation has to be a monologue, and quickly move through what they feel may be a black hole of space. We will cover a wide range of strategies to create more dialogue and involve the people at the other end of the phone or computer.

- Pace and pitch play a bigger role in the virtual environment due to lack of visual cues. The pace needs to be faster in the virtual realm to drive engagement, boost focus and keep progress moving forward.

- Asking for more frequent feedback is important in the virtual domain to ensure the conversation is hitting the mark.

- Small really is beautiful. Numbers in groups are exponential, and each new person brings a new web of layers.

*What similarities and differences do you see in this work? What is going to create an enabling environment for your groups?*

## FOUNDATIONS OF ADULT LEARNING AND EXPERIENTIAL EDUCATION

A second set of ingredients for creating effective virtual conversations is leveraging the best practices of adult learning and experiential education. Unlike the in-person realm, where multitasking is quickly noticed, one of the major challenges in virtual conversations revolves around engagement and capturing people's attention. Without this, it is easy for virtual attendees to fall into the trap of multitasking, which leads to their not paying attention and disengagement. Many studies now demonstrate that our brain is not capable of multitasking, and that thus multitasking creates a cognitive switching load. In layperson's terms, there is a cost to switching back and forth!

As such, in creating engaging and effective virtual conversations, it can be important to keep in mind how adults learn and what they value. Adult learning principles assert:

- We learn what is interesting to us.
- It is important for us to know *why* we are learning.
- It is important for us to connect early on to the topic—(often referred to as the WIIFM—*What's in it for me?*).
- As adults, we want to make the connection between the topic and the application—how we can apply the skills and knowledge gained.

Keeping these principles in mind, we are more likely to capture, and hold, virtual attention, inviting people into the conversation.

## PRACTITIONER'S TIP: ERGA IN ACTION

In the virtual domain, helping people connect early on to their WIIFM helps them engage in the conversation. It's this connection point that will help mitigate against the multitasking habit many people drop into in the virtual domain. Consider, what can you do at the beginning of a virtual conversation to help people connect with:

1. Their WIIFM?

2. What they want out of the call?

3. What success is going to look like to them?

Starting with these questions and listening to the answers creates alignment for virtual groups. While it might take time to verbally hear from everyone on all three questions, it is also possible to poll the participants, get their input via chat or have them comment using annotation.

Experiential education principles also help to create more engaging virtual conversations. In the virtual realm, "being talked to" will quickly lead those on the other end of the screen or phone to turn their attention elsewhere. More experiential approaches invite our conversation partners to get involved in the conversation and be active participants. Experiential education has served as the roots for many disciplines as we know them today—coaching, design, thinking, etc.

At its core, the experiential education process is a four-stage learning cycle. Through this process, we create meaning and learning. David Kolb premised that all individuals learn by looking at their experiences through different lenses, commonly abbreviated as *ERGA*.

**E – We have an *Experience*.** For example, it is the day of my first virtual presentation. I host a call for 10 people who are calling in from 10 different locations in 10 different countries. I leave the call with the impression that it did not go very well, although participant feedback says otherwise.

**R – We benefit from *Reflection*.** In the Reflection phase, we ask ourselves a series of *What* questions that help frame our experience:

- What happened?
- What worked well?
- What didn't work well?

- What did I think?
- What did I observe?
- What did other group members think/want?

Continuing with the example of my first virtual presentation, in the Reflection stage, asking these questions can help me glean new insights. In asking myself, *What worked well?* I may have noticed that participant chat interaction was high, and there were lots of questions that were answered. I may also have observed that people gave a number of positive emojis when I asked them to comment on the question, "Select an emoji to represent how confident you are in putting these ideas into practice." Using this Reflection process may help me begin to realize that it may have been a much better session than I gave myself credit for.

**G – We *Generalize*.** In this stage, we ask ourselves *So what?*

- So what's important about the feedback I received from participants?
- So what assumptions am I making?
- So what's important to note?
- So where else is this showing up in my life?

In the Generalization phase, I can start thinking about what is important about the feedback I've received. I can think about what assumptions I may be making and whether or not they are backed up by the feedback received. In the Generalization stage, I may also be able to access other data points that may further frame my learning and start shifting my beliefs.

**A – We *Apply* what we have learned.** In the Application phase, learning is formed by putting things into practice. We ask ourselves *Now what?*

- Now what am I going to change next time I run the course? Process? Questions?
- Now what am I going to do the same way?
- Now what am I going to do differently in terms of activities?

At this stage, the questions allow me to shift into the perspective that the learning was powerful for the group, and help me think about the changes I will make next time and what I will leave the same.

In creating engaging virtual conversations, questions become an important tool in establishing space for dialogue, reflection, and learning. Consider how you can incorporate the ERGA model and more reflection into your conversation space. You may also want to note how other leaders and facilitators are using it as a tool to stimulate learning, reflection, and action.

## TEAM AND GROUP DEVELOPMENT: ADAPTATIONS TO TUCKMAN'S MODEL IN THE VIRTUAL DOMAIN

Another area imperative for the virtual conversationalist to understand is the life cycle of teams and groups. Anyone who has been part of a small virtual group may have experienced the close connections formed between a group of people that started off as strangers. With the advent of video streaming, we can now also put faces to names immediately, creating connection early on. This allows for much quicker real-time collaboration and learning.

Many of our conversation spaces involve groups and teams. Understanding the life cycle of how teams and groups operate can be useful for those of us who are designing and leading virtual group and team conversations. For many years, those of us who have worked in group development have talked about the seminal research by Bruce Tuckman. His *Forming, Storming, Norming, Performing and Adjourning* model of group development has had significant impact on not only how we lead, but design, group processes. I often receive the question, "Does Tuckman's model hold true in the virtual realm?" I would assert that it *can* play out in the virtual realm—notice next time when conflict surfaces in a second or third call.

The text box reviews some of the important elements in group development at each stage and points to some nuances specific to the virtual realm. It also focuses on what virtual facilitators can do at each stage to support the group or team to ensure an enabling environment for virtual conversations, boosting relationships and results.

NOTE: In the virtual domain, group and team development starts even before the call. Pre-program connection points can be part of the Forming stage and may involve:

- A pre-meeting with the facilitator.
- Connection with other learners though a web portal—whether it's a Facebook group or learning management portal.
- Reflective opportunity through a questionnaire—"What I want to get out of the program" and/or a self-assessment.
- An introductory call to listen to or a welcome video to review.

# GROUP DEVELOPMENT AND TUCKMAN'S MODEL IN THE VIRTUAL DOMAIN

STAGE: FORMING - *In this stage, we are helping the group explore the What?*

**What's Important**

- Safety, expectations, clarity around what the program is about
- Getting people to connect and/or share their WIIFM

**Virtual Nuances**

- Group/team members can't see each other
- Geographically dispersed
- Different realities and priorities
- Notice how people are engaged in the virtual realm—video versus text-only interaction
- Creating of a shared group portal or "go-to place" for resources can be important

**Considerations**

- WOW – Ways of Working
- Focusing on connecting the group
- Choosing platforms and considering synchronous and asynchronous** connections
- How do people want to connect?
- How do you ensure privacy?
- Confidentiality agreements

** Synchronous conversations happen real-time. For example, I can be conversing real-time with someone in London right now through text, chat, or voice from my desk in Toronto. In Asynchronous Learning there is a lag—so, for example, I might post a comment on a shared thread tonight that can be read tomorrow by someone else, somewhere else.

## Things to Make Sure You are Doing

- Clarifying what is expected
- Group norms
- Connections amongst groups
- Reviewing
- Checking how to share personal information with each other
- Discussing confidentiality or how information is shared

## Activities You May Want to Use

- Activities to create trust and connection such as:
  - Personal Logos
  - Coins
  - Vision/Values
  - Assessments
  - Goal Setting

STAGE: STORMING – *In this stage, we are helping the group explore the What? So, who are we? What's this all about?*

## What's Important

- Figuring out roles
- How we want to operate
- How this connects with me

**Virtual Nuances**

- Greater likelihood of disconnection
- Greater opportunity for the *anonymous factor*, or, *They can't see me* to kick in or people to disengage

**Considerations**

- There may be a lot of variances regarding culture and language
- Notice differences in how people approach, and are comfortable with, conflict

**Things to Make Sure You are Doing**

- Normalizing conflict
- Reinforcing the Ways of Working

**Activities You May Want to Use**

- Normalize functions, tasks, decisions
- Appreciation
- Best team
- What's holding the team back?
- How to have difficult conversations or working across differences
- Prioritization
- Style Assessments – MBTI and DiSC

STAGE: NORMING - *In this stage we are exploring What? What's acceptable? Who we are?*

**What's Important**

- Planning, roles

- Figuring out how you really want to work

**Virtual Nuances**

- Individual norms and collective norms
- Making explicit different roles, ways of working, norms
- Is there an evolution of new shared group/team culture?

**Considerations**

- How do we want to operate together?

**Things to Make Sure You are Doing**

- Building trust
- Getting people into deeper dialogue with each other
- Using breakouts regularly
- Clarifying roles and responsibilities
- Deepening identity of the group

**Activities You May Want to Use**

- Values and behaviors

STAGE: PERFORMING - *In this stage we are exploring acceleration. What's working? What will keep momentum going?*

**What's Important**

- Getting the results in place

**Virtual Nuances**

- Participants will be performing in isolation from others and could benefit from pause to look at what support they need

**Considerations**

- Resourcing, roadblocks, enablers
- Systems and structures that will sustain the work

Things to Make Sure You are Doing

- Creating opportunities for reflective pause
- Creating opportunity for people to share their commitments and update each other in a way that does not just have to be a 30-second soundbyte

**Activities You May Want to Use**

- Keeping energy moving
- Troubleshooting
- Planning for celebration
- Use the work (and structures) they are undertaking

STAGE: ADJOURNING - *In this stage we are helping the group articulate*

**What's Important**

- Wrap up
- Sustainability
- Evaluation

**Virtual Nuances**

- Last time together
- Application to local context

**Considerations**

- Closure
- Feedback

- Evaluation
- Lessons learned.

**Things to Make Sure You are Doing**

- How do you want to stay connected?
- Where can you access the materials?
- For how long can materials be accessed?

**Activities You May Want to Use**

- Spiders Web
- Acknowledgement
- Action Planning: One-Page Plan and Commitments
- Evaluation
- Learning takeaways

It is important to note that in the virtual domain, the group doesn't always end with adjourning or the official closure. Consider for yourself how virtual groups may stay more connected after an official close off than an in-person group does.

As facilitators or virtual leaders, keeping in touch with your group members can add an additional benefit in "keeping the learning alive." You may opt to undertake some of the following:

- Post-program evaluation—for example at one, three, or six months after the program.
- Host a group follow-up call to reconnect.
- Facilitate a *Best Practice Call*. These calls give people an opportunity to share what they have implemented and what best practices are emerging in their work, or as they go to apply their learning and insights back at the workplace.

- Encourage group members to consider how they can share lessons learned.
- Get group members to consider the network you have created together and can carry forward.

## THE IMPORTANCE OF INTERCULTURAL UNDERSTANDING

It is likely that those of us who are leading virtual calls will be working with a cross-section of group or team members from different cultural backgrounds. This is an area where a 2016 study completed by Culture Wizard notes that only 22% of respondents had participated in virtual team training, and 34% in global leadership training.[23] In that study, 68% of respondents reported that cultural challenges were the biggest hurdle to global virtual team productivity.

For those leading virtual calls, there is significant value in learning more about the world around you. As someone who has spent their career working in the global context—first physically, and now virtually—I have seen many great professionals impacted by their lack of understanding around culture. For many years as a Program Manager, part of my role was to recruit and train global virtual teams. I will now share some of the practicalities of where I saw virtual team members struggle in the area of culture.

When working in a virtual context, it is very important to check our assumptions based on information received. It's also important to note that relying on stereotypes can also be a danger point. As facilitators and leaders, we have been shaped by our own upbringing and cultural experiences. As someone who worked for years outside of my own cultural home, I learned a lot about the sometimes painful process of "unpacking" and "owning" your own biases, power, and privilege.

This section is not intended as a crash course into a complex field. However, in starting the dialogue for virtual team leaders or facilitators it is important to note some of the differences that exist across cultures. In my almost three decades with intercultural training and briefing, one of the best researched and most easily understood frameworks is that of Geert Hofstede.

Hofstede proposed we can look at culture through six dimensions:

1. Individualism–Collectivism
2. Uncertainty Avoidance
3. Power Distance (strength of social hierarchy)
4. Masculinity–Femininity (task orientation versus person-orientation)
5. Long-Term Orientation
6. Indulgence vs. Self-restraint

Each global culture is located along different parts of these continuums. Recognize that in a virtual grouping, especially one that is global in nature (team or a group), it is likely that members will vary across this spectrum.

In 1980's *Culture's Consequences; International Differences in Work-Related Values*, Hofstede developed a framework through which we can explore both national and organizational culture. Using data from IBM he identified four dimensions of culture:

1. **Power Distance** explores how equal or distributed power is within a nation, team, or organization. A great example is Brazil, where a few individuals control a lot of power and access to resources, versus a country such as Canada, where power is more evenly distributed and "flatter" organizational structures are embraced.

2. **Individualism vs. Collectivism** captures how much we look at issues from an *I* versus *We*. How much do people work or connect individually versus collaboratively? Compare cultures that are more collaborative and group-centric, such as communities in the Caribbean, to the more individualistic cultures of North America.

3. **Masculinity vs. Femininity** explores how competitive or cooperative a culture can be, or how "tough versus tender" it is. As described by Hofstede, "The Masculinity side of this dimension represents a preference in society for achievement, heroism, assertiveness and material rewards for success. Society at large is more competitive. Its opposite, femininity, stands for a preference for cooperation, modesty, caring for the weak and quality of life. Society at large is more consensus-oriented."[24] More masculine cultures prefer and reward "achievement, heroism, assertiveness and material rewards." More feminine cultures value "cooperation, modesty and quality of life."

4. **Uncertainty Avoidance** looks at our tolerance for ambiguity. It can include grey areas, as well as how comfortable we are with uncertainty and ambiguity in things like decision making and taking action within an uncertain context. Countries which are high in Uncertainty Avoidance "maintain rigid codes of belief and behavior and are intolerant of unorthodox behavior and ideas."

Later, two more dimensions were added:

1. **Long-Term Orientation:** Countries low on LTO may be seen as more focused on tradition rather than investing in the future. Cultures may change more quickly if they have higher scores in this category. China, Hong Kong, Taiwan, and Japan have some of the highest scores in this area.

2. **Indulgence:** Countries lower in this are stricter with their codes versus countries that are more focused on immediate gratification.

Part of Hofstede's research includes a comparison between two countries, where national cultures are rated according to the six different factors on a scale of 1 to 100. Even if cultures appear to be similar on the surface, as we look closer through the lens of these six areas, we start to see some important distinctions. This helps to provide insight into the nuances that are not always apparent, but are essential in virtual conversations and global business.

As someone who has been involved in cross-cultural training and executive support for relocations to Canada for more than a decade, I know many times people think that the US and Canada are very similar. And while we are very similar in some areas, we are very different on others. So, for example, if we compare Canada to the US we can see that we are very similar along three of the continua: Uncertainty Avoidance, where Canada scores 48 and the US 46; Indulgence, where we are both 68; and Power Distance, where Canada is 39 and the US is 40.

The two cultures differ more in the area of Individualism, where the US scores 91 and Canada 80. While both countries have strong drives for individual achievement (rather than communal effort), individualism is even more of a common trait in the US than in Canada. This is evidenced in American values like "working hard = success", valuing and fostering entrepreneurism, and a focus on the individual spirit. Both countries vary along the Masculinity continuum as well—with Canada scoring 52 and the US 62. Canadians tend to place more emphasis on work-life balance and time with family rather than solely achievement and success. Finally, there are differences in the area of Long-Term Orientation, with Canada scoring 36 and the US 26. While both countries' scores are on the low side, there is a distinction between the two countries' culture in terms of long-term orientation and planning.

It can be helpful to get this granular around culture as it heightens awareness of our own national values, which shape how we interrelate and what we find valuable. Our national values influence how we hold meetings, communicate, make presentations, make decisions and involve others. Understanding culture also makes us more aware of the conscious and unconscious biases we bring to any discussion or group/ team interaction. As teams and learning events become more global, it is important to keep in mind the role of national preferences and values, as they will impact the types and approaches you use in virtual dialogue.

**Practitioner's Tip: Explore the Culture Scales**

Explore the resources provided by Geert Hofstede including the culture scales. You can receive a customized report on how one national culture compares to another. This may provide some useful clues to you as a facilitator (which need to be backed up or validated by meetings with your group) around how group members may tend to interact (such as preferences for group work, hierarchy, structure). See my corollary below.

## IMPLICATIONS FOR VIRTUAL GROUPS AND TEAMS

In a virtual team or group context it is likely that you will have participants from a wider variety of cultural contexts than you may normally see in your face-to-face work. As in all cross-cultural work, it is very important to avoid the trap of stereotypes or assumptions that just because someone comes from a particular place they will behave a certain way. For example, because I am from Canada, one might assume that I will always say "eh" and be more risk-averse than my American counterparts. While the "eh" part may be true, thanks to my global experience, I am not as likely to be risk averse as many of my Canadian counterparts! As with anything, our socialization and work and life experiences shape how we see and interact with the world.

Practically, in my virtual work I tend to place a lot of emphasis on getting to know group members prior to the start of any program, and to learn more about who each person is uniquely. This helps me understand at a deeper and wider level the impact geographic culture may have on the virtual event, as well as helping me relate to each person as a unique individual.

# CULTURE CLASHES

One of the challenges of working virtually is developing a greater understanding of culture, as well as power, privilege, and impact. In any organization today that spans borders (even regional ones), it is important to have dialogue about how organizational culture and personal culture mesh together. In most organizational settings, it is assumed that organizational culture will trump personal culture. So, for example, as a former staff member of the UN, the organizational values and obligations superseded some of the more Canadian working styles. At the same time, it is important to be aware of larger distinctions, around things such as privacy laws of different countries, or discrimination legislation. So, for example, if I am leading a virtual team and I am allowing jokes that could be perceived as discriminatory (sexist, racist, or seen as discriminatory on any level), a Canadian staff member would have the right to file a complaint aligned with our different legislation around human rights and discrimination.

Taking time to educate yourself on the implications of managing a global team is important. Your HR team should be able to advise you on resources and support around this.

In addition to culture, two other important factors may be at play, influencing the way we prefer to interact—learning styles as well as generational impact.

# KEEPING LEARNING STYLES IN MIND

While there is some debate in the research world that different learning styles exist, I have to say this is a factor I keep in mind every time I get to meet a new group. Chances are that in a group or team, you are going to have a variety of learning styles at play.

**Visual Learners** interact in the world by seeing. They will prefer video streaming platforms over phone-based only. They'll enjoy the eyeball to eyeball opportunities that platforms like Skype and Zoom can offer. They also will love any PowerPoints you throw their way. Visual Learners may struggle in audio only environments where there is no streaming or visual to keep them focused. *A majority, approximately 60%, of adults in North America are said to have a preference for visual learning.*

Questions that visual learners may appreciate include: *What does that look like? What impact do you envision?*

**Auditory Learners** learn by hearing. They will love the auditory nature of a conference call and may find the more individual experience of learning virtually creates more safety and less anxiety than a face-to-face context. Auditory Learners will enjoy supplementary program supports through TED Talks, audios, and peer dialogue.

A question auditory learners connect with is: *What does it sound like?*

**Kinesthetic Learners** prefer to learn by engaging with the world. They may find the virtual world to be the most challenging, especially if you are not including some active, hands-on ways for them to engage and learn. Kinesthetic Learners love to try things out. What are you doing to create a powerful environment for them?

Questions they may appreciate include: *What does it feel like? What would you do?*

## ENGAGING ACROSS GENERATIONS

In our work as virtual facilitators it is likely that we are engaging across generations, each of which have different aptitudes and comfort levels for technology and virtual learning. Additionally, in any group, you may find that some people are more comfortable than others. As we lead virtual calls, it is important to consider the experiences of different generations, not to spotlight differences, but to better understand each generation's comfort level with different types of technology. These shape our preferences for virtual conversations.

Let's take a closer look at each generation:

## BABY BOOMERS (1946–1964)

While this generation is starting to retire out of the workforce, you may still be working with Boomers as Subject Matter Experts (SMEs) and mentors, if not as leaders. Keep in mind that Boomers have historically valued teamwork and meetings in ways that others do not. This can lead to preferences on their part for meetings, which are not shared by others. The Boomers have seen technology emerge in the work place from rolodexes to the first satellite phones that were often housed in a briefcase.

## GEN XERS (1965–1979)

Enshrined in Douglas Coupland's book *Gen X*, Xers have a smaller demographic footprint in the workplace than both Boomers and Gen Yers, due to their size. They bring a variance in their technological savvy. As a member of this generation, I explored DOS programming in Grade Six computer science camp and marvelled at Atari's pixelated games. I wrote my high school papers on a computer, although I had to save them on floppy disks. When I led programming and teams of more than a hundred in South America, we were connected by short-range radio, while my communication with the head office was through the fax, or an email that sat in Trinidad overnight. The need to take immediate action led to high degrees of autonomy in my work as a leader. Gen Xers may be comfortable in the virtual realm as many of us started engaging in "distance learning," as it was called in the 1990s. Not all of us may be as comfortable in navigating the ever-changing platforms, even though we will enjoy the real-time nature of virtual events and focus—as long as it is during work time.

## MILLENNIALS (1980S–EARLY 2000S)

The Millennials are the first digital natives. They value group work and collaboration, influenced by an educational process that was often more group oriented than earlier generations. One of the biggest distinctions seen with Millennials is their fluidity around different forms of digital communication. For many, texting is as common as a verbal conversation. Real-time/just-in-time communication, or instantaneous communication is often expected. Millennials are positioned to offer an important voice around innovation and creativity.

## GEN Z (THOSE BORN AFTER 2000)

Gen Z are truly the digital natives. They have grown up with smart phones and tablets in their hands, and global connectivity. iPads are part of everyday life in classrooms, and, for many, are a toy from infancy. Skype and Facetime have replaced phone calls, and video streaming is their norm. Gamification is an extension of their learning process. The ability to connect immediately with people around the world, getting real-time data and seeing inside each other's households and businesses in a way that no other generation has experienced will no doubt shape what is possible with virtual learning.

## OTHER SOCIETAL FACTORS

At present, there are several other societal factors influencing our digital or virtual conversations.

## DIGITAL OR VIRTUAL

In my work, it's always interesting to notice how language is used in different populations. While a vast majority of professionals are starting to embrace virtual and remote work, what we call it is varying. Corporate environments which are non-global tend to talk about remote teams, while global organizations talk about virtual teams. Small business prefers

47

the term digital conversations over virtual conversations. What do you notice about the language being used in your context?

## "THE UBER EFFECT"

As always, society shapes our experience. Most recently the term *the Uber Effect* has been used to describe our lack of appetite for waiting in a shopping line for a long amount of time. We have become accustomed to a real-time, on-demand environment. What do you see as the impact on your meeting and virtual learning events?

Even in the two quarters I've spent writing this book tremendous changes have emerged—a push for nationalism in some countries and less global focus, as well as even more discussion about the role of automation and artificial intelligence. IBM recently announced they would be co-locating workers in six offices, rather than having them work remote.[25] What do you notice about factors influencing virtual conversations?

In working virtually, or in the digital economy, there can be a few more considerations. We are going to turn our attention to Triad of Safety, Connection, and Trust—three essential ingredients for any virtual conversation.

## THE TRIAD OF VIRTUAL CONVERSATIONS—SAFETY, CONNECTION, AND TRUST

In order to enter into a virtual conversation, we need **to feel safe, feel connected with others,** and **trust.** Trust the process, trust the leader of the call, and trust the others we are with. Without these, it may not be a space for dialogue, merely monologue.

Increasingly, there is research which backs up what exceptional facilitators have known for years. In order to create an engaging conversation space, we need to create safety, connection, and trust. This is a theme we will be returning back to throughout the book, providing different research reference points from neuroscience as well as organizations such as Google. Without safety, connection, and trust, is it unlikely that people will engage in the virtual domain.

## CREATING A SAFE SPACE FOR THE VIRTUAL ENVIRONMENT

*"Consciously managing boundaries in a group setting is an essential way to sustain and deepen the safety that people feel."* [26] *- William Isaacs*

In creating an engaging virtual environment, it is important to ensure that people feel safe, valued, and connected. This is even more important in the virtual realm, to the degree that it is unlikely that people will actively and eagerly participate without this in place. Part of creating safety involves helping people feel connected, as well as letting them know what they can expect. People will also feel more secure if they are clear on what to do if there is a technical issue. Is there a backup? How do they reach out for technical support? Should they be looking to their email, etc.?

The notion of safety continues to be a foundation of high performance. In his book, *Smarter Faster Better,* and the excerpt article entitled "What Google Learned in Its Quest to Build the Perfect Team,"[27] Duhigg notes that creating safety involves a couple of things. He writes, "After looking at over a hundred groups for more than a year, Project Aristotle researchers concluded that understanding and influencing group norms were the keys to improving Google's teams." Good teams also took equal turns in talking, and had awareness of their social impact. Duhigg also notes that a key factor of success for these teams was Amy Edmonston's notion of Psychological Safety, which she describes as a "shared belief held by members of a team that the team is safe for interpersonal risk-taking."[28]

One of the first things to consider in a virtual conversation is answering the question, "What creates safety in a virtual environment?" This includes:

- Clarity in terms of the purpose of the call, what the call is for, end results and what is expected of them (input, interaction, etc.).
- Co-creating shared **Group** or **Team Agreements** or **Ways of Working**—how are we going to operate together?
- Having a roadmap—knowing where you are going.
- Providing an opportunity for all group members to voice concerns.
- Connecting with others in a deeper way.
- Connecting with the facilitator or leader of the call.
- Using language and word choice and approaches that are appropriate for the conversation space.
- Using a platform that is appropriate for the context, and providing instructions on how to access it before the conversation if people are new to it.
- Providing materials that support the learner in moving forward (Job Aids, Discussion Guides).
- Connecting learning and conversations to those in the environment.

## CREATING CONNECTION—WAYS TO CREATE CONNECTION VIRTUALLY

In the virtual realm, creating connection is not only important during the call itself, but also in between calls through peer connection. Consider the platform you are using as well as what is feasible in connecting group or team members between the calls. Ongoing communication channels can range from central repositories which house materials people can access between calls at an IntraNet or Teachable site, to shared and private groups for communication like a Facebook group. It is important to select a platform that is specific, secure, and private to that group.

There are many different ways to build connection virtually;[29] through introductions, breakouts, visuals, and learning partners. Let's look at each one of these:

1. **Introductions** – Consider how you can make introductions a key part of creating connection. Whether you are in person or on the phone/web, consider how you can use introductions to make people feel more connected. What is it that each person brings to the conversation space? What is unique? In later chapters we go through instructions to a number of quick icebreakers that will bring people together. Is there any follow-up (i.e., photos and a paragraph about themselves) you would like people to share after the first session?

2. **Utilize breakouts** – Breakouts make a huge difference in getting people to connect in a larger group setting (even when the group may only be 4-8 people). Think about the last time you were in a face-to-face learning event. How much time was spent in lecture and how much in small group work? Historically, it was only conference calling services such as Maestro Conferencing that allowed you to do breakouts on the phone. Today free services such as FreeConferencing.com allow you to break into up to four separate groups. How might you leverage breakouts for connection?

3. **Bring in different approaches, for example, visuals** – I continue to get amazed at the impact of using visual tools such as Visual Explorer in my work. Several weeks ago, while I was delivering a conference presentation, I brought in Visual Explorer as a conversation sparker around collaboration. The change of energy in the room was instantaneous, which was a lot for 3:30pm! Using visual resources may allow certain participants to connect to the conversation in a different way.

4. **Leave enough time** – Creating connection takes time. A best

practice in any group coaching work is "Less is more." What might you need to let go of in terms of topics, activities, in order to provide the space for people to be in dialogue?

5. **Peer learning partners/buddies** – Creating peer partners (twos or threes) can also provide a significant way to keep the conversation flowing and boost connection between some group members. If you are concerned that these connections may create cliques, rotate the pairings. From my experience, I have found that people have enjoyed building connection with one or two other peers in the group, and that it has allowed them to go deeper in their own goals and plans. Also, it's always interesting to notice what connections people find, even if pairings are done randomly!

## BUILDING COMMUNITY

Part of our focus in virtual conversations is that we are building community. Building community in the virtual space involves creating a **shared sense of purpose** (*Why are we here?*), a **common identity,** along with other things such as **belongingness** (*Do I belong here?*), and **safety** (*Do I feel safe and that I can contribute and will be respected?*).

*What activities do you want to undertake in building community?*

Some examples of what virtual leaders do:

- Have a branded logo to represent the virtual meeting space, for example, having a logo made or designating that as the team's virtual meeting place.
- Take the time for people to explore common ground, as well as what they bring as unique, to the team.
- Create paired partners across the team who meet for support, brainstorming, etc.

## BUILDING TRUST IN A VIRTUAL WORLD

*"Mistrust begets mistrust. Trust begets accomplishment." – Lao Tzu*

Trust is an essential foundation for dialogue, and virtual conversationalists will be aware of the things that they do and don't do in boosting trust within their groups. In the virtual domain, our ability to build trust can be the difference between a one-way conversation and an engaged dialogue. While it can be perceived as being "risky" to speak out in the virtual realm, it can also be more liberating for others.

The Great Place to Work Institute notes, "Trust between managers and employees is the primary defining characteristic of the very best workplaces."[30] While virtual conversations can take place without a level of deep trust, they will tend to skim the surface and not get to the level of vulnerability, frankness, and honesty required in conversations like coaching. When relationships are important, or performance will be measured over the long term, creating trust is essential in any virtual dynamic.

There are a number of activities we can undertake which build trust and some that rapidly destroy trust. Take a look at the following table:

# BUILDING TRUST IN THE VIRTUAL DOMAIN

| TRUST BUILDERS | TRUST DESTROYERS |
| --- | --- |
| Walk the talk | Not setting people up for success |
| Be fair | Lack of follow-through or lack of follow-up |
| Provide clear communication | |
| Build on strengths | Lack of clarity in terms of communication/expectations |
| Take ownership for what works and what doesn't | Hearing at a later date that everything you shared on a virtual call was broadcast to others |
| Clarify expectations | |
| Connect people | Assuming that silence means everything is OK |
| Confidentiality—a safe space to connect | Not acting or responding to feedback given |
| Clarify process—let people know what they can expect | Saying you'll do something during the call and doing something different |
| Set people up for success with pre-work and follow-up | Not being clear on process |

**In building trust in the virtual domain we want to:**

- **Walk the talk.** Walking our talk is about modelling what we say we will do. For example, if we say that we are participatory, are the techniques we are using participatory?

- **Be fair.** Treat all with respect and all equally. Note that fairness is also about perceptions of fairness.

- **Provide clear communications.** Clarity in communication takes a number of forms. Are we communicating in language that is resonant for our groups? Are we checking for understanding? Are we using mediums that work for the group members?

- **Build on strengths.** From Gallup's research we know that strengths-based work boosts engagement, quality of life, and productivity.[31] Bringing an appreciative approach can open people up for learning, exploration, and connection.

- **Take ownership for what works and what doesn't.** Things are unlikely to work as planned in the virtual domain, and it is important to take ownership for what works and what doesn't rather than "blame it" on something or someone else.

- **Clarify expectations.** Creating shared expectations lays the foundation for success for all involved. We will be taking a more extensive look at this in a minute.

- **Connect group members.** It's imperative that people feel connected in order to engage. In your groups, notice where people are not feeling connected. What do they need to do in order to feel like they are connected with you? What grounding do they need? What follow-up do they need?

- **Respect confidentiality.** What is said on the line, should stay on the line. If you are recording virtual calls be sure to confirm how that information will be shared, as well as what will be done in future recordings. Let participants know how recordings will work so they can choose what level of information to share. Some groups may have agreements around not using real names or other identifiers.

- **Clarify process.** Part of creating safety, trust, and shared expectations is clarifying the process of things. Let people know what they can expect around process. This can include:

  - How long you will be meeting
  - What level of engagement and input is being requested
  - What pre-work is required
  - What follow-up is needed

We are now starting to see how trust is an essential ingredient for "opening up the conversation." As we will see from neuroscience to practical approaches, trust is a major foundation in this work.

Consider how you are building trust in the virtual conversations you are holding. What might be destroying trust as well? Take a few minutes to identify both trust builders and destroyers in your work.

Download the trust worksheet from EffectiveVirtualConversations.com.

# SETTING EVERYONE UP FOR SUCCESS—CREATING AN ENABLING ENVIRONMENT FOR LEARNERS

One of the central themes of this book is that effective and engaging virtual learning requires a number of ingredients and focusing on "setting everyone up for success." This includes:

- The facilitator who brings a range of tools and approaches for virtual conversations along the continuum—for learning and leadership.

- Engaging material.

- Using a platform that is appropriate.

- Cued-up learners who are primed, ready to engage, know why they are there, and are an active part of creating the conversation and/or learning space.

- Equipping your group members or peers with skills to have better conversations, including skills in questioning, listening, being curious rather than advising.

- Providing clear instructions. For example, if you are using breakouts, what are the questions people will be discussing? How much time will they have? Assigning roles within breakouts can be a useful strategy in keeping participants on point and on target. In addition to providing clear instructions, provide multiple ways to view instructions.

- Spending time focusing on creating shared expectations for the group.

- Assigning roles so that you may have a time-keeper, a note-taker and a facilitator. Get groups to figure this out, and when they may be working in the same groups for an extended period, ask them to consider how they want to shift the roles.

In addition to these factors, in every program we run we want to keep in mind which factors create a virtual environment that is conducive to learning. This could include thinking through the implications of sounds, time of day and connectivity. Get individual members to think about creating their own environment of learning in their space—noticing things like air temperature and lighting and if/when they take breaks and/or have snacks/drinks on hand.

## CREATING SHARED EXPECTATIONS

Given the range of virtual events that exist today, what are the expectations you as the facilitator have for things such as engagement, focus, interactivity, responsibility of the learning? What are the expectations of the group members? To create deep levels of conversation, co-creating, or coming up with shared expectations together is key to creating a safe and trusting environment.

Prior to the session, take some time and think about what your expectations are, and give people an opportunity to "prime" themselves before the call. As I write later in the book, tricky issues often emerge when expectations are not clarified or shared.

There are several activities we can undertake to create shared expectations in the virtual domain, including:

1. **Pre-calls** – Short pre-calls to each group member prior to a call can be an important way to connect with people and hear more about what they bring to the table and what they want to get out of the conversation. These can play a key role in ensuring people know what to expect and any preparation required prior to the first touch point.

2. **Needs assessment** – Knowing your group members and what

they want and expect is key. If pre-calls with each person are not possible, another form of needs assessment can be undertaken such as a short survey or poll (think Survey Monkey or Google Polls), or a questionnaire that is sent out to everyone which is sent to complete and return before the call.

3. **Designing group agreements** – What are the things that are going to help group members feel that they own the process? Ownership leads to engagement. Spending some time early on co-creating your agreements can also create a sense of safety and connectivity. Some common group agreements include:

   a. Starting and ending on time—very important in the virtual realm, especially with people potentially calling in at different times of the day

   b. Confidentiality—what happens with what you are discussing? What is okay and not okay for people to share?

   c. Expected roles during the call

   d. Clarity on your focus during your time together

   e. Asking for what you need

   f. Asking questions of each other rather than providing advice

4. **Creating a welcome email** – Outline what people can expect from your work together. This should include accessibility (how to join the call), any backup numbers, what participants should do if they have any questions.

5. **Developing a list of Frequently Asked Questions (FAQs)** – FAQs are often underutilized, but are an important resource for group members. Typical questions addressed in an FAQ might include:

   a. What is the program?

   b. What benefits are there from participating in the program?

   c. What will I learn during the program? (include curricula)

   d. What do I need to participate?

    e.   How much time will this take for me each week?

    f.   What's the structure?

    g.   What can I expect in terms of…?

    h.   When do I connect?

    i.   What follow-up will there be? (Are there post-calls, when, how will the structure work?)

    j.   What pre- and post-work will there be?

    k.   Who leads the calls?

    l.   What do I do if I can't access it?

    m.  Is this recorded? How do I access recordings?

    n.   What course materials are provided?

    o.   Anything else?

Take a few minutes to write up your FAQs. FAQs can be posted on your website and/or sent out in advance.

## BELIEF SYSTEMS VIRTUAL FACILITATORS HOLD

There are a number of beliefs leaders of virtual conversations can hold to enable a rich terrain of virtual dialogue. These include:

- Learning can be robust.
- There is value in peer-to-peer interaction.
- I need to trust my group, and lean into them for expertise and insights.
- Technology can be an issue so expect the unexpected.
- Individual learning is important as is group learning.
- There is a role for trainer, facilitators, and coach. I may be needing to wear multiple hats on one call.
- Reflective practices are important (pauses, pre-work).
- Learning is not just a one-off event but a series of learning experiences.

- Pre-work and post-work will help to prime learning and expand the conversation when we do get together.
- Keeping the end result in mind helps with choosing the right platform.
- Be practical—focus on what's needed as we go forward.

## CREATING AN ENABLING ENVIRONMENT FOR VIRTUAL CONVERSATIONS[32]

In addition to the Triad of Safety, Connection, and Trust, there are several enablers or things that help to add to the foundations of success for virtual events. Keep these in mind whether you are leading a virtual team meeting, a virtual training webinar or facilitating a virtual meeting for a team:

- **Being clear about the process and what people can expect.** What's the purpose of the session? What levels of engagement should people expect?
- **Being clear about the outcomes of the call.** What can people expect to leave with? In a training session this may be set by the virtual leader, but in a coaching conversation this may be co-created by asking *What do you want to leave with?*
- **Watching pace changes.** Keeping people focused in the virtual environment is key. You are probably competing with email and other tasks immediately at hand. Adjusting the pace by asking questions, getting people to reflect, verbalize or do something every few minutes turns a dull virtual event into an engaging one.
- **Connecting participants with the WIIFM early on.** WIIFM or *What's in it for me?* is a foundational principle of any engaging presentation. Helping people connect early on with how the topic relates to their work and why it is important creates an environment where people are not just passive acceptors of information.
- **Knowing the platform and being confident with it.** It is

important to be as well versed as possible with the technical side of things, for both the facilitator and participant. If people are not familiar with the platforms you are using, make sure you provide clear instructions. Do you want to send out a tutorial in advance, or provide tips along the way? When people are not as familiar with the technology you may need to adjust the amount and type of content covered, along with the types of instructions and activities you choose.

Consider what other things will help to make your virtual event a success.

## ASSUMPTIONS AROUND VIRTUAL CONVERSATIONS AND VIRTUAL LEARNING

One of the central tenets of critical education is to check your assumptions. Unspoken assumptions can be extremely detrimental in today's global conversation space. There are a few assumptions that are useful to explore as you undertake your work.

- It's just like working in person.
- It's going to be easy.
- Everyone is going to have the same needs.
- Everyone understands what I am saying.
- They will follow up. (Keeping things visible after the training is of critical importance for any facilitated conversation. As discussed in other chapters, the benefit of virtual training can be that people can apply things real-time during the call, or immediately thereafter.)
- They are not going to be tempted to multitask.
- It has to be big!
- You can't learn or connect without a face-to-face connection. (With the advent of Facetime, Skype, and other streaming

platforms we are able to create more closely mimic the in-person context.)

- People will not connect in the virtual space.
- Technology is going to be challenging.
- Death by Conference Call is the only way.
- I can wing it!

Note these statements and see if they are a belief and/or assumption you are leading from. How does that influence the way you are approaching your design and conversations? What are the assumptions you are making around virtual conversations? How are these helping or hindering your work?

## DERAILERS IN VIRTUAL FACILITATION

While we will explore more about tricky issues in Chapter 8, it can be important to consider some of the derailers that can surface within any virtual event—be it a team meeting, webinar, or virtual meeting space. Derailers have the potential to take the entire call off course, and include:

- **A lack of focus** – A strong hand on process plays a key role in great facilitation work, especially in the realm of virtual facilitation. Being clear on the end goal and outcomes, or ensuring you are asking to clarify what these are helps to mitigate this derailer.
- **Different people on different platforms** – Today's virtual meeting realities have blended platforms as a reality. Perhaps there are six people calling in by phone from a conference room in downtown Toronto, and some in Montreal. At the same time, you may have virtual callers on the web from other locations (even down the block!). When facilitating, be aware of what can and cannot be seen by each party. If you are facilitating from a "live" (which really should be called in-person) environment, be sure that you don't only pay attention to those in the room with you.

- **People feeling disconnected** – In instances where you have one or more people calling in from their own location, notice how connected they feel to the larger group. Engage them regularly verbally, and invite comments through chat, annotation, and other virtual features. Providing regular opportunities for smaller group work helps to boost interactivity.

- **Not having the right format for the right purpose** – A lot of professionals think that webinars are the only format available for virtual meetings today. Webinars, especially engaging ones, can be great for a training experience, but may lack the interactivity needed for learning complex skills, building teams, or running a focus group. Leveraging platforms such as Zoom can allow for all participants to see each other and interact. Breakouts also can mimic the traditional small group dialogue, which is so important for the learning and exploration of complex topics. Many facilitators and leaders hesitate to use breakouts due to past challenges using the technology, or concern they won't know what's going on in the breakout room. Trusting your group, the process, and platform is a critical factor.

- **Making it all about the facilitator** – Connecting people early on with their WIIFM (*What's important about me learning? What do I want to get out of the call?*) is critical. There is need to give up control along the way to open up the realm of engagement. That can mean giving group members the ability—and encouragement—to use markers, chat, questions and answers, etc.

- **Finally, the facilitator's *presence*** also has a significant impact on the tone and energy of the room. Consider the tone you want to create, and the pace and pitch you want to set the meeting at. Your voice tone is critical. Notice the energy that exists around the "virtual room." These skills of presence and listening are paramount in exceptional virtual facilitation.

*What derailers do you encounter in your virtual meetings? What's going to help mitigate against these or avoid them altogether?* [33]

## CONCLUSION

This chapter covered the foundations any virtual conversationalist can benefit from. From culture, to generational preferences, to considering how we build safety, connection, and trust, focusing on these elements will enhance any virtual conversation.

---

### END OF CHAPTER QUESTIONS

What are the key actions you are going to take based on what you learned from this chapter?

What do you want to learn more about, or consider as it relates to culture, styles, and the mix of groups and teams you work with?

What is going to hinder—or derail—the virtual conversation?

What is going to help—or enable—the virtual conversation?

Make a note of any action steps from this chapter in the Action Plan Tracker.

---

# CHAPTER 3

# WHAT EVERY CONVERSATION NEEDS: ESSENTIAL ELEMENTS AND CORE SKILLS

*"The most important work in the new economy
is creating conversations."[34]*

*– Alan Webber*

Whether you are leading a team-building session, a virtual meeting or a webinar, there are several core elements included in each virtual conversation, as well as skills virtual facilitators lead by. This chapter focuses on:

- What it means to have an effective virtual conversation
- The role of the virtual facilitator/conversationalist
- Core skills of masterful virtual facilitators/conversationalists

## EFFECTIVE VIRTUAL CONVERSATIONS

At this point, it may be useful to define what is meant by "Effective Virtual Conversations." Effective conversations incorporate:

- A **safe environment** where everyone is invited to contribute and all perspectives are valued
- A **purpose** to the conversation—it is not just to waste time but there is a shared end goal or results
- An **intent**—to gain awareness, to solve a problem, to explore alternative perspectives
- A **process** that will help the group move from point A to point B.

As you will note, there are processes outlined that are more peer-related and others that are more formalized (i.e., teacher to student, mentor to protégé, coach to client).

## THE REALM OF VIRTUAL TODAY

The realm of virtual conversations—what they look like, and how they take place—continues to mushroom. From virtual team meetings to virtual coaching calls to on-line, on-demand learning, virtual learning and conversation takes several forms, including mobile learning and digital conversation. There will be times when we work with groups, and other times we work with teams. Whatever the context, it is clear that the virtual realm is continuing to explode. So the skills and approaches outlined in this chapter are essential to any virtual conversation, regardless of the virtual modality. Even what it is called can vary—small business has a preference for digital, corporate prefers virtual or remote.

Creating engaging and effective virtual learning environments is an art form as well as a science. This chapter explores the question: *What do we need to bring to the table to create more interactive and engaging learning events, meetings, and team sessions?*

Here's a list of some of the top skills which help to make a virtual facilitator shine:

- Flexibility and adaptability (to navigate things that probably won't work the way you think they will).
- Process facilitation skills.
- Exceptional communication skills—being clear and concise, ability to adapt the message for different audiences.
- Listening skills—being able to listen for the nuances, energy, distinctions, and synergies in groups that are remote and often multi-cultural.
- Creating connection with group/team members virtually.
- Understanding different cultures.
- Being a great host—there's an important host function as a virtual facilitator in greeting people, making them feel comfortable and connected.
- Confidence and knowledge of your presence (and the ability to be a chameleon).
- Strong observational skills and ability to integrate multiple pieces of information.
- Technical skills with different platforms.

…and while it is not a skill, a robust toolkit!

## THE ROLE OF THE FACILITATOR

In leading virtual conversations, there are many types of dialogue, including some that take us into the realm of facilitation. As I often share, the word *"facilis"* comes from the Latin "to make easy." Our role as virtual facilitators and conversationalists is also to make things easy—easy for our groups and easy for ourselves. In some contexts, the work will be described as convening. Convent means to "assemble with others; to come together." Looking at our work as a virtual conversationalist, our role is both to bring people together, and to make it easy. In today's virtual space our conversations harness global voices, co-creating common ground. Whether or not we consider ourselves as facilitators, there is a facilitation element to the different types of virtual conversations leaders, coaches, mentors, and other professionals have.

How we develop as facilitators is covered in Chapter 12. For now, we will focus on a number of core skills every virtual conversationalist needs.

## SO WHAT IS FACILITATION?

Consider these two definitions of facilitation:

"The facilitator's job is to *support everyone to do their best thinking*. To do this, the facilitator encourages full participation, promotes mutual understanding, and cultivates shared responsibility."[35]

*Advanced Facilitation Strategies* author Ingrid Bens defines a facilitator as "one who contributes structure and process to interactions so groups are able to function effectively and make high-quality decisions."[36]

 **Content**

# WHAT

Topic/Subject
Goals
Agenda items
Task knowledge
Results, Goals, and Outcomes

 **Process**

# HOW

Methods/Procedures
Group Dynamics
Environment/climate
Flow/sequencing
Relationships

In her seminal book *Facilitating with Ease*, Bens (2002) makes a distinction about the two focus areas of any facilitator: *Content* and *Process* (figure adapted from Bens, 2002).[37]

In the Content realm, we are focused on *the What?* of a conversation. This includes things such as:

- What is the topic or subject of our conversations?
- What are the goals of the individuals on the call?
- What agenda items need to be covered?
- What is the content focus or task knowledge?
- What are the results, goals, and outcomes required by the facilitated session?

The Process side of facilitation looks at *How* the conversation is achieved.

This includes things such as:

- What are the methods, tools, and procedures you are going to use to set agendas and come to agreement?
- How do group dynamics flow?
- What is the environment or climate you want to create?
- What sequencing or flow is going to work best?
- What are the key relationships you and group members need to create?

Depending on our role, sometimes we are more focused on the process—the *How* of the conversation. Sometimes we may ask the group to supply the content, for example, when working as a third-party facilitator. In other instances, we may be both a process and a content expert, such as when we are a virtual team leader. Being clear on which hat(s) you are wearing is crucial in the work that you do.

A nuance in the virtual realm is focusing on the *How* (Process) and making sure that each person is heard and involved in the conversation.

## AM I WORKING WITH A GROUP OR A TEAM?

One of the most common questions raised today is, "Is this a group or a team?" Understanding the difference can help us select the solutions or processes that are going to work best.

Some important distinctions between a group and a team are:

- **Teams have a history and a web of ongoing relationships**. This history and set of relationships infuse the conversation. As a virtual facilitator, you may not be aware of the past alliances and conflicts. It requires that you use your intuition more, and watch for becoming part of a political power play in a team.

- **What's at stake in the conversation?** For a team, their livelihood is at stake, especially when we ask them to speak about challenges and stretch points.

- **The lifecycle of the grouping** is significant. As I wrote in *From One to Many*, "Some groups undertaking a group coaching process may come together for a short period of time, disbanding at the end of the coaching engagement. In contrast, team coaching builds the capacity of the team. The team exists before and after the coaching engagement."[38] Our role as a conversationalist is impacted based on whether the grouping continues after our involvement. How we facilitate and support conversations about next steps will vary depending on whether we are working with a group or a team.

- **What is the role of leadership**? If leaders are not engaged in the process and have not "bought in" to being the steward of the process, then the sustainability of change and impact may be minimized.

- **Teams have established (and often entrenched) roles,** which is not usually the case in a group. This can make it easy for people to get boxed into one role, for example, the person who raises issues is always seen as a complainer.

Consider what the grouping is that you are working with—is it a group or is it a team? This will have an impact on the lens that you are working with. In a team, it is often the collective; whereas, with the group, we usually work to build capacity with each individual member.

# CORE SKILLS OF EXCEPTIONAL VIRTUAL FACILITATORS AND CONVERSATIONALISTS

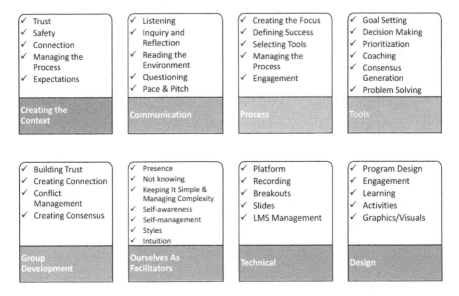

**Core Skills for Exceptional Virtual Facilitators**

In creating and leading effective virtual conversations, there are skills along eight different areas including:

1. **Creating the Context:** Building Trust and Creating Safety, Building Relationships or Connections, Focusing on Process, and Co-creating Expectations

2. **Communication Skills**: Listening, Inquiry, and Reflection, Reading the Environment, Questioning, Pace and Pitch, Clarity

3. **Process Skills:** Creating the Focus, Defining Success, Selecting Tools, Hosting, Engagement

4. **Tools for Conversations**: Goal Setting, Decision Making, Prioritization, Coaching, Consensus Generation, Problem Solving. (Many of these are addressed in Chapter 7 – Building Your Toolkit)

5. **Group Development:** Building Trust, Creating Connection,

Dealing with Conflict, Creating Consensus

6. **Ourselves as the Facilitator/Leader:** Presence, Self-awareness, Self-management and Partnering, Keeping it Simple and Managing Complexity, Noticing our own Biases

7. **Technical Skills:** Mastering the Platform, Recordings, Slides, LMS Management

8. **Design Skills:** Program Design, Engagement, Learning, Activities, PDFs, Graphics/Visuals

Excellent virtual learning hosts require bench strength in these eight areas whether we are training, leading a virtual meeting, or coaching. Let us take a look at these eight areas:

## CREATING THE CONTEXT FOR A GREAT CONVERSATION

The first set of skills we need as great virtual conversations is creating the context. In the host function, we want to create the space for: trust, safety, connection, process, and expectations.

- ✓ Trust
- ✓ Safety
- ✓ Connection
- ✓ Managing the Process
- ✓ Expectations

**Creating the Context**

This involves many of the skills we explored earlier in the last chapter—Building Trust, Creating Safety, Building Relationships (or Creating Connection), and Clarifying Expectations. We have already covered a number of strategies for building the Triad of Safety, Connection, and Trust.

A final set of skills reside in this category of clarifying process. Being more explicit and planned with process (how long things will take, what the sequence is, how you will transition from point a to b) is more important in the virtual conversation and learning space.

## COMMUNICATION SKILLS

| |
|---|
| ✓ Listening |
| ✓ Inquiry and Reflection |
| ✓ Reading the Environment |
| ✓ Questioning |
| ✓ Pace & Pitch |
| **Communication** |

Communication skills are at the heart of masterful virtual conversations. These include the skill sets of *listening* and *questioning*. There are also a sub-set of skills such as bottom lining, articulating/mirroring back/paraphrasing, providing a space for inquiry and reflection, reading the environment and intruding.

### LISTENING

85% of what we know we learn through listening, 45% of workdays are spent listening, yet humans only listen at a 25% comprehension rate. Only 2% of working professionals have taken formal training in listening.[39]

In virtual environments, listening is critical. We want to be listening for the speech patterns, but also what is being said and not being said. Notice the flow of conversation, who is dominating and who is holding back. Listening to the pace and pitch of the conversation is also an important factor. Listening in the virtual realm means that tone, pace, and pitch take on new meanings. This is overlaid as well by nuances including second languages being at play and geographic culture.

It can be important to go back to the basics with listening, including a reminder of where messaging comes from. Approximately 55% of the message of a conversation comes from body language.[40] This is where use of virtual platforms like Zoom, which offer virtual streaming, allow group members to see each other and note body language. When these visual cues are absent (as in phone-only conversations) we need to rely solely on listening for pace and pitch. When we turn to chat or text-only conversations, we lose pace and pitch as well. Words become the only way to understand what is being said.

*What are you listening for?* It can be very important to check the lens through which we are listening. Are we deeply listening for what the other person is saying, or are we listening to formulate our response. When we are thinking of what we are going to say or how we are going to respond, we lose sight of what is important for the other person, and may miss what is really being said.

## PRIMING PEOPLE FOR LISTENING

Because not everyone's skills in listening are developed for the virtual world, it can be useful to support some skill development with your group members. One activity I like to undertake is helping "prime" people for listening. If I am going to have a coaching conversation with one group member in front of the others, I will invite those people who are observing the conversation to be an "active listener" rather than a passive listener. In priming these observers, I encourage them to listen to the coaching conversation (and take notes for themselves) on three levels:

1. Listen to the questions that I am asking.

2. Listen to the impact of my questions on the other person.

3. Listen to what is important for you—what's the impact of the question for you?

Consider how you might incorporate this, and ask your group members after trying it what they find "interesting" or "important" about that process for them. Use breakouts and smaller groups to get feedback.

## CLARITY AND CONCISENESS OF COMMUNICATION—BOTTOM LINING/LASER SPEAK

As mentioned in other chapters, creating connection through word choice and language is very important. One core coaching skill I introduce in most virtual groups I work with is called "laser speak" or "bottom lining." Given the limited amount of time available in virtual calls, it can be important to let people on a call know how much time they have to present ideas or be in discussion. Bottom lining encourages people to get to the core of the message. This can be an invaluable skill when a multitude of group members are verbose. By reminding all group members of the skill, everyone can become more proficient in staying focused and being brief with their comments.

## ARTICULATION/MIRRORING BACK/PARAPHRASING

This set of skills has the virtual facilitator mirror back or re-summarize the comments that have been made. Many facilitators are taught to use the skill of paraphrasing to summarize what they have heard. In re-articulating or mirroring back in the virtual environment, it can be important to use the language of the speaker verbatim, in terms of reflecting back exactly what you heard.

## READING THE ENVIRONMENT

Even though you may not be physically present in a room, great virtual conversationalists—leaders and facilitators—are able to deftly read the environment. While the environment may not be "visible," much is said through the way people are speaking; their pace and how fast they are speaking and the pitch or level at which they speak. Part of reading the environment is also noticing the overall energy of the call. I think we can all recollect times when meeting energy was very low (Death by Conference Call) or when meeting energy was very high.

Next time you are in a virtual meeting, think about how you would describe the energy of the call.

As a conceptual framework it can be useful to keep in mind the framework outlined by Kimsey-House et al in their book, *Coactive Coaching*.[41] The authors make this distinction between listening at three different levels. They include:

- Level 1 listening – Listening to ourselves.
- Level 2 listening – Listening to the person we are talking to. *What do you notice about pace and pitch? Word choice? What is being said and what is not? What is aligned with tone or body language? What is not?*
- Level 3 listening – Listening for the global, or macro level. *What is the energetic arena in which we are holding the dialogue?*

Like coaching, in virtual conversations we want to be listening deeply to the person we are talking to, as well as practicing Level 3 listening, listening at the global level of the conversation.

## THE SKILL OF INTRUDING

Process skills are important in keeping the flow of a group conversation moving—including the skill of intruding, which can be very useful in managing process and flow. In virtual work, there can be a dichotomy that we need to interrupt to support flow of conversation. In a virtual environment where there are no visual cues these interruptions can feel uncomfortable, like the person cutting in doesn't value what the other person has to say. It is important to create shared agreements around what people can expect with interruptions and why they are made. A better practice can be to ensure that people know how much time they have to speak, and set a chime to alert them when their time is up.

## SKILLS OF INQUIRY AND REFLECTION

A downside of current virtual and digital learning is that we don't often take time to pause or go deeper into dialogue. When we fail to do this, we lose the opportunity for individuals to explore the rich terrain of assumptions, beliefs, and other areas.

In *The Fifth Discipline Fieldbook,* Senge et al write, "Two types of skill are central to this work: they are reflection (slowing down our thinking processes to become more aware of how we form our mental models) and inquiry (holding conversations where we openly share views and develop knowledge about each others' assumptions." The authors continue, "The value of these skills is perhaps most apparent in their absence. Individuals who are undisciplined in reflective thinking have difficulty hearing what others actually say. Instead, they hear what they expect others to say. They have little tolerance for multiple interpretations of events because they often 'see' only their own interpretation. In teams and groups, people who have not mastered a threshold level of inquiry skills will spend hours arguing their skills."[42]

For extended work in the virtual space, supporting our team members to develop skills in the areas of inquiry and the art of reflection is critical. If we don't help them develop these skills, they will continue to hear what they expect to hear, rather than what really is going on in the conversation.

### *Practitioner's Tip: Silence* [43]

How much silence do you include in your virtual work? Is there any silence at all?

Many virtual facilitators shy away from providing silence and pause points during their virtual programming. Consider the impact and value of silence in in-person programming. Chances are as you think about it you might consider the real value introverts and those that need a little more time for processing find when silence is given. Why not consider incorporating a little more silence in your virtual programs? This could include:

- A pause point at the start of the call for people to get grounded, or to capture their ideas in a worksheet/online notes.

- A pause point at the middle of the call for people to note what they have learned so far.

- Pause points throughout, or at the end of major sections, when they can capture their learning in a One-Page Plan or a one-page sheet that they will take forward within their work.

- A pause point at the end for people to take notes on their learning.

- A pause point, or 30 to 60 seconds of silence, before you ask someone to speak.

- A pause point at any time for people to notice what their breathing is like (fast, slow, rushed). There is increasing research about the benefit of incorporating more mindfulness training in our work with professionals of all kinds. This does not need to take a lot of time, and may simply involve introducing your virtual group members to pause points to notice their thoughts or what their bodies are saying throughout your virtual calls.

*What pause points do you want to provide during your virtual learning process?*

As you can see, communication is a critical skill set of effective virtual conversationalists. Four core skills Issacs identifies as essential in dialogue are, *Listening, Respecting, Suspending,* and *Voicing*.

Isaacs defines Voicing as "What needs to be expressed now?"[44] This is a very powerful question to ask the groups and teams you are working with, particularly if they are not naturally accustomed to creating pause points and speaking intentionally. There is often a "voice of the system" representing the entire team, or many times "a voice" that represents what wants to be articulated.

Issacs defines Suspension as "To suspend is to change direction, to stop, step back, see things with new eyes. This is perhaps one of the deepest challenges human beings face."[45] He continues, "The absence of suspension…is certainty." What are you doing to create a moment, or moments, for suspension? How are you giving people a pause to see things with new eyes?

*Question to consider: In close-off to listening, take note of your skills. Where are your strengths? What needs attention?*

## QUESTIONING

**"Questions form the backbone to any coaching conversation."**
**– Jennifer Britton**

In the virtual realm, questions play an equally important role. Our questions open the space for exploration or focus, action or awareness, insights or application. In addition:

- Questions help us gain clarity.
- Powerful questions create a pause.
- Questions help us explore assumptions.
- Questions prompt discovery, action, and awareness.
- Questions surface belief systems (empowering and hindering).
- Questions open up options and possibilities.

John Maxwell notes that questions can take a number of forms. In his book *Good Leaders Ask Great Questions*, he writes, "Good leaders ask great questions that inspire others to dream more, think more, learn more, do more and become more."[46]

Here are a couple of things to note as you consider the use of questions in your work.

## QUESTIONS, WORDS, AND VOICE

Our voice is one of our greatest tools as a facilitator. In using your voice, you will want to look at how your voice projects as well as the intonation. Do sound checks regularly to see how your voice is coming through, and/or review past recordings to see what you really sound like. Are you coming through clearly? Are you noticing breathing? Take some time to really notice the tone of your voice. Does it sound like you intend it to sound? Is the intonation right?

## QUESTIONING FRAMEWORKS

The development of a facilitator's question toolkit is a significant focus of any facilitation training process. There are a couple of foundational things to keep in mind around questions:

- Keep questions open-ended. Asking closed-ended questions such as *Who learned something today?* leads to a simple yes, no response. Rephrasing the question as *What did you learn today?* can lead to a more generative statement.
- As Issacs writes, "An estimated forty percent of all questions that people utter are really statements in disguise. Another forty percent are really judgements in disguise: *Do you really think she deserved that raise?* Only a small percentage of "inquiries" are genuine questions. Real questions are often notable for the silence that follows their utterance. People may not know the answer! In fact, it becomes that finding an answer too quickly is not necessarily a wise goal."[47]

In supporting thousands of leaders and team members of all stripes to have better conversations, I've reminded people that in order to be available to conversations we need to go back to the basics around listening. When we are struggling to think about what is the question we next want to ask, we are no longer listening to what the person is saying, rather we are thinking about what we are going to ask next.

There is an art form in learning to ask better questions and trust that the right one will emerge at the right time. One of the easiest questioning frameworks to remember is the *Five Ws and an H*. Here are some examples of questions you can ask during the course of a virtual meeting, or conversations that you may want to consider including in your own work:

| | QUESTIONS TO ASK | AS IT RELATES TO VIRTUAL MEETINGS |
| --- | --- | --- |
| WHAT? | What is this all about?<br><br>What is the purpose?<br><br>What is our focus?<br><br>What is our process?<br><br>What can you expect?<br><br>What will success look like at the end of the call?<br><br>What end results are we looking for?<br><br>What's the one thing we want to leave this meeting with/having explored? | *What* questions help to frame and create process and end results. |

| | QUESTIONS TO ASK | AS IT RELATES TO VIRTUAL MEETINGS |
|---|---|---|
| WHY? | Why is this important? Or, what is important about this?<br><br>Why are you doing this?<br><br>What might get in the way?<br><br>How is this connected to our bigger *Why*? | Note that when ***Why*** questions are asked they can naturally put people on the defense. When trust levels are low it is best to avoid ***Why*** questions as they may inflame the conversation. Notice here how ***Why*** questions are reframed as ***What*** questions. |
| HOW? | Where do I start?<br><br>What is the next step?<br><br>What might get in the way?<br><br>What resources are required?<br><br>What has worked well in the past?<br><br>What will success look like?<br><br>How will I know you are being successful?<br><br>What check-ins do we need?<br><br>What are the major milestones? | ***How*** questions are usually process related. It can be important to get "granular" around the ***How*** of conversations in the virtual realm. Note that ***How*** and process questions do not always need to start with "How."<br><br>Process questions help to clarify next steps, opportunities and derailers. |

|  | QUESTIONS TO ASK | AS IT RELATES TO VIRTUAL MEETINGS |
|---|---|---|
| WHO? | Who can help with this?<br><br>What can they offer?<br><br>What relationships are important to consider?<br><br>What authority or responsibility is needed to make decisions? | Asking ourselves the *Who* questions even in preparation for virtual calls can be significant. In preparation for your virtual work you may be asking yourself:<br><br>Who needs to be on the call?<br><br>What platform is going to work best for each participant?<br><br>Who can provide resources or information to help this call? |
| WHERE? | Where does this need to be visible?<br><br>Where do people go to get the resources they need?<br><br>How are we going to meet? What's the best platform?<br><br>What is the communication channel that will allow us to provide feedback? Input? Changes? | Even in the virtual realm, we need to think about *Where*. Designing repositories for information, considering how and where people connect and share information, are all critical questions to explore. |

| | QUESTIONS TO ASK | AS IT RELATES TO VIRTUAL MEETINGS |
|---|---|---|
| WHEN? | What are the major milestones?<br><br>Who will complete what? By when?<br><br>How will we all know?<br><br>When will there be follow-up? | Be sure to leave the conversation with clarity around **When** and **What** will be the next steps! |

## WATCH YOUR LANGUAGE!

Our language has even greater impact in the virtual realm, especially when the context lacks any visual cues. Avoid words such as *but* and *should*. As we noted earlier, the realm of the *should* takes us into the NEA, shutting down the brain.

Try instead, "I'd like to invite you to…"

Another tweak is to replace *buts* with *ands*. *Buts* automatically negate what you said before. Consider this statement: "You did a great job, *but*…" versus "You did a great job, *and* here's what I'd like you to try next time."

As a facilitator, using the language of the group or team you are working with builds trust and confidence in their abilities. Use the skill of mirroring back where you can, and when feasible, use the language verbatim (word-for-word exactly as you heard). While facilitators over the years have been encouraged to paraphrase, in the cross-cultural context it can be very useful to use people's exact words, given the different connotations words can have globally.

You may also want to clarify that the words hold the same meaning for everyone, especially if the group is very diverse. Coming to a group or team definition for some terms may be appropriate and useful. Ask for clarification, or ask people to elaborate if terms are unique.

# PROCESS SKILLS

✓ Creating the Focus
✓ Defining Success
✓ Selecting Tools
✓ Managing the Process
✓ Engagement

**Process**

Our third "bucket" of virtual facilitation skills includes a focus on Process. A strong focus on process is required in the virtual domain. In the process category, there are five core skills:

- Co-creating the focus
- Defining success
- Selecting tools
- Managing the process
- Engagement

## CO-CREATING THE FOCUS

Edgar Schein wrote, "To the extent we need to coordinate our actions and establish common understanding of what we are trying to accomplish, some form of dialogue must be used if we are to make any progress at all."[48]

In the virtual realm, engagement is created when we co-create the agenda together. As Schein noted, coordination and common understanding are essential. Whether the focus is created before we get on the phone, or in the first few minutes, creating the focus is a key part of virtual meeting success. For longer programs, consider how dotmocracy can be used to ensure a collaborative voice. Dotmocracy is further described in Chapter 7.

## DEFINING SUCCESS

Being clear on the end result of the conversation—what it is and what it looks like—sets the foundation for the call. Is the purpose of this call to expand ideas or make a decision? Success looks different for expansion than decision making. Is success of the meeting being defined by the group? If so, leave time. If success measures are already laid out, note these and remind people of what has been defined already to keep the call moving.

## SELECTING TOOLS

Masterful virtual facilitators have a wide variety of tools at their disposal. Refer to Chapter 7, The Facilitator's Toolkit, and also Chapter 11, which is dedicated to expanding your toolbox in virtual team development.

## MANAGING THE PROCESS

In virtual facilitation, a strong hand on process can go far. Given that we often don't have the same cues as we do in the face-to-face environment, it is important for the leader or facilitator to take a strong hand with process—things such as time allocated, agenda items, start and end times, clarifying decisions and determining where you are going to next.

## ENGAGEMENT

Virtual Meetings can feel never-ending. It's important to engage people throughout the call. Design with the group what engagement can look like (for example, an expectation that you will hear from everyone). The topic of engagement as it relates to this work is covered in Chapter 7.

### *Practitioner's Tip: Interactivity and Pace*

The key to creating engaging and interactive virtual event is pace and interactivity. To avoid the Death by Conference Call mode, consider how you can adjust pacing for maximum interactivity.

Different ways to change pace include:

- Asking a question.

- Getting people to annotate using pens, markers.

- Asking people to comment in the chat box.

- Creating breakout groups. Just like in-person events, many services allow you to use breakout groups. Whether you pair people automatically or manually, these can provide for a deeper level of conversation. Consider what opportunities you can leverage with breakouts and how much time is needed for people to have a good discussion. It can take people several minutes to set themselves up as they arrive in their virtual domain.

- Creating a pause where you invite people to take notes or complete an activity in silence.

- Introducing a different media—i.e., showing a video you have created, or introducing a cartoon.

While pace changes are generally recommended every 7-10 minutes in the in-person realm (Britton, 2009 and 2013), in the virtual realm we may be introducing pace change more frequently to boost engagement and focus. Some authors recommend switching pace every 2-3 minutes. Notice what is an appropriate pace change in your context.

*What approaches do you want to use to introduce different pace changes?*

## TOOLS FOR CONVERSATIONS

The fourth area of skill development for facilitators is around tools. Different conversations have different focus areas leading to the need for a variety of distinct tools and processes for virtual facilitation. Some of the most common ones are:

- Goal Setting

- Decision Making
- Prioritization
- Coaching
- Consensus Generation
- Problem Solving

| ✓ Goal Setting |
| ✓ Decision Making |
| ✓ Prioritization |
| ✓ Coaching |
| ✓ Consensus Generation |
| ✓ Problem Solving |
| Tools |

In this chapter, we are going to zoom into goal setting. Refer to Chapter 7 - Building Your Toolkit for tool suggestions around decision making, prioritization, and consensus generation. Coaching is a skill set on its own and is covered throughout the book.

WORKING WITH GOALS:

Goals are a foundational part of any virtual conversation space and virtual learning process. As coaches, supporting each group member's goals may be the heart of the call, shaping the focus. If you are facilitating a team virtually, helping them articulate their goals may be the focus. In training, goals may take the form of what you are going to do next.

In working with goals virtually, it is important to note that it is likely that each person will have their own goal framework, given that they are remote and in different geographic locations. Practically, this may mean that they have different priorities and different ways to measure and be accountable towards goals.

We are often working on goals on multiple levels including:

- **Length of time** – Goals can be short-term, medium-term, or long-term. What are the timeframes for each one of these categories? Check your assumptions, as short-term could mean over the next week in one context, and over the next year in another.

- **Different levels** – Are we looking at the goal from a strategic, tactical, or operational level?
- **30,000 foot view vs. in the weeds** – What is the lens through which we approach a goal? Are we looking at it from the macro, or what is often called the meta level? From the airplane view or mountain top? Or are we looking at it from the weeds? What value is there in these different perspectives?
- **What is a stretch goal?** What is the goal that is going to help move people forward?

## GOALS AT DIFFERENT ORGANIZATIONAL LEVELS

In organizations today we may find that we are working across goals at three levels—individual goals, team goals, and the more macro-goals of KPIs (Key Performance Indicators) and/or organizational goals.

- **Individual goals** – At the individual goal level we may be hosting calls bringing together a group of individuals from different parts of the world, such as facilitating a planning session for a group of small business owners.
- **Team goals** – When working with teams, virtual facilitators may be facilitating a planning session for a virtual team that is exploring their annual and quarterly plans. At this level, planning and goal setting may have more of a collective lens.
- **Organizational goals** – Sometimes we also wind up connecting with organizational goals, helping individuals, teams and divisions roll up their KPIs to the macro organizational context.

What is the level at which you are exploring goals? How can you remind people to connect their goals to the relevant goal levels?

## DIFFERENT GOAL FRAMEWORKS

There are a variety of goal setting frameworks, some more well-known than others, including the SMART, PURE, and SAFE goal frameworks.

One of the best-known goal setting frameworks is the SMART goal framework, which I often rename the SMART-E goal framework.

**S – Specific:** What specifically do you want to achieve? What will it look like?

**M – Measurable:** How can you track progress?

**A – Achievable:** With some stretch are these achievable?

**R – Realistic:** Again, with stretch are these in range?

**T – Timebound:** What's the timeframe on this - next week, end of June, early next year?

**E** – And most of all, are these goals **Exciting**? If they are not exciting, chances are they might not get done, or may get done only to get them checked off.

Given that some organizational contexts have become fatigued with SMART goals, you may also want to refer to other goal frameworks such as those mentioned by John Whitmore [49] (1992, 2009), CLEAR goals and PURE goals. CLEAR Goals are: Challenging, Legal, Environmentally sound, Achievable, Recorded. PURE goals are Positively stated, Understood, Relevant, and Ethical.

## MAKING GOALS VISUAL

Making goals not *specific and* also visual is a key part of the virtual facilitation experience. One of the frameworks I often share with groups and teams I work with is **The One-Page Plan.**

As a leader, I worked in contexts where the annual plan for my team was 30 pages long, so the act of providing focus in bite-sized chunks was essential in translating our annual plans for each geographic context. The One-Page Plan is an iteration of this—a one-page overview of the top five goals for the next timeframe (i.e., month or quarter).

You can download a One-Page Template at <u>effectivevirtualconversations. com</u>. You will note a section that asks you to consider what are the enablers and derailers of the goal—for what might get in the way (derail) or help (enable) the goal achievement.

## WHERE VIRTUAL TEAM MEMBERS MAY STRUGGLE AROUND GOALS

Some of the common goal pitfalls can include:

- Not being specific enough. One of the benefits of using the SMART-E framework is that it allows us to get granular on specificity. *Rather than just growing sales, I know that I am going to grow sales by 50% in the first quarter.*
- Not setting milestones. Without a milestone, the goal can become too fluid. *Knowing that I am aiming to increase sales in the first quarter, I have an end milestone to work towards and can set short-term check points in getting there.*
- Not thinking about what's needed in order to be successful. Consider the resources required—human, financial, material, other. *What is going to be needed to achieve this goal?*
- Not keeping goals visible. The beauty of a One-Page Plan is that it keeps goals front and center. When we are not regularly referring to our goals, they get out of focus.
- Failing to make goals iterative. A final trap we can find around goals is not making our goals living and breathing. One of the reasons I like the concept of the One-Page Plan is that it allows us to check goals off, put new ones on the list, and see progress. Goals should be living and breathing entities.

## *Practitioner's Tip: 3 Tools to Work with Goals and Problem Solving*

Having a wide variety of problem-solving tools is important for team leaders today. In solving, or even addressing (because sometimes we aren't able to fully solve), today's complex and ever-changing business problems, having a solid grasp of the situation is critical. Having a number of tools in your back pocket is always useful and they do not need to be overly complicated. In this section, I am covering three tools you may find useful to have in your back pocket around goals and problem solving.

### Tool #1 – The Five *W*s and an *H*

In order to get more granular around goals or make a better decision, it can be useful to explore this through the lens of these six questions: *What? Why? When? Where? Who?* and *How?* How can exploring them support a better decision for the team?

### Tool #2 – The Fishbone

One of my favorite visual problem-solving tools is the Fishbone Diagram. Emerging originally from Japan and Toyota, also known as the Ishiwaka Diagram, the Fishbone helps us unpack an issue and explore it from multiple perspectives of People, Process, Materials, Environment, Equipment, etc. This is a very visual tool which stimulates dialogue and sharing across group members.

Take, for example, a challenge of slow customer service response. The Fishbone can be used to identify and explore the different causal factors that may be at the root of this issue. This can therefore help with problem solving and more effective goal setting.

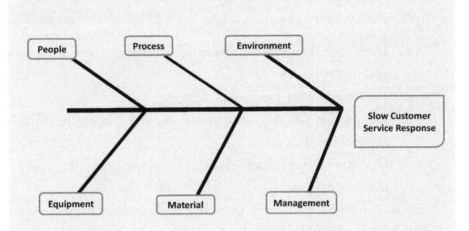

In using this as a tool in a virtual conversation, you could place the fishbone diagram with labels on the virtual whiteboard and have people annotate what they saw as factors contributing to the problem. You could also break the group into smaller pairings and have them generate a more extensive list bringing it back to the larger group. Fishbone activities can run for 10 minutes to several hours depending on the focus and context.

**Tool #3 – The SOAR**

Tools like Strategic Issues Mapping, the SWOT, or SOAR, can also be used in supporting goal setting and better decisions, not only for strategic planning.

The SOAR comes from the realm of Appreciative Inquiry (AI) and reframes the well-known strategic planning tool of the SWOT, which explores Strengths, Weaknesses, Opportunities and Threats. In AI, the SWOT becomes SOAR, encouraging individuals, groups or teams to look at the Strengths, Opportunities, Aspirations and Results.

AI is grounded in the 4-D Cycle of Processes, most commonly attributed to Cooperrider and others. The 4-D model consists of:[50]

1. Discovery: Identify moments of excellence, core values, and best practices
2. Dream: Envision positive possibilities
3. Design: Create structures, processes, and relationships to support the dream
4. Destiny: Develop an effective, inspirational plan for implementation

Refer to Chapter 7 for more planning tools including Strategic Issues Mapping and the SWOT.

## Learning Tip: Retention and Reinforcement

In any learning environment retention and reinforcement is critical. I would say that is especially true in the virtual domain, especially as learners are often doing this in isolation. To boost retention in your work, consider these items:

- **Consider reinforcing key themes several times.** We learn through repetition, and it can be useful to aim to reinforce key messages and themes three times. This could be done once by you (#1), then you could have group members recap after break (#2), and then, before the end of the day, have everyone share the one theme they are taking away (#3). Another favorite end-of-day/session activity is to get groups (usually smaller breakouts) to highlight their top 10 ideas or tools from the session, sharing them with the group. You can get people to use a whiteboard to capture these tools, or have people create a PowerPoint and share it.

- **Accountability and repetition supports reinforcement.** Ask the group, "Who will you share this with?" Enlist supervisors to support learning done virtually, or mentors who can share their experiences as well.

- **Immediate application.** Ask "What's the one opportunity in the next 24 hours for you to share this with someone else or apply it in your work?"

## GROUP DEVELOPMENT

✓ Building Trust
✓ Creating Connection
✓ Conflict Management
✓ Creating Consensus

**Group Development**

Our fifth area of focus is group development. Under the group development umbrella, we have core skills including:

- Building Trust
- Creating Connection
- Conflict Management
- Creating Consensus

Masterful virtual conversationalists are well aware of key group development processes including building trust, creating connection, dealing with conflict, and creating consensus. As highlighted earlier in this chapter, trust and connection are essential for creating a "safe" space for conversations. It may also be useful to refer to the stages of group development outlined in Chapter 2, along with the Triad of Safety, Connection, and Trust.

Chapter 8 addresses dealing with conflict. Given the diversity of people and perspectives on calls, conflict can be a real possibility. Equipping leaders and team members with different tools and resources for working across differences and working through conflict can be invaluable. It can also be valuable to provide some training or an assessment like the

TKI for helping people understand their natural approach to conflict, especially when they are under stress and pressure.

Tools for creating consensus are also important. Making sure you are leaving calls with a decision made, or having input is critical.

The 2016 Virtual Team work study[51] from RW3 found that the key characteristics for "good virtual teammates" remained relatively unchanged from their 2014 study. Characteristics that were identified by survey participants as what made "good virtual teammates" included:

- Being collaborative (19%)
- Willingness to share information (19%)
- Being proactively engaged (18%)
- Being organized (15%)
- Providing useful feedback (11%)
- Having good social skills (10%)
- Offering assistance to teammates (8%)

Chapter 11 explores how we can support team and group development more in-depth.

## OURSELVES AS THE FACILITATOR/LEADER

Our sixth area of development as a virtual facilitator is knowing ourselves. Under the umbrella of knowing ourselves, we find a variety of skills which need to be well defined in the virtual domain. These include:

- Presence
- Being comfortable with not knowing
- Keeping it simple and managing complexity

| |
|---|
| ✓ Presence |
| ✓ Not knowing |
| ✓ Keeping It Simple & Managing Complexity |
| ✓ Self-awareness |
| ✓ Self-management |
| ✓ Styles |
| ✓ Intuition |
| **Ourselves As Facilitators** |

- Self-awareness
- Self-management
- Styles
- Intuition

## PRESENCE

According to Amy Cuddy, presence is "knowing who you are and being able to access that when you most need to."[52] Our presence is how we show up in a virtual conversation. It's not just about how we speak, or words we choose, but also the deeper level of who we are choosing to be in a conversation. Masterful virtual facilitators bring a range in their presence. They are able to travel with groups to the highs and lows of work and the world.

It can be useful to poll our group members as to how we show up in our calls. What are the three adjectives they would use to describe your presence?

## COMPLEXITY AND BEING COMFORTABLE WITH NOT KNOWING

*"We do complicated for a living." – NANOWRIMO 2016 Sprint*

Being comfortable with not knowing is a key skill for the virtual facilitator. Edgar Schein talked about the ability to "access your ignorance." Sometimes we are facilitating groups who have content knowledge we know nothing about. Other times we may not really know what others are thinking or feeling (particularly in a phone-only context) and we need to lean into our intuition.

Part of being comfortable with not knowing is keeping things simple. In virtual learning, "we do complicated for a living" is part of the context in which we operate. There may be several different areas in which things are less than simple and there are several layers of complexities. These include:

- **Cultural complexity** – In the virtual realm it is likely that we are working with multiple levels of cultural complexity, often more than in other contexts.

- **Group level complexity** – For more on this, refer to the information on how groups form and the Tuckman model. While some may think this is not relevant in the virtual domain, it is!

- **Complexity due to lack of visual cues** – The lack of visual cues can make it much harder for facilitators to "really know what is going on."

- **Complexity due to the ingrained nature of the Death by Conference Call mentality** – We may be competing against ingrained habits. Habits are often dopamine related, and when things feel good—like getting two things done at once—it's harder to unwire this.

- **Complexity due to the different platforms we operate in** – There are technical complexities that can exist including making the technology work,

The more complex the topic, the more need there may be for interactivity, engagement, and deeper dialogue. For example, leadership training on collaboration is not a passive task. Sitting and learning about it is one thing—actively engaging in case studies and scenario-based learning is another. We can also send out materials in advance to our learners, just as we might do in a classroom.


## SIMPLIFICATION

*"Simplifying is the manager's most neglected art. It opens the door to solving previously intractable problems, enabling the team to surround them. To simplify is to lead."*[53] *– Richard Koch*

Simplification is an important part of what we do as virtual facilitators and virtual team leaders. It's important to note that simplistic does not equal simple, nor does it mean that we make things too simplified.

It is important to remember that the complexity is often because of the group—how they interact, their learning styles, and the differences in how people process and see the world. Just as I said at the start of this chapter, we need to embrace the chaos, given the complexity that exists. If we try to control everything or even plan for everything we will wind up in a place of "Analysis by paralysis."

## SELF-AWARENESS

Self-awareness on the part of the virtual conversationalist is critical. Rick Warren wrote, "Humility is not denying your strengths. Humility is being honest about your weaknesses."[54] As virtual facilitators, it is important to know our strengths and styles, as well as our weaknesses and blind spots. It is often said that a blind spot is a strength overused. For example, a virtual leader who is great at process may go overboard to the point of creating complexity when simplicity is needed. What strengths do you overuse? In self-awareness, it is also important to recognize and avoid assumptions we might carry. Cross-culturally, these assumptions can be very dangerous.

We are shaped by our experiences, socialization, education, and upbringing. Notice the conscious and unconscious bias we can bring to our conversations. Bias can occur across multiple layers—age, gender, race, class, sexual orientation. This topic warrants further exploration by virtual facilitators. Much has been written in this area. Some recent articles linking this topic to performance include:

- "Consciously Overcoming Unconsicous Bias" by Beena Ammanath, CIO Magazine www.cio.com/article/3161713/leadership-management/consciously-overcoming-unconscious-bias.html

- "You're More Biased Than You Think" by Jane Porter, Forbes www.fastcompany.com/3036627/youre-more-biased-than-you-think

## SELF-MANAGEMENT

Managing our emotions, checking our assumptions, and noticing our impact are all part of self-management. Part of masterful virtual facilitation is also being able to notice when we get triggered by something a participant may say that impacts us directly, or may be in conflict with what we believe. If your role as a facilitator is to be neutral, what do you need to do to self-manage?

## STYLES

As virtual facilitators, we may become chameleon-like over time, as we look to adapt and adjust our styles and approaches for different contexts.

Wilkinson notes that facilitators should speak no more than 40% of the time. For those that are more naturally coaches, this number may drop more to 5-15% of the time. Our ability to adjust our styles for the various types of groups that we work with is very important. What does each group need from us along the way?

Adjusting our styles is also about our ability to adjust our language, pace, tone, and other nuances. Consider running a leadership development dialogue for a group of North American leaders. Now consider running the same dialogue for leaders who are based in Asia. Our sensitivity to the differences in culture scales are essential in building trust and rapport within a virtual group. That trust and rapport is critical to the learning process.

To learn more about your style inclinations, you may want to explore the Everything DiSC or the MBTI (Myers Briggs Type Indicator). Doing some self-work around strengths can also be useful.

*What else is important for you to notice around styles?*

## INTUITION

Being able to access and act on your intuition is another key characteristic of masterful virtual facilitators. This in part connects with our ability to listen at a global level—to use our "Spidey sense" to pick up on the subtle nuances. Intuition is about going with your gut. As Dag Hammarskjold wrote, "The more faithfully you listen to the voice within you, the better you hear what is sounding outside"[55]

# TECHNICAL SKILLS

✓ Platform
✓ Recording
✓ Breakouts
✓ Slides
✓ LMS Management

**Technical**

There are also four skills required in the technical vein including knowledge of platform (which we turn to next in Chapter 4), recording, breakouts, managing a Learning Management System, and slide design.

These technical skills are dependent on the platforms you choose to use. Refer to the platform for more information on how to set up recordings, breakouts, navigate the Learning Management System, etc.

# DESIGN SKILLS

The final set of skills required by virtual facilitators is in the area of design. These include:

✓ Program Design
✓ Engagement
✓ Learning
✓ Activities
✓ Graphics/Visuals

**Design**

- Program design skills
- Engagement skills
- Learning design
- Activities
- Using graphics and/or visuals

Chapter 5 explores program design skills, and Chapter 7 looks at engagement and different activities.

## CONCLUSION

Throughout this chapter, we explored more than two dozen skills required by virtual facilitators. These skills are not innate, but are built up over time, through practice, feedback, and more practice. If you are not able to practice these skills, take note of how the skills are used by others who are leading calls. What do you notice about their process skills? What tools are they using? What do you like? What is having an impact—positively or negatively?

### END OF CHAPTER QUESTIONS

Complete a self-assessment of your skills based on this chapter. Where are your strengths? What could use attention?

Make note of any action steps from this chapter in the Action Plan Tracker.

# THE ECOSYSTEM OF VIRTUAL CONVERSATIONS: THE RANGE OF DIFFERENT APPROACHES IN VIRTUAL LEARNING

*"As competitive environments increase in speed, complexity and volatility, organizations and individuals are compelled toward a dynamic learning mindset. Dynamic learning is defined as rapid, adaptive, collaborative and self-directed learning at the moment of need."*[56]

*– Timothy Clark and Conrad Gottfredso*

This chapter explores the range of different approaches in the virtual conversation space—from learning to leadership approaches. Specifically, we are going to look at:

- Nine different types of virtual conversations that vary along a continuum of conversation versus learning, or focus on self versus peers

- Different platforms for this work

## THE CONTEXT OF VIRTUAL LEARNING TODAY

Virtual conversations can be viewed as an ecosystem that reflects the wide variety of learning and conversation approaches in the virtual realm. Since 1995, with the advent of the internet, learning, leadership, relationships, and conversations have changed significantly, influencing the type of learning that is undertaken, the role of the "facilitator" and the level of control available to the "learner." We've moved from solely a classroom-based or hands-on experience to a just-in-time, on-demand learning experience in which the learner has multiple avenues and locations to explore.

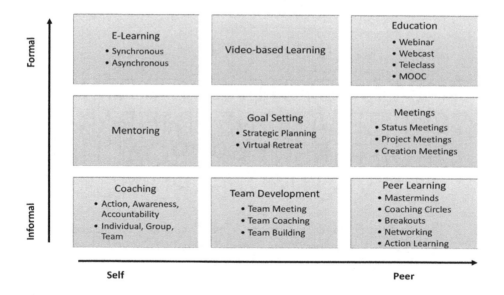

From mobile learning to digital learning to video-based learning, just-in-time learning approaches are flourishing. Regardless of platform, many of the same philosophies exist when creating exceptional virtual learning events.

This chapter explores the range of virtual learning options—the ecosystem—as well as some of the different platforms available for this work. We will start the chapter by looking at the current context and then explore the range of different approaches that make up the ecosystem of learning and dialogue.

In the virtual domain, there are several different approaches we engage in across a range—from individual to peer processes, conversational to formal education. These include:

- E-learning synchronous or asynchronous training
- Virtual educational events – instructor/facilitator led through webinars, e-learning, webcasts
- Video-based learning
- Virtual meetings of all stripes – conference calls
- Goal-setting via strategic planning sessions and virtual retreats
- Mentoring
- Coaching
- Virtual team development
- Peer-to-peer learning – masterminds, breakouts

This chapter also looks at some of the core platforms that are available for learning.

Consider these statistics:

- In 2014, 74% of companies used learning management systems (LMS) and virtual classroom/webcasting/video broadcasting.
- According to *E-learning Magazine*, the training delivery methods for 2014 were as follows[57]:
  - 47% of training hours were delivered by instructor-led, classroom-only setting—an increase of 3% as compared to previous year;
  - 29.1% of training hours were delivered with blended learning methods—an increase of 0.8 as compared to 2013;
  - 28.5% of training hours were delivered via online or computer-based technologies (no instructor)—an increase of

2.6% compared to the previous year;

- 15% of training hours were delivered via virtual classroom/ webcast only (instructor in remote location)—a decrease of 1% compared to the previous year;
- 4.2% of training hours were delivered via social learning—an increase of 0.9% compared to the previous year;
- 1.4% of training hours were delivered via mobile devices—a decrease of 0.5 compared to the previous year.

## THE RANGE OF VIRTUAL CONVERSATIONS

Across the virtual conversation and learning space, there are a variety of different modalities, from mobile learning to social learning to blended learning. These modalities also span the range of training, facilitation, and coaching.

In this book, we are using the term "virtual learning" to represent the spectrum of different learning approaches including mobile learning and blended learning, as well as informal approaches such as mentoring and coaching via phone, MOOCS, and video-based courses.

## SOCIAL LEARNING

Bandura's 1974 Social Learning Theory stressed that we can learn by observing others. Social learning approaches continue to spring up in organizational contexts. From mentoring approaches to sharing curated content, social learning approaches are shaped by peers, typically in formats that work best in the context they operate from. Social learning can take a variety of formats—from Intranets to shared collaborative wikis.

## MOBILE LEARNING

Mobile Learning has expanded tremendously in the last decade with the advent of the smart phone. Mobile learning can include app-based learning such as MOOCS (Massive Open Online Courses) offered through EdX or Coursera. Foundational to mobile learning strategies is that learning can take place anytime, and real-time. Mobile learning has changed how we are consuming learning, making it shorter, and more real-time. This has had significant impact on the context of remote and virtual teams as well. These topics are addressed further in Chapters 10 and 11.

In 2016, Google found that "Micro-moments occur when people reflexively turn to a device—increasingly a smartphone—to act on a need to learn something, do something, discover something, watch something, or buy something. They are intent-rich moments when decisions are made and preferences shaped."[58] Google/Ipsos, "Consumers in the Micro-Moment," March 2015.

Consider this:

- 62% of smartphone users are more likely to take action right away toward solving an unexpected problem or new task because they have a smartphone.
- 90% of smartphone users have used their phone to make progress toward a long-term goal or multi-step process while "out and about."
- In 2016, more than 64% of Americans owned a mobile device that would facilitate this kind of learning.

## BLENDED LEARNING

Blended Learning usually combines online learning, mobile learning, and classroom-based learning. In blended learning approaches, some of the programming is delivered in face-to-face settings, while some is delivered online. It is often considered the "best of the best," providing real-time *engagement* and real-time *application* opportunities. Part of making blended learning work is that it prepares people, or "primes" them, for the conversation. For example, a blended learning program might include a series of short video modules watched by participants, followed by one or more live calls where the material is discussed with peers.

The U.S. Department of Education's "Evaluation of Evidence-Based Practices in Online Learning: A Meta-Analysis and Review of Online Learning Studies" notes: "Students in online conditions performed modestly better, on average, than those learning the same material through traditional face-to-face instruction," and, notably, "Instruction combining online and face-to-face elements had a larger advantage relative to purely face-to-face instruction than did purely online instruction."[59]

In your work, consider where a blended approach might work well.

## INFORMAL APPROACHES TO LEARNING – THE 70/20/10 MODEL

One of the more common training models today is known as the 70/20/10 model, which emphases the three types of learning: experiential learning, which is said to occur 70% of the time; social learning, which occurs 20% of the time; and formal learning, which takes up 10% of the time.

Training Industry.com indicates that the 70/20/10 model of learning, "holds that individuals obtain 70 percent of their knowledge from job-related experiences, 20 percent from interactions with others, and 10 percent from formal educational events."[60] What are the main modes of learning in your organization?

The 70% of learning that happens in the experiential realm can include things such as job shadowing, as well as day-to-day job experiences, projects and tasks.

The 20% includes the social learning practices of peer learning, coaching, mentoring, and other collaborative learning. The final 10% comes from formal classroom learning.

This theory is being challenged by the increasing amount of informal learning that is occurring today. With increased emphasis on coaching, mentoring, and other forms of informal learning, the ratios are changing. It is often asserted that formal learning works best when information is being absorbed and informal learning strategies are best with tacit learning (learning things such as innovation, leadership, intuition) and complexity. Increasingly it is these areas of tacit learning, which are hard to teach, which are becoming competitive advantages for organizations.

More information about the 70/20/10 can be found at www.702010forum. com/Posts/view/podcast-background-and-early-research-part-2?fw

## ACROSS THE ECOSYSTEM: FACILITATION, TRAINING, COACHING, MENTORING

Throughout the ecosystem of learning, there are a variety of different modalities including coaching, facilitation, training, and mentoring. Before we delve further into this chapter, I want to make the distinction between these modalities, which virtual leaders may find themselves working within. When virtually facilitating, we may move back and forth between different disciplines. Let's take a look at what skills a leader of virtual conversations would require in each one.

### FACILITATION

Facilitation is characterized by a focus on helping a group or team get to a result. The stance of the facilitator is usually neutral, and their tool box includes tools, frameworks, and practices to help a group or team move through a series of processes towards an end result.

Core skills facilitators lead from are:

Questioning, listening, paraphrasing, summarizing, and using tools to help groups move from A to B. Facilitated processes may support groups in goal setting, generating consensus, prioritizing, or generating new options.

Examples of facilitation processes include the dotmocracy approach to prioritization, Lewin's Force Field Analysis, and the Fishbone exercises, to name a few.

## TRAINING

Training is all about equipping the group or team members with new content and/or skills. A trainer leads from their objectives, which may be set by the organization. Training can involve deliberative practice, which we know from research is a core component of developing new skills. In the virtual realm, training programs often take the form of webinars, webcasts, or teleseminars. The differences amongst these are explored in the following section.

## COACHING

In the coaching process, the person being coached is the one shaping the focus of the conversation, which often is geared to results and relationships. For example, a group of new leaders may come together to explore styles and strengths and how these are getting in the way of their own leadership approaches with their team.

## MENTORING

Mentoring pairs a more seasoned employee or expert with another (or others) to pass on their own practical insights and approaches.

# THE RANGE OF VIRTUAL EVENTS

There is a range of different types of facilitated virtual events across the domains of individual to peer experiences, conversations to formal learning. In this next section, we are going to explore what these look and sound like.

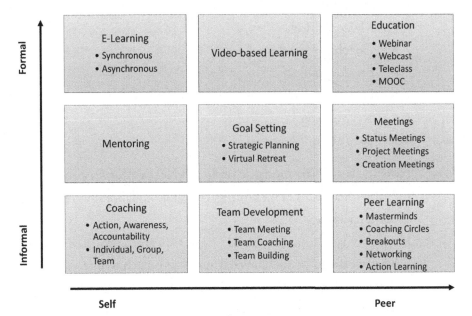

The nine areas we are going to explore are:

1. E-Learning: Synchronous and Asynchronous
2. Educational Events: Content or training pieces including webinars and webcasts, teleclasses and MOOCs
3. Video-Based Learning
4. Meetings:
   - Planning Meetings – i.e., strategic planning, team meetings
   - Status Meetings
   - Creation Meetings
5. Goal Setting: strategic planning and virtual retreats
6. Mentoring Conversations: Where a more seasoned and experienced professional is paired with another
7. Group or Team Coaching: Focused on action, awareness, and goal setting and ongoing accountability. Coaching may be delivered by internal or external coaches.
8. Virtual Team Development: From virtual team meetings to virtual retreats and team coaching. Each conversation takes on a very different flow.

9. Peer Learning:
   - Masterminds
   - Coaching Circles
   - Breakouts
   - Peer Partners
   - Networking

Each of these vary along two continua:

1. How focused is the modality on individual or peer learning—from the individual focus of mentoring, to a more collaborative experience of team coaching;
2. How conversationally based versus learning-focused is the modality—from more conversational approaches like mentoring and coaching, to structured educational events like e-learning.

Let's look at each one of these in turn:

## CATEGORY 1 – E-LEARNING: DEFINED AND IN DECLINE?

When people think of online learning, many think of the traditional e-learning, with a self-paced program delivered online, such as a health and safety program, or a self-paced program to learn a new language. Learners move through the program on their own time, usually with quizzes or other checkpoints to ensure that they have completed and understood the content.

E-learning approaches can be either synchronous or asynchronous. Synchronous learning takes place in real-time in the virtual world. An example is a leadership development training session delivered live via WebEx. Participants are expected to attend and actively engage with other group members—answering questions, using chat and breakouts. The focus of this book is on boosting these approaches of synchronous learning where everyone is in the room at the same time.

Asynchronous learning provides learning opportunities "real-time" at the convenience of the student. Students can participate 24 hours a day, 7 days a week at their convenience, accessing the same material as their colleagues from different parts of the world. We have moved quickly beyond traditional, self-led e-learning to much more interactive types of asynchronous learning such as MOOCs (Massive Open Online Courses) provided by universities and colleges where lectures are pre-recorded and released at a certain time each week. Students have assignments, but there is no live component.

In fact, self-led e-learning continues to shrink in terms of growth. Here's what Sam Adkins of Ambient Insight wrote in August 2016:

"The worldwide five-year compound annual growth rate (CAGR) for self-paced eLearning is distinctly negative at -6.4%; global revenues for self-paced courseware are dropping fast. In 2016, global revenues for self-paced eLearning reached $46.6 billion, down slightly from the $46.9 billion in 2015. By 2021, worldwide revenues for eLearning will plummet to $33.4 billion."[61]

### Practitioner's Tip - Making Learning Stick

One of the main challenges when you have learners taking programs at their own pace is making asynchronous learning "stick." Perhaps you are leading a course on business development or growing your leadership capacity. Some considerations to make this learning "stickier" are to:

- Create application opportunities to help learners link what they are reading and viewing to their world of work or life.
- Consider what will keep the learning "alive." How will people be reminded of what they are learning and what's next? The use of email autoresponders can keep the learning visible. For example, during a three-month group coaching process where the group met bi-weekly, students received three emails a week with quotes regarding the business issues they were exploring. These helped to maintain a focus between the "real-time" touchpoints.

- Provide opportunities for real-time engagement. This could include quarterly calls where people drop in for a Q&A, or holding office hours—a monthly call where people are invited to attend live and ask their questions.
- Provide different ways for people to engage in learning and dialogue between the calls such as discussion boards, secret Facebook groups, or short individual one-to-one calls (on a monthly basis).

# CATEGORY 2 – INSTRUCTOR-LED EDUCATIONAL EVENTS

The environment of instructor-led educational events continues to shift. From traditional 60-minute webcasts which push information to students, we have seen the advent of MOOCs, where instructors from a range of colleges, universities, and other individual experts can deliver short, video-based lectures to "massive" numbers of students. Students usually have short assignments that can be automatically graded or graded by fellow classmates. Some of the major platforms are EdX, Coursera, and SkillShare.

The corporate realm is where most individuals are likely to have participated in a range of webinars and/or teleclasses—and most of the principles discussed in this book are specific to the webinar and teleclass realm. While webinars often get a bad rap for being dry and one-way, consider how you can retool this format to offer interactive approaches to learning and dialogue. Webinars and teleclasses can be either synchronous or asynchronous.

| TYPE OF MEETING: |
| --- |
| Webinar or Teleclass |

| PURPOSE: |
| --- |
| To pass on information and/or skills. |
| **DESCRIPTION:** |
| Webinar or teleclass (with or without video). Typically 60 minutes in length. |
| **ROLE OF THE FACILITATOR:** |
| To pass on information and content to learners. |
| Depending on the platform, they may stimulate conversation amongst group members. Webcasts are typically a one-way passage of information versus an interactive webinar where chats and breakouts are used. |
| **TOOLS YOU WILL WANT TO USE:** |
| Chats, PowerPoint, Media |

**Teleseminars** became popular during the 2000s and are historically phone-based only. They may involve a phone-based presentation or a more interactive dialogue between the facilitator and leaders. During their heyday, teleseminars were regarded as a great way to connect with large groups and/or pass on information to many.

With the advent of more mainstream video modalities, the webinar platform has increased in popularity in recent years. However, some professionals such as coaches are still utilizing teleseminars for their coaching work to provide more focus on the individual, without the visual distractions video can create.

**Webcasts** are a web-based presentation that provide a one-way passage of information, although there may be chat functionality for people to include their questions. Webcasts provide the benefit of more visual learning—they are usually on the larger end of the spectrum, although they can use the same platforms as smaller, more interactive webinars. With the explosion of different platforms including WebEx and Adobe Connect, there are now a variety of possible webinar formats. Webinars can be one-way directed or small and interactive, leveraging breakouts.

Facilitators of teleseminars and webinars will usually find themselves leading from a training stance, leading with skills such as content expertise, program design, questions (usually to create new knowledge and or insights), and group dynamics.

### Five Tips for Creating Impactful Teleseminars[62]

While video streaming is replacing a lot of teleseminars, this is still a perfect modality for hosting larger calls. In creating impactful teleseminars:

1.  **Consider what's important for your learners**. Focus on them, their learning, and in creating opportunities for them to connect their learning to real life.

2.  **Provide useful content, resource links, and materials** that members can sink their teeth into (many of you may note how I consider teleclasses to be more content rich, and group coaching more conversation rich).

3.  **Provide an overview of the call.** Provide an agenda or overview of the topic at the start of the call. Let people know where you are going. Recap regularly.

4.  **Provide visual anchors**. I regularly speak with trainers, coaches, and facilitators regarding the importance of these anchor points in the virtual domain. What will keep a visual focus for group members during the program? Will you create a handout? Have a slide deck? Integrate video?

5.  **Be familiar with the technology, and most importantly, know how to mute callers**. Test out your technology prior to the call, know how to overcome the invariable echoes, dogs barking and other audio distractions by knowing how to use mutes, "raised hands" for questions, and other bridgeline tools.

## CATEGORY 3 – VIDEO-BASED LEARNING

According to Cisco Systems, 84% of internet traffic will be video content by 2018.[63] With the proliferation of smart phones, tablets, and other video-based devices, video-based learning continues to expand. In recent years, there has been an explosion of video-based learning—from the MOOC experience of online courses being delivered by world-class universities, to educators and experts being able to lead their own courses through Teachable and Udemy.

**Why video-based learning is important**

Video-based learning takes learning new things to a whole new level. It visually allows anyone to demonstrate a skill or idea. Video-based learning can be the virtual world made visible.

At present, YouTube has surpassed TV viewing for younger generations. Consider these statistics:[64]

- Total number of hours of video watched on YouTube each month (as of September 2016) – **3.25 billion**.
- **10,113** YouTube videos generated more than **1 billion** views.
- 80% of YouTube's views are from outside of the U.S.
- The average number of mobile YouTube video views per day is **1,000,000,000**.

**Different ways you can incorporate video learning**

When incorporating video learning consider these ideas:

- **Create simulations or animations of activities in motion**. For example, in designing an E-Learning program on Coaching and Mentoring Skills, I created a series of animated scenarios, which brought to life the coaching conversation. Rather than just passively listening to the audio, animated characters moved their lips and arms. Course participants indicated that the animated characters helped with attention, engagement, and retention of

117

the skills.

- **Keep it short.** Modules in the video world are much shorter, with core tips videos often being only 1-2 minutes in length. Most platforms like Udemy or Teachable cap video length at 20 minutes.
- **Provide additional learning supports to video courses.** One of the things I love the most with video-based courses is the ability to include multiple modalities with many of the learning platforms today. For example, a course in goal-setting could include the videos themselves, PLUS:
  - A chat functionality – connecting learners for dialogue and discussion is another part of the learning process. Several platforms such as Udemy and Teachable have these integrated in.
  - A workbook to accompany the video – providing a workbook or worksheets for people to take notes in and work along with provides the best of both worlds.
  - Space for additional material to be uploaded – this allows you to update things with time—for example, a new webinar you created, an article you found, etc.

Platforms such as Teachable provide the space for you to create a repository for multimedia resources for learners (text, audio, video, chat) making asynchronous learning a more engaged learning environment. Consider supplementing this with live calls—quarterly, monthly, etc.

## Ten Considerations with Video-Based Learning

On-demand, video-based programs are increasingly becoming a popular additional offering for professionals of all types.

Whether you are creating programs for full video-based platforms like Udemy, or whether you are creating programs as an add-on to your current programs, video-based programs are destined to grow with the introduction of 3D video and other platforms.

These are ten items you will want to consider when you go to launch or design a video-based program:

### 1. Consider your topic

As you go to design your first video-based program, consider your topic. What is the purpose of the program? What are the top 3-5 takeaways you want people to leave with?

Make a list of what you want to include in the video-based program.

### 2. Consider your audience

Consider the audience of the program and rewrite the objectives according to what they find important. What are the issues keeping them up at night?

Each audience group will shape:

- What they want
- What topic areas are important to them
- The optimum length of course—do they prefer long or short?
- Their preferred lecture length
- What program support elements they want—workbook vs worksheets, audio posts, regular communication and interaction between sessions
- Amount of streaming video vs PowerPoint only
- Community interaction—chat room, Facebook group (secret), or other
- Amount of interaction with your email access, 1-1 time, group calls

Go ahead and make a list of what you know about your clients and their preferences.

3. **Consider your platform**

    There are several platforms on which you can host your program, each with its own pros and cons. Explore these different platforms:

    - Udemy
    - Teachable
    - Skillshare
    - Other

    Go ahead and do some research.

4. **Map it out**

    Once you have thought through the different program elements, map it out. You may first want to start with a MindMap. What are the main lessons or lectures? Further define these with the content for each session.

    In terms of mapping it out, you might want to use the Group Program Design Matrix in conjunction with a tool like Trello, which is a very visual way to see your content and capture it all in one place.

    Go ahead and get mapping!

5. **Write your script and/or design your slides**

    Once you finalize your block of content, start writing your script for what each session will include. You may also want to design your slides. Do your research, capture quotes, and add images to bring the different content to life.

In tandem with this you may want to design your worksheets, or add this as a step after recording.

Some designers like to do everything in bullet form, others use the notes section of the PowerPoint or Articulate software, while others write out a full-blown script. Experiment with what is going to work best for you.

**6. Record**

It is good practice to do some test recordings to see what the end result is going to look and sound like. Record then review. Look at it on a couple of different platforms. You may need to tweak your audio and/or lighting. Even if you don't have it all mapped out, do a test record and notice what it looks—and sounds—like.

There are a variety of do-it-yourself recording options for videos from recording software such as Camtasia, to mobile video (using your phone), to recording on a Zoom line. Budget and your comfort with the technology may dictate the platform you choose.

Consider your own style in terms of whether you want to design and script all modules and then do a recording from start to finish or if you want to record the videos in blocks.

One consideration with video-based programming is the effort you need to take to ensure continuity (the way you set up the recording and lighting, wearing the same clothing, etc.) if you want the end result to look like a start-to-finish process. If you design in modules (which can be taken in blocks), if may not be as important to make it appear seamless.

7. **Edit**

Editing always takes more time than you think it will. Consider if you want to do all the editing and/or listening to the entire recording yourself. You may want to bring in others to help you, especially if there are any sound quality issues.

In the final edit, make sure your design matrix and program outline is complete, especially if you want to transpose it to other platforms over time. It can be useful to have a final document outlining the lecture name, length, video and audio supports, worksheets, etc.

Go ahead and download the Video-based Program Outline template.

8. **Run-through**

Once you have done the editing you will want to do several run-throughs—by yourself and/or having others listen in. Make any final edits needed.

Make sure everything is uploaded and the related worksheets are attached.

9. **Marketing**

Marketing should actually occur earlier on this list if you are thinking of it chronologically. Filling the program that you have worked so hard to create is just as important as designing a powerful video. I have created a separate program that addresses the topic of Marketing. For those interested in some key marketing tips around group and team programs, you may want to check out a digital chapter that accompanied my book, *From One to Many: Best Practices for Team and Group Coaching*. You can access digital chapters at www.from12many.com/downloads.html (use code 4411).

Take half an hour and map out a strategy for how you are going to get the word out about the program.

Go ahead and get your marketing plan drafted and into motion!

**10. Communicate**

Finally, schedule time to communicate and build relationships with your learners. Some online courses offer drop-in calls, while others have vibrant message boards.

Consider how you want to keep in touch with your group members. Remember they are often your repeat customers, so the more you can build a connection with them, the better it is long term.

# CATEGORY 4 – MEETINGS

When we think of virtual events, for many, the idea of meetings comes into play. This topic is further delved into in Chapter 9 – In Focus: Virtual Meetings.

## TYPES OF MEETINGS

| TYPE OF MEETING: |
| --- |
| Conference Call |
| **PURPOSE:** |
| To share information and make decisions |
| **ROLE OF THE FACILITATOR:** |
| To keep to process and ensure everyone is able to be heard |

> **PROCESS OUTLINE:**
>
> Welcome to call
>
> Purpose
>
> Overview of agenda
>
> Agenda items discussed and agreements
>
> Recap of main focus areas and next steps

Conference call meetings do not have to be boring or ineffective. Here are some tips for avoiding Death by Conference Call:[65]

1. **Have an agenda**: Create an agenda with clear start and end times, as well as time frames for each item. Make sure you have all the right people at the table. If things are not working with agendas, switch them up.

2. **Create interactivity every 5-7 minutes**: Part of the Death by Conference Call mindset is shaped due to the monotony and length of time we need to stay focused. The human brain can only focus for about eight minutes before it needs a change of pace. Creating a shift or change every 5-7 minutes—hearing from another speaker, asking a question or switching a slide—can create greater levels of engagement on the part of learners.

3. **Keep to time:** Many meeting facilitators fail to keep an eye on the time. If facilitating the meeting and keeping an eye on the time is too much, assign the timekeeper role to someone else. You might also benefit by having an alarm at hand to prompt you for the next item.

4. **Create visual anchor points:** If you are only on a conference call bridgeline, it can be useful to provide a number of visual anchor points. Consider what can be sent out prior to the call in terms of visuals, which might include an agenda and/or a work sheet. When you get on the call, you can invite everyone to create a map or draw a table marking who is who on the call. This will

be useful to you and group members to track who has had input and who hasn't.

5. **Highlight agreements and next steps:** At the end of the call, or as you go through, summarize and capture agreements and next steps. Soon after the meeting, send out an email that captures what was agreed to. Regularly revisit how effective your reporting structures are. Many times meeting management systems are duplicated or overly detailed. What is sufficient, yet detailed enough, for your purposes? Before the next meeting, send out agreements and a summary so you don't need to spend half of the meeting recapping. Get people into the practice of checking in succinctly.

# CATEGORY #5 – VIRTUAL EVENTS FOR PLANNING AND GOAL SETTING

The virtual realm has made it possible to involve more voices in planning and goal setting. This can be extremely valuable when you consider virtual teams, regional teams etc. With the advent of technologies like Zoom that make breakout work possible, we can now leverage the best of the in-person environment.

## GOAL SETTING

Goal setting can take place on a couple of different levels including:

- Individual goal setting
- Team goal setting – development of an annual or quarterly workplan, reviewing departmental plans
- Organizational goal setting – annual plans, strategic plans

As previously indicated, most goal models adopt a SMART approach.

In Chapters 7 and 9 we explore several different goal frameworks and processes you can utilize including the SWOT, the SOAR, Strategic Issues Mapping, and One-PagePlans.

Here are six questions to help with goal clarity:

1. What are the top priorities right now? In the next quarter? The next year?
2. Who will help you be successful with these?
3. How do your goals connect with individual goals? Organizational goals?
4. How will goals and achievements be measured?
5. How do your priorities impact others?
6. If we shift our goal horizon from the conceptual level to the practical and tactical levels, what do we notice? (If we move to look at our goals from the big picture or 30,000 foot view, what do we notice?)

| TYPE OF MEETING: |
| --- |
| Planning Meeting |
| **PURPOSE:** |
| To create an annual or strategic plan |
| **ROLE OF THE FACILITATOR:** |
| To help the group move from A to B and have a developed plan |
| **PROCESS OUTLINE:** |
| Ranging from one-hour sessions to half-day or multi-day sessions, virtual planning meetings can take a number of forms. There are several different processes we may undertake including the SWOT, SOAR, or Strategic Issues Mapping. One-Page Plans also provide a space for individuals to capture their most important notes. |

**THINGS TO KEEP IN MIND:**

Planning and goal setting can take place on multiple levels; short-term, medium-term, and long-term or local, regional and national. Define the appropriate level with the groups you are working with.

In planning, it is important to make the link between the plan with why people are doing it or else planning can become a "Check Box Activity." One way to get people to connect their plan to the bigger picture is to be exploring the *Why? Why is this important? What's the compelling reason we are doing this?*

If you notice things slowing down it is likely that the team has lost sight of the *Why.*

Individual versus collective goals – Depending on the group you are working with, you may be working on more collective goals (when working with a team) versus individual goals (when working with a group that is not interdependent on each other).

Accountability – In the book, *The Oz Factor*, authors Connor, Smith, and Hickman write, ***"Accountability is the guiding principle that defines how we make commitments to one another, how we measure and report our progress how we interact when things go wrong, and how much ownership we take to get things done. It is, in essence, the nerve center that runs throughout every part of the organization and through every working relationship to every member of every team."***[66]

What are you doing to create accountability with the teams and groups you are working with around goals?

Key to accountability success in the virtual domain is building in time to discuss:

- Who is going to do what?

- By when?

- How will they let the team/group know about their progress?

## OTHER TYPES OF MEETINGS

In addition to planning meetings there may be status and creation meetings.

| **TYPE OF MEETING:** |
| --- |
| Status Meeting |
| **PURPOSE:** |
| To provide a forum for updating how projects and tasks are going |
| **ROLE OF THE FACILITATOR:** |
| To provide the space for a facilitated process where everyone can receive updates and project tasks are clarified |
| **PROCESS OUTLINE:** |
| Group members may submit a formal written status report prior to the call, so that the call is spent troubleshooting issues and identifying appropriate next steps. Depending on the type of project, status meetings can range from 15 minutes to multiple hours.<br><br>One popular project status framework is the Red, Yellow, and Green Light framework. In this approach, each team member reports on their different project tasks according to:<br><br>Things are good – GREEN<br><br>Things need attention – YELLOW<br><br>Things require immediate support – RED |

| **TYPE OF MEETING:** |
| --- |
| Creation/Innovation Meeting |
| **PURPOSE:** |
| To create something (a new product or program), or may focus on special projects |
| **ROLE OF THE FACILITATOR:** |
| To create the space for creativity, innovation, experimentation, and action |

**Process outline:**

Sprints and hacks are mushrooming in the realm of meetings—face-to-face and virtual. Widely used in the tech sector, virtual sprint meetings focused on creating new products or services can range from 45-minute, virtual program hacks to multi-day sprints where teams are engaged in prototype development around a burning business issue.

Over the last year, I have been experimenting in leading design hacks for group program developers (coaches, trainers, and facilitators) through facilitated 45-minute blocks. It is very interesting to see the intensity and action created in a short time. Rather than spending four hours on a similar process, it is interesting to note how much can be captured and designed in a compressed amount of time.

## CATEGORY #6 – MENTORING IN THE VIRTUAL SPACE

Mentoring conversations are usually geared to passing on tips, information, and ideas based on personal experience. Mentors for leaders at all levels are quite common in workplaces today. Leveraging the virtual network by pairing people across geographic locations or two sites can expand networks and experiences.

### In the Spotlight: Making the Most of Your Mentoring Experience

Mentoring plays a key role in the development of talent within organizations, and is often overlooked or underutilized. Increasingly organizations are viewing mentoring as an important part of their succession and talent management process, in addition to being a useful approach during onboarding. While many mentoring programs focus on growing the next generation of leaders, mentoring programs can also support career transition across industries and diversity initiatives within organization.

Mentoring plays an important role in building relationships across an organization and/or industry.

Throughout the mentoring relationship mentors provide opportunities for the protégé to learn based on real-life experiences. A powerful tool for understanding organizational culture. Mentors also help protégés understand how things really get done, as well as the politics in an organization. A mentor can be a powerful—and positive—person in your network.

As you start to establish mentoring within your organization and formalize a mentoring process, there are several areas you will want to consider. These include:

**Clarify the roles and responsibilities of mentors and mentees/ protégés** – In successful mentoring relationships, expectations are clear. The roles and responsibilities of both the mentor and mentee are discussed at the start of the mentoring conversation. Pairings know who will be initiating meetings, and what type of support each party wants and can provide to the other. Mentoring can benefit from a clearly defined start and end to the process. Create expectations early on around how frequently partners should meet and how long. As part of the process of mentoring, it can be useful to hold a short kick-off session, which may also involve some training and expectation setting for the wider group of mentors and protégés.

**Have mentees set the goals** – Having two or three specific goal areas in focus helps to structure the mentoring conversation. Mentees should spend time at the start of the process identifying and sharing key areas they would like support in with their mentor. It will also be useful to have the mentee set the agenda for each conversation. Some mentors may ask protégés to email focus areas a few days before the session; whereas, others may be more comfortable addressing the mentee's needs in the moment.

**The life cycle of the mentoring relationship has several distinct phases** – In the first meeting, mentors and mentees will want to share their backgrounds and their expectations for the mentoring process. At this time, it is also very useful to identify together when, where, and how you will meet. Be clear with each other on what's going to work best for both of you. Some compromise and flexibility may be required on both of your parts. Another alternative may be to schedule some of your meetings by phone or Skype, particularly if you are situated in different offices or geographic locations. Discussion around topics such as confidentiality are also important as the mentor will likely be sharing real examples based on their experience.

As you get to know each other and connections progress, check in around what's working well with the mentoring relationship and what is not. It is important to be honest and frank with each other, particularly if expectations are not aligned.

As the mentoring relationship comes to a close, build in time to have the mentee identify their learning from the process. We often say that mentoring is a two-way street and hopefully mentors will learn from their experience as well. As a mentor, consider what your greatest learning has been throughout your conversations. At the end of a mentoring process in your organization it can be useful to bring mentors and mentees together, even virtually, for the sharing of lessons learned, best practices, and other evaluation feedback. This can feed forward into the next cohort of mentoring conversations. Some protégés may even opt to become mentors in future program rounds.

**Core skills in the mentoring process** – There are several skill sets that enhance the mentoring process. As a mentor, lead with core skills such as listening and asking powerful questions. Mentoring is not just about sharing your experience, it is also about supporting the mentee with new insights and perspectives around their work. Listen closely for what they need. Do not assume you know.

Mentoring is also a conversation to support the mentee in identifying what they know and where they want to go. In asking questions it is often useful to lead with a *What?* For example, *What's another perspective around that?* Or, *What did you learn from that experience? What* questions invite conversation and dialogue, *whereas Why* questions may put people on the defensive, *and How* questions often lead us into process and thinking about how things are done.

Other core skills that mentors may use include sharing observations and providing feedback. Sometimes mentees may also want you to be an accountability partner. Others may want to be acknowledged. Ask what they would like from the mentoring process and what role they would like you to play. Finally, inquire about the approaches they would like you to incorporate—providing stories, leading them to resources, providing links to best practices.

**What's different about mentoring in the virtual space?** Many new to virtual mentoring wonder how to make it work. Some tips to keep in mind are:

- Have a plan – just like in the in-person environment, create a roadmap of where you want to focus each conversation.

- Ask for feedback as you go.

- Incorporate streaming approaches if that works for both of you.

- Blend face-to-face and virtual meetings where feasible.

Successful mentoring partnerships benefit both the mentor and mentee. It is an underutilized approach for growth and development. Consider how you can expand mentoring within your organization or industry.

## CATEGORY #7 – COACHING APPROACHES

Coaching is all about supporting a journey of enhancing awareness, and expediting results. The coaching conversation leads from goals, action, awareness, and ongoing accountability. It is unlikely that coaching is a one-off conversation. The coaching may be undertaken by a leader, or an internal or external coach.

The 2017 Sherpa Coaching Survey[67] has found that more coaching conversations are taking place virtually. 8% of coaching conversations are taking place by HD video, 22% by webcam, 28% by phone, and 34% in person. Contrast this to 2008 figures that found 48% of coaching conversations happened in person, and 40% by phone.

Coaches create pause points to support a focus on what's important for their clients. Those clients may be individuals, like a business owner looking for help opening 10 new offices over the coming year, or groups or teams. Coaches work with existing teams as well as teams that are newly forming or coming together after a merger and acquisition. Meeting together via phone, Skype, or Zoom, the coach will work with each client or group on moving towards their goal, perhaps generating a series of options and a robust action plan, exploring strengths, values, and areas for improvement.

Coaches lead from "powerful questions" geared to help clients discover new insights, expand their knowledge, explore new perspectives, or generate new options. The coaching conversation is usually grounded in one of eleven coaching competencies.

Coaching approaches differ from training because the coach leads with a core focus on the client, who sets the agenda and focus, whether that client is an individual, team, or group.

| TYPE OF MEETING: |
|---|
| Group Coaching |
| **PURPOSE:** |
| To support group members in enhanced goal setting and action; or to promote greater understanding and awareness about the self or professional issues. |
| **DESCRIPTION:** |
| A series of conversations undertaken by phone or video streaming (Skype or Zoom). Group size is typically four to eight group members, with a maximum of 15. |
| **ROLE OF THE FACILITATOR:** |
| To support the group members in setting and moving towards their goals, as well as in developing enhanced awareness and understanding. |
| Research indicates that optimum group size for pure, virtual group coaching is approximately 4-8. Credentialed coaches have the provision to work with groups of up to 15. Working with larger groups is considered facilitation. |

**PROCESS OUTLINE:**

Group coaching conversations typically last 1-1.5 hours with a focus shaped by the group members. Groups often come together to explore topics of common interest, such as a coaching group for entrepreneurs who want to expand their businesses, or leaders who want to expand their awareness and impact.

Group coaching sessions meet for multiple conversation touchpoints, with ongoing action steps and accountability between each session.

Team Coaching conversations focus on coaching the entire team—sometimes as a series of individuals, but often as a system. Coaching the team takes place across multiple conversation touchpoints. Common themes in team coaching may include creating a vision, exploring values, or holding difficult conversations.

**BENEFITS OF THE PROCESS:**

There is a range of benefits that organizations, participants, and coaches experience from a group coaching process. As I wrote in Effective Group Coaching,[68] some of the core reasons group coaching has become a popular modality includes the:

- Leveraging of time and resources (for clients and coaches)
- Economies of scale (more impact with less time and money)
- Effecting change
- Harnessing the collective wisdom of the group
- Scalability
- Making it stick

## AVOIDING THE TRAPS IN TEAM AND GROUP COACHING WORK

There are a number of traps or pitfalls that coaches should keep in mind around coaching groups and teams, many of which become magnified or augmented in the virtual realm. Five of these traps are:

## TRAP #1: UNCLEAR EXPECTATIONS

I can't say enough about the importance of setting expectations that start *before* you step into the room—physical or virtual. In a coaching process, there are a number of expectations you need to set including:

- What coaching is and what coaching is not?
- What are the goals for the coaching process?
- What is the role of the coach? The role of each group member?
- Activities that can be undertaken to clarify expectations include:
    - Pre-program 1-1s
    - Developing Ways of Working with your group
    - Establishing Coaching Agreements – Formal written Coaching Agreements will include sections on: What coaching is and what coaching is not, the role of coach, the role of the clients, and the responsibility of those being coached
    - What is important for group/team members to know about you? What are your expectations, and their expectations, around:
        - Ownership of the process and focus of the group
        - What is done in between sessions
        - The role/responsibility of the group members
        - Who is responsible for setting the focus, and taking action

*How are you creating agreements together? What needs clarification? What changes do you want to make in future programs?*

## TRAP #2: TOO MUCH!

Often we want to include as much as we can in service to the client without recognizing that sometimes it is too much. Consider weaning out some of the following:

- Theme areas
- Field work
- The number of action items you ask people to focus on—one may be enough
- Number of coaching questions
- How much material you provide at the start
- Number of activities you include
- Different program components (i.e., having live calls and videos, and peer partners and…)

*What will simplify your current program?*

## TRAP #3: UNRULY PARTICIPANTS

There is a range of participants who show up in our rooms (physically and virtually). Addressing unruly behavior is a key issue for many new virtual facilitators.

People can become unruly when they do not feel safe, heard or valued. Setting everyone up for success often begins with how we set things up—creating shared expectations, Ways of Working, and also being clear on what is acceptable and not in the room/on the phone. What can you do to ensure these needs are being met?

*What are you noticing about your current participants? What issues have emerged?*

Tricky issues and different participants are covered in Chapter 8.

## TRAP #4: NOT TRUSTING YOURSELF AND YOUR SKILLS

As group workers, we operate in a context where "uncertainty" is the norm. Uncertainty is created by not knowing where a conversation may go, or how much time a conversation may take. We need to be comfortable a lot of the time in *not knowing*. We need to develop a deep trust in our skills, that what we need will show up in the moment, and also that the people we are working with will bring what is needed to create a great experience.

## TRAP #5: UNDERESTIMATING OUR PRESENCE

Our being, or *presence*, as a coach is an important instrument in our work. How we show up influences so much in our work—from how the group feels to the environment we create. As you think back to recent conversations,

*What adjectives would you use to describe your presence? What do others say about you and the space you create?*

# CATEGORY #8 – TEAM DEVELOPMENT

In the virtual realm, there are several options for virtual team development, ranging from regular team meetings and ongoing team coaching processes to one-off team-building sessions. Team development initiatives in the virtual realm range from short, regular team meetings, to ongoing team coaching conversations which can help newly forming teams create clarity on goals, directions, and practices. Virtual team-building events bring teams together to strengthen connection and clarity around where they are going.

We know that high performing teams excel when they have shared team practices for sharing information and communication. For more on developing teams in the virtual realm, refer to Chapter 11.

Two of the more common team development approaches are team meetings, virtual team-building events, and team coaching.

| TYPE OF MEETING: |
| --- |
| Team Meeting |
| **PURPOSE:** |
| A vehicle for communication, connection, and updates. |
| **DESCRIPTION:** |
| Regular meetings across the team—from brief, daily 15-minute huddles, to hour-long, biweekly meetings. |
| **ROLE OF THE FACILITATOR:** |
| To keep the meeting on track by setting the process and creating an agenda. |
| Leaving space for dialogue and confirming agreements and next steps. ***Who will do what? By when? How will we know?*** |
| A precursor to successful team meetings is a focus on developing trust and connection. Without trust and connection, it is unlikely that teams will feel comfortable exploring their core issues. |
| **PROCESS OUTLINE:** |
| Refer to tools in Chapter 11. |

| TYPE OF MEETING: |
| --- |
| Virtual Team-Building – i.e., Virtual Retreat |
| **PURPOSE:** |
| To build connection across the team. May also include a focus on productivity—goal setting, clarity around projects, etc. |

**DESCRIPTION:**

Usually a one-off activity such as a virtual retreat or team-building as part of a team meeting. Virtual retreats are as the name implies—retreats held virtually. Especially for teams who are distributed and can't get together, virtual retreats bring people together for extended dialogue and a "pause point" for the day. They leverage the opportunity to video stream across the team creating full team conversation, use breakouts for smaller group discussion and include real-time team-building events delivered online. Consider how some of your favorite retreat items could go virtual!

**ROLE OF THE FACILITATOR:**

To support the team in creating better connections, energy, and possibly goals. To create a pause point for the team for conversation, reflection, and planning.

**PROCESS OUTLINE:**

Virtual team-building events can range from weekly team development sessions as part of a team meeting (such as the **What's Outside Your Window** exercise in Chapter 7) to a full day virtual retreat where traditional team retreat sessions focusing on building connection and trust and exploring roles and goals are delivered online.

---

**TYPE OF MEETING:**

Team Coaching

**PURPOSE:**

A longer, facilitated process usually consisting of multiple touchpoints between the coach and team. Team coaching can benefit teams that are newly forming, during a merger and acquisition, or when a team is struggling.

**ROLE OF THE FACILITATOR:**

Adopts the role of coach, holding the team "creative and whole," meaning that the team is capable of solving their challenges with additional dialogue, skills or changes. The coach supports the team in creating behavioral norms, leading from the skills of goal setting, accountability, action, and awareness. Coaching is not a one-off conversation, rather a sustained series of conversations, with a heavy focus on accountability as a differentiator.

**PROCESS OUTLINE:**

Team coaching engagements often start with an assessment such as a DiSC or Team Diagnostic to help the team understand their strengths, challenges, and/or blindspots. These assessments usually point to where teams will benefit from more dialogue and exploration. Whether it is developing trust, or exploring perspectives and limiting beliefs, the focus of team coaching should be co-created by the team. The following textbox outlines key stages of the team coaching conversation.

**BENEFITS OF THE PROCESS:**

In *From One to Many: Best Practices for Team and Group Coaching*[69], I wrote that some of the benefits of team coaching are:

1. Space for the team to pause and reflect
2. Prioritizing the need for focus
3. A non-judgemental sounding board/space for dialogue
4. Ability to mirror back to the team what is going on
5. Strong focus on the outcome
6. Accountability focus

### Key Components of the Team Coaching Process

## Contracting

- With sponsor and/or leader
- Key focus areas, logistics, fees
- Outline process
- Confidentiality
- Roles of different parties

## Pre-Program

- Meeting with leader - discuss role of leader
- Diagnostic/Assessment
- Pre-program 1-1s: Role, Needs of Team, Personal Objectives
- Welcome Email: Team Coach Role, what to expect,

coaching process, confidentiality

## Offsite/Kick Off

- Kick off and launch of program
- Agreements - Ways of Working, Team Contract, Expectations (2 levels)
- Review/presentation of key diagnostic
- Identify key focus areas and measures of success
- Coaching work begins

## Ongoing Coaching Conversations

- Work around key themes identified - deepening awareness and taking action
- Iterative goal setting, check in on commitments
- Action and accountability
- Capacity building/development - transfer of key skills and processes

## Wrap Up

- Inventory of new skills, processes, and awareness
- Evaluation
- Sustainability - How will you continue this work? What might lead to slippage? What might get in the way?
- How do you sustain this?
- Identification of other areas of focus - book future tune-ups

A key focus area for team coaches is enhanced awareness for the team. Use the following questions to support deepened awareness around issues as part of a team coaching conversation:[70]

- What's your most important priority right now?
- What's really clear about _____ right now?
- If there was one change you could make in your work to boost results/relationships/impact/other right now, what would it be?
- What is giving you most of your results?
- What is working really well?

- What needs some (or more) attention?
- What are you committed to 100%?
- Where would collaboration benefit this?
- What makes your contributions unique?
- What's strategic?
- What will support your growth?
- A year from now, what do you want to say you have accomplished?
- What do you need to say *no* to, so you can focus in on the most important tasks? What would this take?

## CATEGORY #9 – PEER APPROACHES

The final category we are going to differentiate is peer approaches. A virtual event provides an opportunity for peers to be involved in the learning process together. Sometimes the learning is richer at the peer level than it is from facilitator to learner. Virtual events can be a great networking and learning opportunity for group members with their peers.

There is a range of approaches where the peers themselves lead the conversation. Two examples are *MasterMinds* and *Peer Coaching Circles*. Peers can also play a key role in breakouts and serving as peer partners in between sessions. This section takes a look at these approaches, as well as some tips for setting peers up for success, including skill development for peers. We'll also talk about the unique networking opportunities provided by the virtual realm.

## DIFFERENT WAYS TO LEVERAGE PEERS

Peers provide an important learning resource in the virtual realm. While many trainers think they must provide it all, facilitators may see their role as drawing the learning out of the group, and coaches will look to the group members to partner in co-creating the conversation together.

A key principle in making peer work possible in the virtual domain is to consider how we set people up for success.

## EQUIPPING PEERS FOR SUCCESS

There is a series of skills that can be very useful for peers working in learning environments, including:

- **Listening** – If you are on the phone in the virtual space, you may not have a lot of visual cues. In this case, it can be useful to help people learn to listen for the tone, pace, and pitch. It can also be useful to encourage peers to listen for what is really being said rather than thinking about the question they are going to ask.

- **Questioning** – Questions form the backbone of any facilitated experience. Great questions in the realm of learning and discovery are open-ended, meaning they usually start with one of the *Five Ws and an H* (*What, Why, Where, When, Who,* or *How*). Note the many questions scattered throughout this chapter and the book.

  As peers, it can be important to listen first from curiosity rather than with a focus on problem solving. A learning environment is rich when it is geared around discovery. Unfortunately, in many contexts peer partners want to move to a role of advisor, rather than using the tool of questions or inquiry to help others glean new insights, make connections, find focus and clarity. If we lead too quickly with problem solving, we may shut off the opportunity for people to really learn and discover for themselves. Developing a wide assortment of powerful or strategic questions can be an important part of the learning process for peers. You may want to spend some time getting them to provide each other feedback on what was useful in the coaching conversation.

- **Presence** – Part of being a great peer partner involves learning more about ourselves and how we show up in relationships and conversation. It is communicated in the virtual world through our being, our tone of voice, how quickly we speak, and even our word choice. Every group has its own rhythm, so notice what presence is required. If we move too slowly, we may not be fast enough for a busy Type A leader. If we move too quickly in our pace, and pitch, we may shut other conversations down. As peers, it can be important to learn more about our presence and how we are perceived by others. Get group members to think intentionally about the space they want to create, and encourage them to seek out feedback from their partners on what energy and presence they bring to the conversation.

Peer dialogue can take place on a number of levels, including:

- Breakouts
- Peer partners in longer learning programs
- Masterminds
- Peer coaching circles

Let us look at each one of these in turn:

## BREAKOUTS

Many virtual platforms enable you to use breakouts, including Web Ex, Zoom, Maestro Conferencing, and others. Just like in the in-person realm, being able to spend time in smaller conversation spaces (typically 2-4 people) can foster connection and focus.

Some guidelines when working virtually in leveraging breakouts or virtual pairs include:

- Consider breakout groups of 3-4 group members. When breakouts are too small, one person may be left hanging if the other person has technological issues. When breakouts are too big, usually more than 4-5 people, it is natural for people to feel disconnected. If video streaming is a possibility, invite people to use it, as it allows for deeper connection and more flow of conversation in less time.
- Consider the benefit of pairing the same people throughout the learning process. This can further strengthen trust and connection, especially if the group is meeting for a short period of time.
- Think through how people can view instructions explaining what they are supposed to do. If they miss your instructions the first time around, and if they can't see your screen when they go to breakout, how will they know what to do?
- Consider assigning roles before you have people move off into rooms. Possibilities include a note-taker, a time-keeper, and a facilitator of the dialogue (who writes the question(s) down before you go!). What roles will support your group best?
- One or two questions are usually enough to get people into sharing and dialogue. Make sure you provide enough time for people to connect, figure out their plan or process, and then move into dialogue.
- If you can, "drop in" the first couple of times people are doing virtual breakouts to check and see if they have any questions or challenges. Many platforms allow the facilitator to "drop into"

the different virtual breakouts with a click of a button.

- Walk through instructions a couple of times before you send people off and pause to see if they have questions.
- And most of all, have fun! If you are stressed, it's likely your group will be too. As facilitators, we set the tone, so if you are not comfortable with breakouts, practice these with friends, colleagues and even loved ones.

## PEER PARTNERS

When working with peers on longer programs, you will want to consider how peer partners can meet between sessions to continue the conversation around application, learning, and insights. For example, in longer-term virtual leadership development processes, pairs or triads may meet in between sessions to discuss how they are applying that month's focus in their work.

### Breakout and Partner Questions

Here is a list of questions team members may want to incorporate to help focus the virtual conversation when working in pairs or breakouts:

- What would be most useful for you to explore today?
- If you were successful with your goal, what would it look like?
- What's important about that?
- What's the greatest opportunity for you right now?
- What else?
- What's getting in your way?

- What support do you need?

- What options are available?

- What are the pros? What are the cons?

- Why? Why not?

- What's becoming clear for you, as you talk about this issue?

- What are you next steps?

## KEY TIPS FOR BUILDING THE PEER NETWORK

Creating informal peer connection points between calls or webinars creates a rich dialogue and learning space between peers, and can add value to virtual programming without adding additional time. Some key tips in making peer dialogue and networking work:

1. Be clear and provide written instructions for peer partners for what they should do, in a place they can access during their peer call.

2. Get everyone's approval to share their contact details and circulate a list of contacts.

3. Provide additional worksheets such as contact forms and module worksheets, including discussion questions or peer assignment.

4. Set up a portal where people can connect—i.e., Teachable, a secret Facebook group, a bridgeline.

## MASTERMINDS

Masterminds are very popular in both the entrepreneurial and small business realms, as well as with executives. Masterminds provide collaborative peer conversation, sharing, strategizing, and networking.

| TYPE OF MEETING: |
| --- |
| Mastermind |

| PURPOSE: |
| --- |
| To expand awareness on current business challenges and opportunities. |

| DESCRIPTION: |
| --- |
| Groups of 6-12 may meet virtually once a month for six or twelve months, for anywhere from 1.5 to 2 hours or more. The mastermind host is the one who usually brings the group together and group members are responsible for identifying the issue they want input around. Typically, each member shares their idea and welcomes feedback and insights from others. |

| ROLE OF THE FACILITATOR: |
| --- |
| To ensure everyone has a chance to share their issue. To ensure that there is a space to brainstorm new ideas, collaborate, share resources, and network. |

## PEER COACHING CIRCLES

Peer coaching circles are another popular peer approach. Coaching circles often form around areas of shared interest. For example, parents who want to focus on becoming a better parent, or leaders who want to be a better leader. In peer coaching circles, each group member gets an opportunity to be coached on a topic of their choice. Each session may focus on working with one or more group members. This coaching process is typically focused on issues like goal setting, action, and awareness.

| |
|---|
| **TYPE OF MEETING:** |
| Peer Coaching Circle |
| **PURPOSE:** |
| To provide a space for individuals to bring important issues that they want coaching around, as well as support from their peers. |
| Coaching circles are different from Mastermind groups. In Mastermind groups the primary focus is on peer advising rather than on peer coaching. Peer coaching is grounded in the belief that the client knows their answer, and is naturally creative, resourceful and whole. The focus in peer coaching is around developing awareness, and take action around their most pressing goals. |
| **ROLE OF THE FACILITATOR:** |
| The facilitator adopts the role of coach, placing an emphasis on goal setting, action, awareness, and accountability. |
| **PROCESS OUTLINE:** |
| Each person brings a focus area they would like to look at. This can be done in a rotational fashion or as a collaborative series of smaller breakouts. Questions are usually asked of the person in the coaching chair, with questions geared to create discovery, insight, and connection. |
| **THINGS TO KEEP IN MIND:** |
| Note core coaching skills listed below. |

Some of the key peer coaching/communication skills we will want to foster and develop in any peer coaching process are:

- **Mirroring**: Reflecting back what you have heard. In mirroring, it is important to use the language as the original speaker did, verbatim. Mirroring often creates new insights for the speaker.

- **Listening**: In a coaching conversation, it is important to listen at several different levels. What do you notice about the pace and pitch of the speaker? What is being said and what is not being said? What is being said between the lines? What do you notice about the words, as well as the tone?

- **Questioning:** In coaching, we want to use questions that are open-ended, that do not invite a yes/no response. In any coaching conversation (peer coaching, team coaching, leader as coach), it is important to use questions that open up awareness, prompt a new perspective, invite discovery, or support action.

- **Direct communication:** Use language that is consistent with, and impactful for, the person being coached.

- **Curiosity:** In the coaching process, the person being coached is the expert. This can feel like a 180 from our typical process, where the leader is the expert. In supporting peers to become better coaches, it is important to encourage them to ask questions from a place of curiosity, rather than be an advisor.

- **Assumption busting and perspective shifting:** Throughout the coaching conversation it is likely that you will be exploring and "busting" assumptions as well as shifting perspectives.

- **Support for goal setting and achievement:** Coaching is grounded in core goals as set by the person being coached. A starting place for any coaching process is to have this person identify the goals and the focus of the conversations. The peer coaching conversation should provide an opportunity to move towards those goals, as well as identify blockages.

- **Creating accountability supports:** Creating support for accountability is essential. As John Whitmore wrote in his seminal *Coaching for Performance,* accountability is about getting people to specify "*What* will you do? By *when*? And *how* will I know?" Holding people accountable, including yourself as a leader, is foundational to the coaching approach.

## ACTIVITIES ACROSS THE DIFFERENT MODALITIES

There is a wide range of activities, tools, and processes virtual facilitators may want to tap into during the course of their work, including activities in these focus areas. Refer to Chapter 7 for more on building your toolbox. Having a variety of different approaches to use across the different modalities can be very important. Consider these options:

| TYPICAL FOCUS AREAS: | ACTIVITIES AND RESOURCES TO EXPLORE: |
| --- | --- |
| VISION: | Creating a vision (at either individual or collective levels)<br><br>Simon Sinek - What's your Why? (TED Talk)<br><br>Series of questions - 10 years from now, think about: What you are doing? What you are known for? What have your achievements been?<br><br>Visual card decks such as Visual Explorer from CCL, Points of You - The Coaching Game, the JICT Deck available at CoachingToys, or Conversation Sparker Cards™ from me<br><br>Creating a vision board |
| VALUES: | Peak experience and mining for values<br><br>Values clarification exercise<br><br>Values checklist<br><br>Values cards<br><br>Word string |
| STRENGTHS: | VIA strengths (positive psychology)<br><br>StrengthsFinder 2.0<br><br>Wheel of ....(leadership competencies) |
| STYLES: | DISC<br><br>MBTI<br><br>Personal Style Inventory (PSI)<br><br>Emotional Intelligence (EI) assessment<br><br>Undertaking a deeper dive with a coaching call around the outcome of the assessment<br><br>Application - how to use "findings" and apply the insights gleaned from the assessment undertaken |

| PERSPECTIVES: | Frame of Reference |
| | Visual Cards |
| | Perspectives |
| | Assumptions |
| | Reframing |
| | Six Thinking Hats |
| | Balance Coaching (CTI Model) |
| | Link to discussion around roles |
| GOAL SETTING: | SMART process |
| | CLEAR Goals – John Whitmore |
| | Objective Setting - Link to business goals, KPIs, Organizational Goals etc. |
| ACTION PLANNING: | Call to action - between sessions |
| | Identify action |
| | Accountability |
| | Follow-up next session before moving on |
| | Journaling (paper copy or online tools such as Journal Engine) |
| GENERATING AND EXPLORING OPTIONS: | MindMapping |
| | Brainstorming |
| | Post Its |
| | Fishbowl |
| | Six Thinking Hats |

## CHOOSING YOUR PLATFORM

The choice of your platform is a strategic one. Your choice of virtual platform depends on:

- The purpose: is it marketing, teaching, coaching, etc?

- Size of group
- Interactivity of the process
- Is it synchronous or asynchronous?
- Level of peer interaction—one-way or dialogue based?

Below is a list of some of the common platforms which are currently being used for phone and video calls. Appendix A has more details about the features of each of these platforms. These items are current as of publication of this book, and given the vast changes which happen, please check out what current features may exist.

- FreeConferencing.com
- FreeConferenceCalling.com
- FreeConferenceCall.com
- Skype
- Maestro Conferencing
- WebEx
- GoToMeeting
- Hangouts – Google
- Adobe Connect
- Zoom
- Join.me

## CHECK IN WITH JANE

Jane has been tasked with leading a high-impact, one-day virtual retreat for the global leadership team. It's high stakes and high impact. Jane is exploring the different options available to her for facilitating the program. She knows that the team may struggle to stay engaged all day long, so she wants to ensure that there is ample opportunity for smaller group work and breakouts. As she considers her options, she realizes that the phone-only options are not going to be sufficient for the level of team interactivity, focus, and dialogue she is hoping for.

She considers some of the more popular webinar platforms such as WebEx, but is concerned that these are heavily used for webinars. As such, people may automatically go into "Death by Conference Call" mode and start multitasking as they may expect more of a one-way conversation. She ultimately settles on Zoom as her platform of choice. The paid version gives her the ability to video stream as well as host virtual breakouts. This allows for a very interactive four-hour virtual retreat session. Even with people dialing in from different locations, they are all able to meet in the main room, as well as undertake small group work and paired discussions in breakouts. The four hours whiz by!

### END OF CHAPTER QUESTIONS

What different types of modalities are you considering using?

Do some research into the platforms you think you may use. What are the advantages and disadvantages of your choices? Set up any accounts you think you will use.

Make note of any action steps in your Action Plan Tracker.

# CHAPTER 5

# DESIGN: CREATING THE CONTAINER

*"You can design and create and build the most wonderful place in the world. But it takes people to make the dream a reality."*[71]

*– Walt Disney*

This chapter explores the process of designing virtual events from start to finish. We will look at design on two levels—first, the macro level from program idea to implementation, and second, from start to finish in a session.

In this chapter, we will also explore:

- Best practices for designing and implementing virtual programming
- Tools program planners and facilitators can use to "shape the container" for engaging and effective virtual calls
- Various macro steps of program design

- Core elements of the granular level of a program design from start to finish

## BEST PRACTICES IN DESIGN AND IMPLEMENTATION OF VIRTUAL LEARNING

There are a number of best practices we can leverage when designing virtual programs. Whether we are creating a one-hour webinar or leading a half-day retreat for a virtual team, always design with the following principles in mind:

### KNOW YOUR PEOPLE

*"Start with your people at the core. All else will flow from there."*
*– Jennifer Britton*

A central theme in creating and running effective and engaging virtual learning is that the people you are working with (your groups, your teams) should always be front and center. Their needs and preferences should be at the core of everything you do, and will shape everything from when you meet, to what platforms you use, to how engaging and interactive your conversations are.

Designing engaging and effective virtual conversations involves more than just undertaking a needs assessment. The more pre-connection, the better. Taking time to get to know your people pre-program includes meeting with them, perhaps through focus group discussion or one-on-ones.

In virtual learning, we want to make sure that we are designing with our group's needs in place, busting any assumptions that may be held, identifying any obstacles they may have with learning, and tailoring the learning for their participation and active application. This pre-work is absolutely imperative in creating engaging and effective virtual programming. What may work in one context may not work in another. What works well with one group may not work with another.

# PEBBLLES ETC

In looking at design and implementation principles and best practices for virtual learning I have developed the mnemonic PEBBLLES ETC. I spend a lot of time in the summer leading calls from the beauty of Muskoka. Surrounded by lakes, rivers, and trees it is not uncommon to see both kids and adults spending time skipping stones. This inspired me to start thinking about design and implementation best practices using the acronym PEBBLLES ETC (note the double L!). Because, taken collectively, these individual items, or "pebbles," create a more engaging and effective virtual program.

**PEBBLLES ETC stands for:**

**P** Preparation and Practice

**E** Expectations

**B** Breakouts

**B** Brain-based

**L** Less is More

**L** Loop back/Link back to the Workplace

**E** Expect the Unexpected

**S** Set People up for Success

**E** Embrace the Chaos

**T** Tools and Resources

**C** Clarity

Let us take a look at each one of these in turn:

## PREPARATION AND PRACTICE

Preparation is essential in virtual programming. Regardless of how much experience you bring to the table, it is not enough to show up and wing it. Any great performer knows that the sound check is an essential part of a wow performance. Similarly, knowing your material, the end result you want, and various engagement points along the way are all part of the preparation process. Later, we'll look at how tools like **MindMapping** and the **Design Matrix** can help you to prepare your plan and identify areas of concern.

Going hand-in-hand with preparation is *Practice*. We've all heard that practice makes perfect. In order to develop the fluidness and confidence of an experienced virtual leader, it is important to practice this work regularly. This does not mean simply getting a handle on the content, it's also about practicing technical things like starting a recording, moving people into breakouts, and putting people on mute. It is this practice that allows you to multitask with ease.

## EXPECTATIONS

Creating shared expectations (Ways of Working) with the group or team you are working with is foundational for virtual program success. Creating shared expectations often begins prior to the start of the program during pre-calls and involves reminding everyone of these shared expectations regularly. Because we don't have a flipchart we can keep bringing back to the conversation week to week, it is important to ask people to print the Ways of Working after call #1 and keep them in a visible place or review them at the start of each call. Alternatively, we can include a slide at the start of each streaming conversation, which reminds people of the agreements they have made to each other. Co-created Ways of Working are more powerful than those dictated to the group.

## BREAKOUTS

As covered in earlier chapters, creating an engaging environment for learning is about creating space for dialogue and breakouts. Breakouts are often the thing that get people engaged. Even more than chat, breakouts help people deeply connect with their WIIFM. While there might be some perceived risk to undertaking a breakout in the first session, helping group members gain clarity and connection early on can lead to much more engaged conversations. Consider the size of groups that are working in breakouts. Many times they will not be able to see each other, so smaller is better. Five or less people per breakout group is usually a good rule of thumb to keep the conversations flowing.

## BRAIN-BASED

There is an evolving recognition of the need to be more aware of and intentional with incorporating the neuroscience of what makes conversations and learning work. At a baseline, you will want to keep in mind your group's learning style preferences, as well as the latency and recency effect, to make powerful starts and finishes. Priming also allows us to set the stage for future learning. It might involve some pre-work reading or watching a video around the topic. This helps participants begin to connect with their WIIFM and make them active participants in the process of learning. Our Practitioner's Tip Text Box explores the brain, neuroscience, and great virtual conversations.

## Practitioner's Tip: The Brain, Neuroscience and Great Virtual Conversations

There are a number of ideas from the growing field of neuroscience that are important to keep in mind as we approach learning and virtual conversations:

### Different Neuroscience Concepts and Virtual Conversations

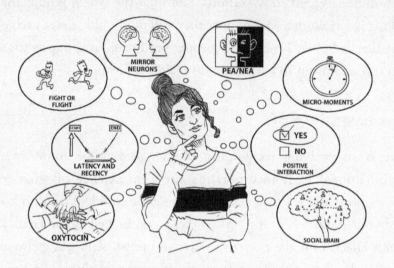

1. **Oxytocin** – the bonding glue

   The neurotransmitter oxytocin is responsible for feelings of connection and bonding.

   In the journal abstract *Oxytocin the Biopsychology of Performance in Team Sports,* the authors write: "We argue that oxytocin is related to biopsychological processes aimed at convergence of emotions and moods between people, and in doing so it is a critical neuropeptide involved in the shaping of important team processes in sport such as trust, generosity, altruism, cohesion, cooperation, and social motivation, and also envy and gloating."[72]

Increasingly, research is focusing on this neurotransmitter, which was originally found in the connection between a mother and her child. The impact of oxytocin is now being explored in the context of teams, and their ability to create further connection. Given that oxytocin is usually passed between two individuals (which is not possible in the virtual realm), we may need to become even more intentional in how we create connection in virtual groups and teams.

2. **The latency and recency effect** [73]

The brain tends to remember the start and end of things. What happens in the middle often is forgotten or murky. In designing effective virtual conversations ask yourself, *What are the core takeaways I would like people to leave with or remember after the program?* Make sure you are highlighting this at the start and end of calls, possibly recapping in the middle.

In the team and group coaching process, this is one of the key reasons why a *check-in* (*What have you done since we last met? What have you accomplished? What do you want to focus on?*) and *check-out* (*What have you learned? What are you taking forward? What are you committed to doing before our next conversation?*) helps to keep a focus on what's really important for the client.

3. **Fight or flight**

When we are under stress, we can experience an "amygdala hijacking," which some researchers say takes us back to the reptilian brain. When we perceive a threat, we may move to an innate response of fighting or running away. In a team or group coaching process, it is important to notice when stress reactions may occur, triggering people's flight or fight mechanism. This may happen due to conflict, people moving out of their comfort zones, or when trust and connection is not present. In terms of program design, think through how group and team members are going to get to know each other and trust each other so they can move into deeper and more challenging discussions. Sequencing—moving from lower risk to higher risk (for the group and/or individual)—is another consideration.

4. The role of **mirror neurons**

In his *Forbes* article "The Neuroscience at the Heart of Learning and Leading,"[74] Joshua Freeman writes about the discovery of mirror neurons that are significant in the "imprinting" of others—for example, the role of mentors and others who have significant impact. Freeman quotes some of the researchers in this area as, *"'Mirror neurons seem to be a bridge between our thinking, feeling, and actions—and between people,' says Iacobini. This may be the neurological basis of human connectedness, which we urgently need in the world today."*

Like several other areas where conflicting or limited research exists, considering the role of mirror neurons in learning, and relationships between people, those platforms where we can see each other (i.e., Zoom, live-streaming) may facilitate their activation at a greater level. More research is needed in this area.

5. The **PEA** and **NEA**

The work of Richard Boyatzis has explored two neural networks called Positive Emotional Attractor (PEA) and

Negative Emotional Attractor (NEA). Supporting people in a coaching conversation or dialogue into the PEA provides "PNS (parasympathetic nervous system) arousal—feeling positive and hopeful; thinking about the future, dreams and possibilities."[75] It also leads to "being optimistic, focusing on one's strengths," being "excited about trying something new, experimenting," and being in "resonant relationships." When we activate the PEA we "open people up" to possibilities and relationships. Coaching questions which are geared to invite exploration about what's possible help to open up the PEA. As we will see with virtual conversations, questions frame our dialogue. Using more open-ended questions may help to activate the PEA in virtual conversations.

By contrast, the NEA occurs when there is "Sympathetic Nervous System arousal. It leads to feeling negative and fear; thinking about the past or present; expectations of others and problems." It also takes us to the world of *should* and *expectations by others*. It leads to dissonant relationships.[76] By activating the NEA we literally shut people down. Notice how that occurs in calls you lead, possibly through the questions asked, a lack of safety being perceived by members, or norms being imposed.

As facilitators and conversationalists, we want to see what moves people into the NEA versus the PEA. The NEA shuts us down and inhibits conversations; whereas, the PEA opens us up to possibilities and dialogue.

6. **Micro-moments**

In 2015, I spent a lot of time working with both clinical and non-clinical leaders in a hospital setting. As you can imagine, the space and time for extended conversations was not always available. Over the years as a coach trainer, I have seen the power of laser-like conversations with focus. In 2015, I connected deeply with the work of Barbara Frederickson, learning from her in a Positive Psychology MOOC, seeing how her focus on the role of micro-moments was translating to the context of real-time micro-conversations happening in the hospital.

Frederickson writes, "Love, as your body experiences it, is a micro-moment of connection shared with another. And decades of research now shows that love, seen as these micro-moments of positive connection, fortifies the connection between your brain and your heart and makes you healthier."[77]

She has also noted that "face-to-face interactions enable greater synchronicity and shared positives between two people (shared smiles and laughter), which can improve health and the capacity to empathize."[78]

Notice in your virtual work how these short, sacred moments (micro-moments) can create trust and a sense of well-being. In addition, notice how face-to-face interaction like those on Skype or Zoom (when streaming) also create a sense of deeper trust and connection.

7. **The power of positive interactions**

Across different types of relationships there is a growing body of research about the importance of positive interactions.

John Gottman has been studying the effects of communication between romantic partners for decades, and he and his team of researchers discovered the importance of a five-to-one ratio of positive communication interactions versus negative interactions. Couples who are able to maintain this balance of positivity are typically in longer-lasting relationships. Those couples don't often divorce.

In 2004, Losada[79] published his findings on teams, finding a positivity ratio of 5.6 for high performing teams. In other words in high performing teams, five positive comments are made for every negative one.

While there has been some recent dispute around these exact calculations, anecdotally notice what happens in your team when they provide more positive comments to others. Take a look at HappierHuman.com's website, which goes into greater depth around these different studies. You can visit www.happierhuman.com/losada-ratio.

Barbara Frederickson also explores this topic in her book *Positivity*. You are also able to explore your own Positivity Ratio on an individual basis at PositivityRatio.com. In her work, she asserts that individuals who experience a 3:1 ratio of positivity can flourish. You can read what she wrote in 2013 about Positivity Ratios here in light of critique on Losada's calculations.

*Questions to consider: Notice the interactions that are occurring on the team. How would you characterize them? What do you notice overall? What impact does it have on the team?*

## 8. The social brain

The concept of the social brain has evolved over the years, grounded in the belief that the brain needs and thrives through interaction with others. If we go back to Bandura's work in the 1970s, he posited:[80]

- Learning can occur by observing others' behaviors and the resulting outcomes
- Learning can occur cognitively without a corresponding change in behavior
- Modeled behavior is reinforced by producing desirable outcomes (for both the observed party and the learner)
- Three variables in the social learning context—the learner, the behavior, and the environment—can influence each other

As Matthew Lieberman writes in *Social: Why our Brains are Wired to Connect,* "We have spent 10,000 hours learning to make sense of people and groups."[81] Recent studies have shown that social pain from rejection can be as significant as physical pain.

There are many other frameworks that are emerging that will no doubt influence the virtual conversation space. Take for example, C-IQ, and the work of Judith Glaser in *Conversational Intelligence.*

Judith Glaser's work has primarily focused on the intersection of conversation and neuroscience. She writes, "This 'chemistry of conversations' is why we need to be more mindful of our interactions. Behaviors that increase cortisol levels reduce our conversational intelligence or C-IQ—our ability to connect and think innovatively, empathetically, creatively, and strategically with others. Remember: behaviors that spark oxytocin boost C-IQ.

Positive comments and positive conversations also produce a chemical reaction. They spur the production of oxytocin—a feel-good hormone that elevates our ability to collaborate, communicate and trust others by activating networks in our pre-frontal cortex. Since oxytocin metabolizes faster than cortisol, its effects are less dramatic and sustainable."[82]

Interested in learning more about neuroscience? Here are some resources you may want to check out:

- The Learning Brain: From Baylor College of Medicine
- A May 2010 white paper by the Maritz Institute entitled "The Neuroscience of Learning: A New Paradigm for Corporate Learning. www.themaritzinstitute.com/ perspectives/~/media/files/maritzinstitute/white-papers/ the-neuroscience-of-learning-the-maritz-institute.pdf
- David Rock and Linda Page's *Coaching with the Brain in Mind*
- Judith Glaser's *Conversational Intelligence*
- Matthew Liebermann's *Social: Why Our Brains Are Wired to Connect*

## LESS IS MORE

Less truly is more in virtual facilitation. First, everything you do, especially the first time, is likely to take more time than you expect. Even pace changes take more time than in the in-person realm. Since it is a natural impulse for most of us to try to pack as much into a program as we can, this can lead to overwhelm.

In design work we talk about the 80/20 rule. This is not the Pareto Principle, which states that we get 80% of our results from 20% of our efforts. Rather the 80/20 rule in design is a metric to get us thinking about weaning down or synthesizing the materials we want to include. Rather than trying to cover all 100% of content, focus on covering just 80% of it. As you consider your design, look for the 20% that can be removed and perhaps made part of another program.

Numbers play a key role in virtual learning, and smaller groups are the norm for many virtual facilitators. Breakouts often work best with five or less group members. Overall, your larger groups may range somewhere between 12 -15 for training, and 4-8 for virtual coaching groups. In the virtual realm it is not always about the numbers, but rather the quality of the conversations. Fewer numbers, generally allow for more dialogue.

## LOOP BACK AND LINK TO THE WORKPLACE

An essential part of learning today is closing the learning loop and linking learning back to the workplace. This is done though goal setting and action planning. It also can be supported by adding an additional call after the series of the initial calls to check in and see what people are using and applying. If you do not prefer to add another call, encourage your group to identify their own accountability partners who will help them link their learning back to the workplace. One of your best allies here is likely the supervisor. What can you do to involve the supervisor in some way?

In several programs I've run we have created discussion guides for the supervisors of the attendees. These guides provide an overview of the virtual training that their staff member(s) went through. They also include suggested application opportunities of how they can support *transfer back to the workplace*. The guides also provide coaching questions the supervisor can pose to their staff to foster continued dialogue and focus. Key to successful integration and support is making it easy for the supervisor to keep this learning, and application of new knowledge, alive.

Another key focus in our virtual programming is the inclusion of action planning into most of our work. Attendees are encouraged to share their action plan with their supervisor and/or team.

## EXPECT THE UNEXPECTED

Whether it's smaller numbers than anticipated or a technology issue, having a backup plan and being fluid and resilient is key to a virtual facilitator's success. Always expect the unexpected. Resilience is key. What is your contingency plan for what might happen?

### Resilience, Recovery, and Renewal as a Facilitator

The concept of resilience is key as a virtual facilitator. Having a backup plan AND being able to "adjust on the fly" are critical in this work. Plan for the contingencies that may happen. This could range from:

- What to do if internet access doesn't work.

- What backup computer systems you have in place in case one goes down or can't connect.

- What if you get triggered by something someone says?

It is inevitable that what you hope won't happen in a virtual call, will. Recovery is important—as is the old adage, "Don't let them see you sweat." Lack of confidence or lack of certainty can be devastating to a group that is just starting out. What will help you get grounded or recover as quickly as possible?

We don't often talk about "burnout" for facilitators, but perhaps we should. I have met a number of internal facilitators who do this work five days a week. Facilitation requires a lot of energy, and each of us has a different appetite, endurance, and range for facilitation.

What are the signs that tell you it's time to take a break? What's the best blend of facilitation support for you over time, both for in-person and virtual events? What do you notice about the energy you expend as a virtual facilitator compared to your work in an in-person program?

## SET PEOPLE UP FOR SUCCESS

Designing from a place where everyone is set up for success is part of masterful design. In setting people up for success, consider these issues:

- What **barriers** will people face in their learning process or discussion? It could be that technology might get in the way, it could be lack of clarity.
- What **pre-work** will support people being ready to learn?
- What **goals** are people wanting to work on?
- What **accountability** will sustain the conversation?
- What **other things** are going to set people up for success?

In the virtual world, learning is more individualized. Getting people to not only identify their goals for learning but also their specific success measures is critical in creating more engagement and buy-in in their work. As a facilitator, it is important for you to note how one group member's success measures may be different than another's. Making sure people are clear on the expectation that virtual learning is not a passive event helps to redirect the focus and ownership of the learning to each participant. Questions to support clarification on success measures could include: *What will success look like for you at the end of the call? What is the tangible takeaway you want? How will you know this call has been useful?*

## EMBRACE THE CHAOS

Rather than fighting the inevitable chaos, what do you need to embrace? Plans will change, so being as resilient and nimble as possible will be useful.

## TOOLS AND RESOURCES

Masterful virtual facilitators have a robust kit of tools and resources to support them in their work. In Chapter 7 we will look at tools ranging from decision making, to consensus generation, to supporting groups with goal setting, team development in the virtual environment. In what areas do you think you will need more resources?

## CLARITY

In the virtual domain, everything revolves around clarity. This includes clear, concise communication in the way we speak and our word choice. It is also about having a robust selection of crisp, clear questions that resonate with the groups and teams we work with.

It's also about ensuring clarity around what's expected. So, for example, if people are on a breakout, what is the question they are discussing? How are they going to be reminded of it?

Clarity also takes place on the level of norms for the group—refer to our earlier discussion around Ways of Working.

As you prepare for your next program, be sure to download the PEBBLLES ETC worksheet. Consider how you want to incorporate each of these eleven best practices. This can be a useful checklist as you go to prepare your design.

# DESIGN QUESTIONS

Design of the space for an exceptional virtual facilitation starts well in advance of the event. This is shaped primarily by your group members and the purpose of the program.

Key questions to consider:

- What's the focus?
- What's the intended outcome?
- What activities and approaches do you want to incorporate?
- What environment do you want to create?
- What level of interaction do you expect?
- What is going to be accessible to the vast majority of participants? What won't? (note platform options)
- How much time will people have to participate?
- What is their appetite for pre-work? Post-work?

Additional questions to keep in mind when designing are:

- What is the size of the group?
- What level of interactivity is required?
- What connection do you want to create?
- What might get in the way?
- How similar is the group?
- What will each person value?

Note your responses to these questions each time you go to design.

## FOUR DESIGN PRINCIPLES

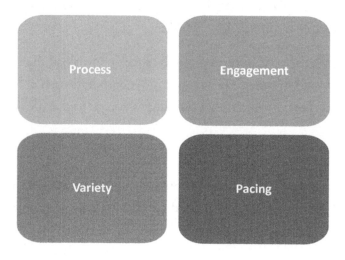

Process

Engagement

Variety

Pacing

Regardless of the type of virtual event, there are four key design principles for virtual facilitation, including:

1. **Process**

   A strong focus on process with the main elements of our design will give you the flexibility to adapt in the moment as needed. In the virtual environment, it is important to let people know what they can expect and where they are going.

   Process pieces you will want to make explicit include:

   - Overall elements/sections of the training or call/webinar
   - When to expect breaks
   - What to expect around engagement (see next point)
   - How visual anchor points will be created through slides and/or participant materials

   *What process pieces are important to consider or refine in your upcoming program?*

2. **Engagement**

   Providing multiple opportunities for members to connect with what they are learning is a key principle in adult learning. Virtual engagement opportunities should be ongoing and often more frequent and varied than in the in-person environment. Consider creating pace changes and different ways for participants to engage with the material through different strategies such as:

   - Polls
   - Chats
   - Use of whiteboard
   - Breakouts
   - Annotation
   - Handouts, worksheets, and/or participant guides sent prior to the call

*What engagement opportunities do you want to include in your upcoming work? What prep will you need to undertake to make this work? What transitions do you need to build in to make these successful with your platform?*

3. **Variety**

Webinars and virtual learning do not have to be a one-way, passive flow of information. From an interactive introduction where people mark their location on a map to breaking people into virtual breakouts, which can mimic the best of classroom-based dialogue, variety really is the spice of life.

Consider using the engagement techniques listed above to boost variety and how different parts of the module can be presented and/or reinforced in different ways.

*How much variety do you want to include?*

4. **Pacing**

Pacing is a key factor for success in any virtual environment. Consider how you can mix activities—from lecture, to breakouts, to using the whiteboard, to chats and individual reflection. Each group will have its own pace, so asking the group to identify how things are going using an emoticon as a pulse check at various points throughout the session, particularly longer ones, can be important.

*What pace will work best for your current group? How do you keep energy flowing?*

# OTHER KEY DESIGN PRINCIPLES

### SIZE MATTERS!

Less is more. Small is beautiful. Whichever cliché appeals to you, the fact is that group size in the virtual realm does not always have to be large. Again, think back to the level of engagement and interaction you want to foster. In developing trust and connection, smaller is definitely better—so if you are a coach reading this book, aim to create your virtual groups on the smaller side. As I mentioned previously, optimum group size from my experience has been around 4-8 members for virtual groups. While we can support more than that on a call, the more voices we have in the room, the more exponential the differences. We're not just adding one person—we're adding a whole new web of relationships.

This has been reinforced by research done by Richard Hackman—mentioned by Keith Ferrazzi in his article "Getting Virtual Teams Right." Hackman found that it only takes 10 conversations for every person on a team of five to touch base with everyone else, but when the number of team members increases to 13, the number of conversations necessary jumps to 78![83]

### TRANSLATING CLASSROOM-BASED LEARNING TO THE VIRTUAL REALM

As part of the move to a virtual culture, it is likely that you may be translating or transferring in-person classes into the virtual model. Some considerations in making this shift include:

- Consider pacing—what needs to change?
- How do in-person groups become breakouts—same questions or different?
- What pre-work if any do people need to complete?
- What elements can be combined or shortened?

- Is there a need for something to be done pre-call?
- What issues are relevant?
- What can people do real-time?

*Note the differences you see. What else do you want to consider as you move from virtual to in-person?*

## SEVEN STAGES TO DESIGNING A VIRTUAL PROGRAM

There are several stages in the program cycle, including activities to undertake prior to the session, at kick off, during the session, and after. This section explores the seven stages of any virtual process:

Briefly, these seven steps are:

### STEP 1 – WHO IS YOUR GROUP MEMBER?

In designing a powerful program, we want to start with our client in mind. They influence content, interactivity, platform choice, as well as the length of the call and when it is offered.

## STEP 2 – WHAT IS THE PURPOSE OF THE CALL?

There are many different reasons to host a virtual call including training, mentoring, meetings, or coaching. What is the purpose? What are the three end results you want people to leave with? What is going to be the best format?

## STEP 3 – BRAIN DUMP

During the design process, get all your ideas on paper. MindMapping can be a very useful tool to capture all of your ideas on one page. Or, if the MindMapping structure does not work for you, grab a set of index cards and capture your ideas, using one card for each idea. Afterwards lay them out on a table or floor and notice the patterns that emerge.

Take 10 minutes to capture all of your ideas either in a MindMap or through a set of index cards.

## STEP 4 – UNDERTAKE INITIAL PROGRAM DESIGN

One of the tools I like to use is the Design Matrix. The matrix serves as a framework to lay out the elements and sequencing of a call. Refer to EffectiveVirtualConversations.com to hear me talk about this tool.

## STEP 5 – NEEDS ASSESSMENT/PRE-MEETINGS WITH GROUP MEMBERS

Pre-meetings or pre-program questionnaires provide valuable data about the unique needs and preferences of your group members. It is harder to pull things together "on the fly" in the virtual realm, so pre-meetings can really help to ensure you've got the right platform, right content and right program. If you can't meet with the participants, discuss with the organization what has and has not worked, around virtual facilitation in the past.

## STEP 6 – CONSIDER THE WELCOME SUPPORTS

In bringing together people there will be a number of different supports you will want to keep in mind, including:

- A welcome letter or package
- A Frequently Asked Questions (FAQ) page
- Any pre-reads, or videos/audios you want people to view before they step into the virtual room

## STEP 7 – MEET THE GROUP AND KEEP ITERATING

Once you meet the group it is likely that there will be ongoing changes needed to initial plans and design.

Let's take a look at each one of these steps in greater depth. You are encouraged to work through the activities as you go:

## STEP 1 – WHO IS YOUR GROUP MEMBER? KNOWING YOUR AUDIENCE

Knowing your audience is key and will influence everything from when you meet, to what platform you use, to how you structure your program. Before moving on, take a few minutes to complete the Knowing Your Audience worksheet. You can download a fresh copy at www. EffectiveVirtualConversations.com.

| KNOWING YOUR AUDIENCE | |
|---|---|
| My participant is….. | |
| What is their WIIFM? | |
| What they will find valuable? | |
| What are the top three questions they have about this topic area? | |
| What is the biggest challenge they face? | |

| | |
|---|---|
| What is their comfort level with technology? | |
| How do they want to be supported going forward? | |
| How will they be applying what they are learning? | |
| What are their expectations coming into the program? | |
| Preferences for materials: hard or soft copy (paper, electronic, USB key)? | |
| What considerations are unique to this group? | 1.<br><br>2. |

**Creating connection prior to the session: How to get to know people –** As previously mentioned, creating connection is key in creating engaging virtual conversations. If you have time it can be a great approach to spend a few minutes on the phone meeting with everyone and hearing about what brought them to the program.

You may also want people to send a quick introduction about themselves. Provide a model so that they know what level to share at. You may also provide some key questions to prompt responses, such as:

- What brought you to the program?
- What are your key goals for taking this program?
- What is important for us to know about you?
- What do you bring to the group that's unique?

Another introductory activity can be to have each person share a photo or icon.

You can also set up a secret Facebook group where people can introduce themselves and share one thing they want to get out of the learning. This forum can be very useful in keeping the conversation going between touchpoints. Note I have indicated using a secret rather than closed group as closed groups are searchable online. If you are maintaining confidentiality of your group members, a secret Facebook group is more appropriate.

## STEP 2 – CONSIDER THE PURPOSE AND BEST PLATFORM FOR THE CALL

Your purpose and the platform(s) available will help to shape the actual design of the call. They will help you choose the platform as well as the level of interactivity. Refer to the platform choices from Chapter 4. As you start up, note whether people prefer communicating via print versus voice (i.e., chat versus microphones on) and how they want to connect.

## STEP 3 – BRAIN DUMP/MINDMAP

Our third step takes us deeper into the realm of design work. There are several design tools that you may find very useful in your preparation phase. These include:

- The MindMap
- The Design Matrix

MindMaps are a great starting point as they provide the benefit of capturing many evolving ideas on one page.

From a one page MindMap, the different components of a program can then be chunked out. For example, I might notice that I have six major topic areas which would translate nicely into spending one module for each of the six-module program. Keeping in mind who the client group is, I'll have a sense of the amount of time I have with the group. This could range from six one-and-a-half hour sessions spread over six weeks to a full six-hour training day with a group.

As we look at a design MindMap, we may start to see some defined modules emerging. For example, if you're working with a group of global leaders, you may see modules forming around topics like time-management, team leadership, and/or stakeholder engagement. Once modules are identified, you can then move onto fleshing them out in the Design Matrix.

## STEP 4 – INITIAL DESIGN

The Design Matrix provides a mini-roadmap of what will be covered in a learning event. In this step, you can start to map out the different activities and conversations you are going to have in each one of the sessions. I have included a blank Design Matrix I use in my work.

### GROUP COACHING DESIGN MATRIX

Topic Name:

Topic Length:

Overall Goals or Objectives of the Topic (*or What people will take away from the conversation*)

| DURATION | CONTENT/LEARNING POINTS/COACHING QUESTIONS | ACTIVITIES/METHODS | MATERIALS NEEDED |
|---|---|---|---|
| | | | |
| | | | |
| | | | |
| | | | |
| | | | |
| | | | |
| | | | |
| | | | |

You will note that there is space to outline:

The topic

Topic length – how long you have

Overall goals – what you want people to leave with

In addition to noting the individual activities/focus areas, there is space for you to note the duration (how much time it will take), what activities or methods you will use (breakouts, large group discussion, lecture, scenario), and any materials needed.

You may move through several drafts of the matrix, which captures key elements of the timeline, any questions, content or learning points, and materials needed to run the session.

Depending on your style, you may include more or less detail in your matrix as you design. With a virtual event, consider the fact that activities and transitions may take longer. You will need more time to provide instructions, more time to move people, and more time for groups to get connected.

### Designing for New Experience: Neuroplasticity

Neuroplasticty refers to the brain's ability to create new connections and expand in size. It was once believed that the brain stopped growing during youth, but now we are seeing even adults in their 90s experience brain changes. In creating learning environments, what are we able to create? As Wendy Suzuki writes, "Deprive your brain of new stimulation or bore it with doing the same thing day after day, and the connections will wither away and your brain will actually shrink."[84]

You may be familiar with the studies done by McGuire on the brain size of London taxicab drivers. Their research found that the taxicab training actually lead to a larger posterior hippocampi.

They measured the drivers' brain size at the start of training and at the end, also comparing the brains of those who passed with the brains of the drivers who failed. The drivers who passed had actually expanded the size of their brain!

## CAPTURING ATTENTION AND CREATING ENGAGEMENT THROUGH YOUR DESIGN

*"Repetition engages the neural networks related to our attention system; in other words, we tend to remember what we pay attention to." – pp 75, Suzuki*

According to Suzuki, there are several factors that make things memorable. We make things memorable when things are ***novel, surprising, emotional, and attention-grabbing.***[85]

What can you do to incorporate these approaches into your design? Make a list of these items.

### The ACCORDION

In my books, *Effective Group Coaching* and *From One to Many: Best Practices for Team and Group Coaching,* I introduced the concept of the accordion—a principle that gets us thinking about what areas could be "collapsed"—like the folds of an accordion—if people are enjoying the conversation. It also gets us thinking about what can be stretched out if things are moving more quickly than planned. The next time you co-facilitate on a virtual call, think about the accordion points. When you start to map out your design, earmark those areas that can be elongated or shortened.

There are a number of different design tools to support you in creating your programming, including traditional design tools. Just remember that things tend to take longer in the virtual domain.

# DESIGN TO-DOS AND NOT TO-DOS

A lot of different elements go into good design. The following table captures some of the key elements around questioning, storytelling, feedback, activity choices, engagement and interactivity, activity choices, tricky issues, breakouts and availability during a program.

| TO-DO | NOT TO DO |
|---|---|
| **QUESTIONING** ||
| Ask open-ended questions to invite exploration. <br><br> Call on people. <br><br> Remember people may want to engage in questions in different ways: <br><br> - Small group <br><br> - Large group <br><br> - Individual reflection <br><br> - Chat response <br><br> - Raised hands <br><br> Give people time to write it down and then respond. | Not ask questions. <br><br> Ask questions that are unclear. <br><br> Ask closed questions. <br><br> Leave the silence hanging. |
| **STORYTELLING:** ||
| Storytelling can be perceived in many different ways by different cultures. When trust levels are low, or connection is not there, storytelling on the part of the facilitator may be seen as boastful by some cultures. ||

| | |
|---|---|
| Keep it brief. | Go on and on with stories. |
| Keep it relevant. | Not make the link to what you are discussing. |
| Share a range of stories or case studies, not just your own. Ask your clients for examples and build off of these to bring examples to life. | Use it as an opportunity to showcase how great you are. |
| Make sure there is a direct connection to what you are discussing. | |
| Encourage others to bring in their own stories. Providing them with an outline of how long the story should be and some key elements can be useful. For example, the iconic "Hero's Journey" moves through a mutli-step process. A piece of homework between calls could entail having everyone identify their journey. | |
| **FEEDBACK** ||
| Ask for regular feedback such as a show of hands or emoticon. | Listen for dead silence. |
| Have a structured process, for example, incorporating feedback rounds framed as *"I appreciate…,"* *"I see your strengths as…,"* *"I need more of…,"* etc. | Not ask for feedback or wait to the end. |
| | Assume that everything is fine. |
| | Not act on feedback received. This will reduce trust levels. |
| Act on it! | |
| **ENGAGEMENT AND INTERACTIVITY** ||
| Make pace change regular–every 7-10 minutes schedule a pace change. | Speak in a monotone or lecture for a long stretch. |
| Incorporate real-time application opportunities where people can "do it now" or write it down. | |
| Use the tools available—chat, emojis, annotation. | |

| ACTIVITY CHOICES | |
| --- | --- |
| Have a range of approaches. | Bring in unrelated items to the theme. |
| Link activities to the topic you are exploring. | Avoid things that are complicated or take a lot of time to complete. |
| Test it out before you use it by doing a walk through. | Overcomplicate activities. |

| TRICKY ISSUES | |
| --- | --- |
| Address issues as they emerge. | Allow group members to dominate the conversation, use inappropriate language, be disrespectful. |
| Mute. | |
| Address them offline. | |
| Maintain respect and safety for everyone. Minimize involvement of that participant. | |

| BREAKOUTS | |
| --- | --- |
| Use liberally. | Shy away from breakouts because they may be too difficult to set up or may not work technically. |
| Provide key instructions on time allocation, what questions you should discuss, and what people should come back to you with. | |

| AVAILABILITY | |
| --- | --- |
| Be clear on how people can reach you – mobile or email. | Be offline or turn off alternative modes of communication. |
| Have another phone line they can access during the call. | |
| Include your contact details in signature lines. | |

## STEP 5 – PRE-MEETINGS AND NEEDS ASSESSMENT

Pre-meetings or needs assessments are key to making sure your program is adapted to the needs of the group you will be working work with. They help you further refine your design. If a pre-meeting is feasible for a program you are running/coordinating, consider asking questions along the lines of:

- What do you want to get out of our work together?
- What do you want to learn?
- What are your expectations?
- How will you know you have been successful at the end of our calls?
- What should I know about how you learn best in the virtual environment? What has been your experience with technology? Are there any tech issues I should be aware of?

If you are working with an internal program that is going to be virtualized, key questions might include:

- What do you want people to get out of their virtual experience?
- What has been your past experience in virtual-based learning/ conversations?
- What platforms do you use?
- What pre-work is feasible for this group?
- Tell me a little more about the participants, their roles and priorities. What will be important about this topic for them?
- How does this connect to other learning modules?
- What else should I know about your experience with virtual conversations?

## STEP 6 – WELCOME SUPPORTS

As indicated in earlier chapters, welcome supports could include:

- A welcome letter
- A Frequently Asked Questions (FAQ) Page
- A Coaching Agreement
- A materials list

*What welcome supports do you want to pull together?*

### The Myth of Multitasking

There is a myth that we are able to multitask. In fact, multitasking is not feasible or possible. Here's what Dr. Joanne Deak writes in her book, *Your Fantastic Elastic Brain*:

"When you try to multitask, in the short-term it doubles the amount of time it takes to do a task and it usually at least doubles the number of mistakes. In the long-term it changes the brain from being able to focus deeply on a single task well, to being what we call a rifle, that wants to jump around a lot." She continues, "Ideally, teacher instruction—or input—should be in short bursts of 10 or 20 minutes, each followed by the students expressing what they have learned, either through discussion, notes or actions—the output... Research shows that ending each section with some form of output is the best form of learning."[77]

*How can you support your group in achieving deeper focus and avoiding a Death by Conference Call scenario?*

## STEP 7 – MEET GROUP AND ITERATE

Finally, you will meet with your group, begin your program, and continue to adapt your design throughout the facilitation process. Remaining open to change is a critical success factor for facilitators.

# THE PROGRAM CYCLE

Every program cycle is comprised of several stages, including activities to undertake prior to the session, at kick off, and during the session. Let's take a look at each of these.

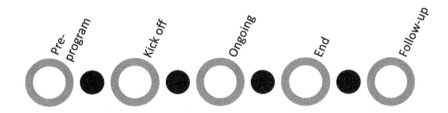

# PRE-PROGRAM

These are the steps we described in our last section, including pre-meetings, platform choice, and design issues.

To make sure you have your bases covered, download the pre-program checklist found at www.effectivevirtualconversations.com.

# KICK OFF

The start of the call sets the stage for the rest of the call. Be sure to always include:

- An introduction of each group member including their sharing around what they want to get out of the program and/or what will success look like at the end of the program.
- An overview of where you are going.
- Expectations/Ways of Working.
- Introduction to any technical issues. This can be on an introductory slide before you start.

**Top 10 Questions to Open a Session**

1. What brought you here?

2. What's important about this topic for you?

3. What do you want to focus on today?

4. How will you know we've been successful?

5. What do you want to get out of the session?

6. What do you bring that is unique to the group?

7. What is your biggest question to explore today?

8. How do you see yourself contributing to our group?

9. What's one thing you'd like everyone to know about you?

10. How engaged do you plan to be today?

# ONGOING CALLS

While every call will be different, there are several items you will want to keep in mind for each call such as:

- Use breakouts.
- Balance the time you spend speaking with group interaction, content, and process.
- Read the room for energy, conflict, questions.
- Ask for feedback.
- Leverage engagement opportunities via polls, breakouts, chat function.

There are several issues that you will likely navigate during your ongoing calls including connecting people between sessions, dealing with the *troll mentality*, visuals and other prompts, real-time action, and what to do when people join from different platforms. Let's take a look at these.

## CONNECTING PEOPLE BETWEEN SESSIONS

In some programs, there will be an opportunity to have ongoing dialogue between the sessions. One effective way to connect people outside formal sessions is to designate paired partners. Then provide group members with a relevant question to meet and dialogue around with their partner. Scheduling these peer calls of anywhere from 15-60 minutes in between sessions can keep the focus alive. It can also be used to create accountability partners, where pairs or triads work together throughout the course, sharing their goals and focus on a regular basis.

*What approaches do you want to use to connect people between and during sessions?*

## THE "TROLL MENTALITY"

Unfortunately, the virtual world can bring out the negative side of people: hence, the *troll mentality.* It's important to shut any negative or abusive behavior down immediately. Having an overall code of conduct that outlines procedures for dealing with abuse, discrimination, etc. may be something worth putting in place before people get on line.

### Visuals and Other Prompts[87]

We live in an era of data. In late March 2017, it was estimated that Google received 3.5 billion searches per day[88]—or 40,000 per second. Within this framework, learning is no longer only about obtaining and processing new information. It is also about making connections.

A 1986 study found that the human brain processes visuals 60,000 times faster than text.[89] How are you incorporating visuals into your work? In the virtual realm, gearing the focus of conversation toward a visual element can be an added advantage. Consider these questions as you think about your programming:

- What are the elements you could convert from text to visual?
- What might you do to incorporate more photographs?
- Could you include more visual media such as TED Talks? Videos? Cartoons?
- What opportunities can you create to encourage the creation of more visuals?

When I work with teams, one activity I like to do at the end of the team day is have each participant create a model of what they learned through our time together...using tin foil. It's pretty amazing what can be designed and created with tin foil!

*Consider three things that you might bring in or adapt in your next virtual presentation that are more visually oriented than text-oriented.*

## WE CAN ONLY REMEMBER SEVEN THINGS

Our brains are only able to retain a finite number of things, and research has shown that number is seven (plus or minus two things).[90] This is why phone numbers used to be seven digits long.

In the virtual domain, anchor points and reminders of where you have been and where you are going are important. While you may be tempted to "overdeliver" with a long laundry list of ideas, keep in mind people may not be able to retain all that information.

Consider the top seven ideas you want to communicate. What's important about them? How are they connected? What is the order in which they are important?

Now, can you simplify that list down to three?

These three big ideas may become the core focus of the call you lead. Consider how you can build in time to share and reinforce these topics with your group, chunking the call down to three overall segments: start, middle, and end.

There you go—it can be as easy as that to chunk down your next training or call.


REAL-TIME ACTION – DO IT NOW!

A beauty of virtual programming is that people are often connecting from their normal life and work environment. This makes it incredibly easy to DO IT NOW. What can you get people to do "in the moment?" Some examples could include:

- Getting people to note their next steps in their calendars right away.
- If you are focusing on time-management and organization, giving people 10-15 minutes to complete a task they have been putting off.
- If you are focusing on time-management and organization, giving people 10-15 minutes to spend drafting their presentation out real-time, followed by another block of time dedicated to having them write their slides or prepare their flipchart.

*What could you do to support your learners in moving into action?*

## WHEN DIFFERENT PEOPLE JOIN FROM DIFFERENT PLATFORMS [91]

Another issue to consider is when different team members join from different platforms. These days, it is quite common to have different participants join a call via different platforms, while some are calling in together from the same room, and others may be calling from the road. This can cause some disruption and is a tricky issue for new facilitators—especially if you have staff who travel, versus those who may be connected online. At the same time, you might have a group of people dialing in from one locale with or without computer access.

Consider the following pre- and post-meeting tips to make multi-platform sessions less disruptive:

- Be aware of the different platforms your group members are located on. What accessibility and interactivity options do those platforms provide? What changes are needed?
- Consider what can be sent out prior to the session and how. If you are referring to slides or a presentation how will you provide the handout before the session? Should you email it or upload it to a part of the Intranet (internal internet or network)? If you cannot send material prior to the session, how can people access it? Recognize that they may need the material before the call, or in a way they can access offline.
- Be as descriptive as possible, especially if some people cannot refer to a screen or notes. Note the pace and time this takes. Adapting in the moment and considering what core essentials should be covered real-time, supplemented by follow-up can be key. Too slow a pace may mean losing the entire group.
- Be aware of what the different platforms look like and what accessibility people will have. Be comfortable troubleshooting or designate someone on the team to help with technical aspects as everyone gets familiar and begins coaching each other.
- Consider any follow-up needed as a result of the call.

*Questions to consider: If you are tasked with leading an upcoming virtual meeting, what are the key steps you want to take note of? When will you complete this?*

# ENDING

There are two layers of closure in programs—one at the end of each session, and another at the end of a program. Consider this:

## LAYER 1: CLOSURE IN A SESSION

Closing a session is just as important as opening the session. You may want to focus on:

- What have you learned?
- What are your next steps?
- Who is responsible for what? By when? How will you follow up?
- What's been important for your learning?
- What's a metaphor that represents what you are leaving with?
- If you could only do one thing, what would it be?
- If you could only explore one thing what would that be?
- What is the one thing you will do in the next 24 hours?

Questions to create clarity or focus at the end of the call include:

- What's important?
- What did you notice?
- What's clear?
- What's the priority?

## LAYER 2: CLOSURE IN A PROGRAM

Closure at the end of a program is often overlooked. Consider what are the ways you want to review the highlights, hear about learning and next steps. Consider techniques such as getting people to identify their "roadmap going forward" such as a gallery walk of whiteboards created during your work, or using breakouts for participants to share their detailed next steps with a colleague, returning to the main room for a large group micro-share of one key learning.

## PRE- AND POST-LEARNING

Virtual Learning is not just about the call time, it is about the larger process, which includes those things that happen before and after the call. How can pre-work, and between-session assignments, keep the conversation and connections going? The following is a list of eight things you can do with pre-work and in-between-session touchpoints:

1. As pre-work, have group members share a brief bio and what brought them to the program. This can be posted on a central home page.

2. Create a closed or secret Facebook group, connecting individuals between sessions. These can be very popular with some groups. Take into consideration access to Facebook and other social media sites.

3. As pre-work, have the group members consider an example, or several examples, of where things worked well and not-so-well as it relates to the focus of the program. For example, if you are leading a virtual session on conflict management, have group members note a time when they navigated conflict well, and a time when conflict management did not go so well.

4. Create learning partners and provide weekly questions for partners to come together and discuss.

5. Create learning partners and create structured assignments for them to complete together—this can be linked into work application and debrief.

6. Create pre- and post- self-assessments so individual group members can track their skill development and new insights.

7. Create a reading and resource list with group members throughout the course of the program. Again, hosting this at a central repository can be useful. This could be a wiki, a Facebook page, or part of your LMS.

8. Each week, have a different group member take the lead on posing a daily or weekly question for the group to consider. This provides an interesting approach to peer collaboration and learning.

*What are the elements you would like to include before and after the program?*

### Four Killer Mistakes Virtual Facilitators Can Make[92]

What are the key mistakes virtual facilitators can make? There are four things to keep in mind, regardless of the size or time of your next virtual event.

**Mistake #1 – Not being prepared.** A lot of things are going on when you lead a virtual meeting, training session or event. Keeping people's focus is #1 and because group members may not see you, they may be more attuned to the nuances of your voice. If they can see you while you are streaming, they will pick up on everything.

Prior to any virtual event, consider what is going to support you in your preparation. How well do you know your materials?

**Mistake #2 – Not knowing the technology.** Every virtual platform has different nuances. Being confident and knowledgeable about your platform is a best practice. Take time in advance to check it out, even if it is only you on the line. Most platforms come with detailed video tutorials and FAQs. Have these on hand and consider what could possibly go wrong, and if so, what you will do about it.

**Mistake #3 – Not knowing the audience.** Knowing your audience and helping them connect early on with their WIIFM sets everyone up for success. In the virtual domain, trust and connection play an even more critical role in engagement. What can you do to meet or connect with the audience before you get started? This could be as simple as a personal email introducing yourself and the purpose of your meeting, or as elaborate and time-intensive as short pre-calls with each person.

Watch out for these assumptions you might be holding about your audience:

- They know what the purpose of this call is.
- They came prepared.
- They are not multitasking.
- They know how to use the technology.
- They all have the same needs.
- They will follow up immediately with what they have said they would do.
- Silence means they are getting it.
- Silence means they are following you.

**Mistake #4 – Not having a contingency plan in place.** Masterful virtual facilitators operate within the realm of contingency planning. *Expect the Unexpected* is the mantra of many masterful virtual facilitators and virtual team leaders. What are the possible things that could happen with your program and what will you do if the unexpected occurs?

A reminder of the accordion principle to facilitation. Where can you shorten the program if things are taking too long, and where can you elongate the program if you need more time? The accordion becomes an important part of your planning. Review your design to note things that might happen. What contingencies do you want to put in place?

Preparation – consider what you will do if A or B happens. In the spirit of contingency planning, what is Z in the plan? Operating in a VUCA environment usually means we wind up quickly moving beyond the A and B of our plan.

Don't let them see you sweat!

They won't know what's happening if you don't tell them. So, for example if you forget to do an activity, do not draw attention to it—your group may not even know they missed anything. Cover that at a different time.

## FOLLOW-UP AND EVALUATION

**Evaluating your virtual event:** Thinking about evaluation from the start can provide you with the opportunity to identify metrics you can track along the way. While it may be tempting to send out an evaluation form after the event, it's always best to get real-time feedback on your program. Evaluation is a key part of making sure that you are being effective in your work.

I usually like to do a couple of quick evaluations and feedback loops throughout a one-day program, including check-in questions like:

- Who got something valuable out of that section?
- Give me a show of hands if you just got a tip you can apply.
- Type in the chat what you have found valuable so far.

At the end of the first session or mid-day I will ask for more detailed feedback such as:

- What worked well?

- What are you taking away from your learning?
- What are you going to put into practice right away?
- What should we do differently next time/this afternoon?
- What approaches do you like best?

Two other tools can be useful in capturing information:

- Emojis – Emojis are a quick and fun way for people to share how they feel. Asking people to comment on their experience using emojis can be a quick pulse check before a break.
- Use of polls – While polls require some pre-planning and set up, they're also a great way to boost interactivity.

In asking these questions you will likely get a sense of the pace, pitch, and tone of the call and how it is meeting needs.

## EVALUATION MID-POINT

Mid-point evaluations are important in longer programs. This could include a self-evaluation such as:

- A self-assessment of the key skills involved in the training, and noting where you were at the start, and where you are mid-point
- Weekly journal prompts
- A one-pager where people make a running list of what they are learning

In coaching, we talk about the importance of creating structures of learning to remind people of their commitments and what is important. In virtual programs, it can be very important to get people to think about what's going to keep the learning alive and visual. This could include things such as:

- Post-it notes
- An alarm or ring tone which will signal it's time to do something

- A vision board

## FOLLOW-UP

Virtual programs don't usually just end with the final call. There are a number of ways you can follow up a virtual facilitation event including:

- A group follow-up call
- Peer partnering
- Worksheets
- Another program

In creating these follow-up opportunities, determining when they will happen and what they will look like, consider:

- Who are the participants?
- What did they find valuable?
- How do they want to connect?
- What partners do they want to be accountable to?
- What do you want to automate in terms of availability and other things?

I typically meet with a group sometime between two and six weeks after the event to see how things are going, usually via a one-hour call. Ideally the group size is less than 10 people (otherwise it can become very cumbersome). We use this as a chance to check in and see what people are doing and give people the chance to:

- Share best practices they have evolved or put into place.
- Share what's working and what's not.
- Identify any roadblocks they may be facing in their work.
- Lock in the learning.
- Identify next steps.

In this chapter, we've explored many different tools and best practices for design of overall programs, as well as individual sessions. Let's see how Jane is going to apply what we've learned.

## CHECK IN WITH JANE – DESIGN

Jane has been tasked in leading a special session for new virtual facilitators at the organization. Part of her mandate is to help them develop. She realizes that she is going to need to do some research on what is really needed so she pulls out the **Seven Step Approach to Design**. Her first starting point is to do some research about the audience, which she realizes is global and really craving a venue to connect, see each other, and share resources. She realizes that a traditional, one-way webcast is not going to be the right modality for this environment, so she goes back to her list of different platforms and realizes that Zoom is going to be the best choice in terms of screen sharing for both herself and the other participants, stability, and easy set-up of breakouts.

In terms of her own preparation, she decides that she is also going to highlight six main points for herself with this program, including:

1. The best practices of PEBBLLES ETC
2. Reminder of Less Is More and the 2:1 ratio
3. When thinking about design keep in mind: Process, Engagement, Variety and Pace
4. Spending time getting to know the group members (pre-calls to ensure that proper platforms are chosen)
5. Pre- and post-program touchpoints
6. Make a list of some of the great questions

She also notes the following tips and questions for herself in her notes:

- Consider the start and end – that's what people remember!
- How will we keep the learning alive? (to discuss with the group)
- What opportunities do I have to get people to "do it now!" during the call (maybe prepare for a difficult conversation, do a self-assessment)?
- What will I do to follow up after the program?
- What will I do to evaluate the program?

## END OF CHAPTER QUESTIONS

What is going to cement design for you? You may want to move through Steps 1 – 7 using our worksheets.

What will jazz things up for you?

Make note of any action steps in your Action Plan Tracker.

CHAPTER 6

# PREPARING FOR BLAST OFF: FOCUS AREAS FOR NEW AND EXPERIENCED FACILITATORS

*"We cannot discover new oceans unless we have the courage to lose sight of the shore."*[93]

*— André Gide*

Setting people up for success is one of the most important things a virtual facilitator does. Preparation is a key success factor for virtual programs. This chapter explores key activities and tasks for "blast off" or program launches.

In this chapter we reconnect with Jane, who brings to life more of the characteristics and skills of virtual facilitator. The chapter also explores topics such as:

- Preparing yourself for your virtual event

- Key activities as you prepare to launch a program and sessions
- Setting yourself and your group up for success
- Habits of exceptional facilitators
- Key activities for first-time facilitators

## JANE –THE TYPICAL VIRTUAL FACILITATOR

Regardless of who we are—whether we're new or seasoned facilitators—many of us are like Jane. Virtual facilitators share several key characteristics including being:

- Tech savvy
- Able to work on our feet
- Able to build connections with people we have never met
- Able to leverage a breadth and depth of experience
- Well-read
- ESP—the ability to use intuition to sense what your group members mean and what's important to them
- Comfortable communicating with people we cannot see
- Good trouble-shooters
- Optimistic

- Able to multitask, including talking and working with technology at the same time
- Confident despite not having all the answers
- Able to pass things over to the group
- Great hosts!

Because technology is always changing and evolving, virtual facilitators by nature are accustomed to ongoing learning. They are adaptable and open to feedback and have the ability to change over time. These qualities are essential in a context like the virtual world that is ever-changing and not in the facilitator's control.

### Five Hallmarks of Exceptional Virtual Facilitators

1. **Hosting capability** – Being a good host to the people you'll be working with is a huge part of the virtual facilitation world. It starts with welcoming people as they "enter the room" and log on, as people get connected. Just as a host functions in a party, this creates safety and connection, laying the foundation for the triad to emerge.

2. **Clear communicator** – This is important especially when we operate only in the phone-based realm.

3. **Intercultural understanding** – We've already explored how exceptional virtual facilitators are aware of the different cultural nuances that can play out with dispersed groups. This includes cultural differences that exist not only when we move outside of our borders, but even to different regions across our own home countries. It's not only time zones that make us unique but also what we value, how we work, how we dress, and how we prioritize. Great virtual facilitators will have a broad understanding of some of these regional nuances as well as the

urban/rural differences that can exist.

4. **Flexibility** – As virtual facilitators, we need to be flexible in terms of:

- Meeting the group where they are at
- Changing pace
- Changing gears
- Changing focus
- Being unflappable—whether it's a bridgeline that goes down or a group that gets dropped, it's important as a virtual facilitator to let things roll off your back and be able to problem solve on the spot. Virtual facilitation is not for the faint of heart, or for anyone who expects everything to work perfectly all the time!

5. **Ability to create a pause point** – Many of us operate in contexts where we are constantly on the go. Virtual calls may provide your attendees with a valuable pause at various levels including:

- At the start of the call to get grounded or capture their ideas in a worksheet/online notes[94]
- At the middle of the call to note what they have learned so far
- At various points during or at the end of major sections to capture their learning in a one-page plan or one-page sheet they can then take forward within their work
- At the end for people to take notes on their learning
- A pause point or 30 to 60 seconds of silence before you ask them to speak

- Periodic "mindfulness" pause points at any time for people to stop and pay attention to their breathing, noticing whether it is fast, slow, shallow or deep. There is increasing research about the benefit of incorporating this type of mindfulness training into our work with professionals of all kinds. This does not need to be time-consuming, and may simply involve introducing these pause points for group members to take note of their thoughts or what their bodies are saying.

*What pause points do you want to provide during your virtual learning process?*

## PREPARING FOR YOUR VIRTUAL EVENT

*"Success depends on previous preparation and without such preparation there is sure to be failure." – Confucius*

As you prepare for any virtual event—your first or your thousandth—there are several key things to do to prepare yourself, have a game plan around content, as well as be ready for whatever shows up in your virtual space. Whether you are a new or seasoned facilitator, it is essential to know the value of making sure we, too, prepare for the conversation.

Preparation includes logistical preparation, preparation for ourselves as facilitators, and tactical preparation.

## LOGISTICAL PREPARATION

What you'll need to have on hand for your calls:

- Microphone
- Timer/stopwatch
- Email and phone numbers of participants (in case you have to get through to them during the call itself)

- Water and drink in hand (in a cup!)
- Backup computer and materials
- Materials for the call—hard and soft copy
- Internet access
- Any required passwords
- Contact names and emails of your group members

Check for these when you are setting up your room:

- Lighting
- Echo
- Speed
- Level of screen
- Ambient or external noise (fans/alarms/etc.)

*** It is important to minimize distractions for yourself. Turn off your phone (if you have a technical backup who can troubleshoot tech issues) or set it on vibrate. Remove any confidential data or information that may be nearby and can be viewed on the screen. Also turn off any unnecessary, or confidential, applications on your device if you are screen sharing.

## OURSELVES AS FACILITATORS

On the personal front, it is important to always remember that we are "leading from self." This is particularly important because in the virtual domain, we can sometimes feel like our own "island." Leaders new to this realm may find that they need to be more self-reliant than when they lead in the in-person domain.

*What do you notice about your energy? What might you find challenging with this call? What do you think might be easy?*

## TACTICAL PREPARATION

As you go to prepare there are several tactical areas to keep in mind:

- Managing your time – What's the roadmap for the call? How much time will you be spending in each area? What are the accordion points that can be expanded if things are going fast, or condensed if things are moving slowly?
- Dealing with difficult issues – Consider how you might address any challenges that might surface. This could include difficult group members, any areas that are not appropriate, technology challenges or a slow connection speed.
- What cultural sensitivities need to be considered? In a virtual environment you are likely to be working with a wide variety of cultures—globally, nationally or even regionally. Be aware of how you are communicating, and make adjustments as needed. Who might know English as a second, or third, language? What adjustments do you want to make around this?

## ESTABLISHING CREDIBILITY

Just as in the in-person world, establishing credibility as part of building rapport is key. In fact, in a phone-only environment, establishing credibility and connection may be even more important, given our nature to automatically multitask. Prior to each session, consider how you want to introduce yourself. This could include:

- Who are you?
- What's your connection to this topic area?
- What can people expect from your role or leadership?
- What can they "count on you" for?
- What are you hoping to create with them?
- What's your WIIFM or intended outcome for the day?

## CREATING TRUST AND CONNECTION IS KEY

Your group will also want to feel confident that you are credible and going to be responsible. They will be looking for:

- How you speak, including the use of slang and swear words
- Word fillers like ums and ahs
- Your intonation – One of the funniest and most famous scenes in the movie *Ferris Bueller's Day Off* (a blockbuster when I was in high school) was the famous scene where the teacher took attendance in a nasal, monotone voice, repeating the name, "Bueller...Bueller...Bueller..." over and over. In virtual calls, especially when visual cues are not present (i.e., teleclasses), your speech, and its natural peaks and valleys, are an important tool. Listen back to any recordings you have of yourself for your intonation, pauses, and energy. What do you notice?
- Your self-management – Knowing ourselves, our strengths, and triggers is important as a facilitator. If you perceive that a session might provoke your emotions, how do you want to handle it? What might trigger you around this topic? What will you do to get focused or grounded?
- How you are standing or sitting – Make sure your posture and gestures are appropriate and applicable to the context in which you are working. In some cultures, trust is eroded when you cannot see someone's hands—i.e., when they're hidden in pockets or under the desk. Gestures can be an important tool to keep energy and engagement levels on the move. Standing desks are a great way to "get the energy up" in virtual calls. If you are leading a number of virtual events throughout the day, you will want to take note of the impact extended sitting has for you, as well as your group members. What is the stance or seating arrangement you want to use to create/transmit the energy you want your event?
- The smile on your face – In the early years of only phone-based work, in some customer service areas it was common for people to have a mirror hanging in the cubicle. When we talk on the phone, our voice and tone changes when we smile, so the mirrors

were a reminder for people to smile while they talked. Your facial expressions do get translated to your group members even if they can't actually see you.

- How you will handle questions you don't know – In the virtual world trust is built by making sure follow-up really happens. Who can you direct questions to? If you don't know this, find it out before you go on your call.

## MANAGING YOUR OWN EMOTIONS

We get impacted by our group members' experiences. We may find that we get triggered emotionally by something someone says that we may vigorously disagree with. At other times fatigue may make us snap. Our inability to read the room may also make us uneasy and unsure of ourselves. It is important to find what's going to ground you and how you can "self-manage" your emotions. It may also be very important to find a release valve for yourself after the calls where you can debrief and process, especially when you may have been triggered by an experience with a group member. Depending on the level of triggering, you may look to a coach or a counselor for support.

## MANAGING YOUR ENERGY

It's important to notice your own circadian rhythms in your work. There are likely to be times of the day where you are more at your peak as a facilitator. When are you at your best? What is your low point of energy? What will help you move through your natural peaks and valleys? As you consider your program, what energy is required for each part of the session? While I have focused on higher energy levels, it's important to also calibrate our energy for the types of emotion our group members are working through. For example, when dealing with a challenging topic, it may not be appropriate for the facilitator to be a "Cheerleader." Notice when you are at your best and how you can maintain your energy.

## Mistakes Made by Virtual Facilitators

These are some common areas new facilitators struggle with. Note for yourself areas that might be a "trap" for you and what you want to do to avoid them.

### Program Design

- Trying to cover too much
- Including too many activities: Not heeding the 2:1 Rule (leaving as much or double time for people to be in discussion with others about their learning and how they will apply it)
- Trying to demonstrate too many concepts
- Thinking that everything you do in person will translate virtually

### Program Delivery

- Consistently running over time
- Starting calls late
- Offering sessions at an inconvenient time
- Not adapting your pace and style for different groups
- Not adapting your language/word choice to fit the group you are working with
- Program materials have extensive typos or formatting issues
- Failing to have online feedback (start and end of call, and in the middle for longer calls)
- Not adjusting your style and approach
- Not considering how pre- and post-work could add value to the program delivery

## Group Management Faux Pas

- Not being aware of group process (Storming, Norming, Performing, Adjourning, and building in sessions as appropriate)
- Allowing someone to dominate or "hog the airtime"
- Allowing someone to be offensive in their speech or actions
- Assuming everyone is an extrovert who will contribute comfortably without bring prompted
- Assuming that everyone processes verbally—provide pause points for people to take a few minutes to write their thoughts down
- Failing to consider learning styles in terms of delivery approach, support materials, and exercises slated
- Not taking time at the start of the program to design Ways of Working that create shared expectations

## Marketing

- Assuming that groups will fill themselves
- Trying to market too many programs at once
- Focusing so much on marketing that you leave too little time to produce a quality product/program
- Thinking that you have a product that is going to be appreciated but is not
- Not asking for testimonials
- Not recognizing that it takes 7-11 times for people to start developing brand recognition, which means sending a message out just one time will not register

# GETTING IT INTO YOUR BODY, BRAIN, AND VOICE— PRACTICE MAKES PERFECT

Regardless of your level of experience and knowledge of content, it is important to do a "walk through" prior to the session. This may take several hours if it's new to you, or 15 minutes if you've done it several times. Inevitably, there are always issues you find before you get on the line.

## WHAT TO WATCH FOR IN A PRACTICE SESSION:

- Is everything there? Is the material ready? Are there any mistakes in any slides or media you will be using?
- How will I start the program? You have .07 seconds to make a first connection. What is the kick off and environment you want to create? How will it engage and connect people from the start?
- Do I have too much content or too many activities?
- What are the top three items I want to reinforce?
- What engagement points are there?
- How much time is allotted for each section?
- How does the flow work from section to section? (Note you may want to go from big picture to little picture.)
- What transitions do I want to use to move from section to section?
- What level of interactivity is there? Is it frequent enough? Am I varying up approaches, i.e., polls, chat, breakouts?
- What's the call to action? What will the attendees do? What are they learning? What new insights do they have?
- What will I do to end the session?

Make note of what is important for you in your walk through.

## A REMINDER OF THE PROGRAM CYCLE

In Chapter 5, we reviewed the phases of the program cycle:

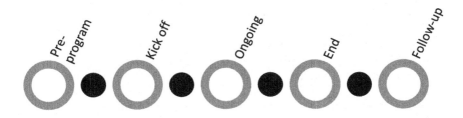

Let's take a closer look at the activities specifically designed for pre-program and the first session kick off.

## CHECKLIST – BEFORE THE FIRST SESSION

Key things for getting the group going:

- Pre-calls, pre-surveys, or other needs assessments—review these again. What key issues are people excited about? What do you notice about their experience?
- Have all materials been sent out?
- Do you have a backup copy? Where is it housed for people to access if they need it?
- What size is the group?
- What is the roadmap of your call?
- What is the end result you are aiming for?
- How have you included Ways of Working/group agreements?
- What are your interaction points?
- What platform are you using? Any issues to note? What access codes are required?
- What are the contact details for group members?
- Any other issues to note?

## CHECKLIST – DURING THE FIRST SESSION

**10 Essential Activities for Any Virtual Facilitator to Blast off at the Start of the Session**

There are ten essential activities any virtual facilitator will want to undertake during your session - particularly as you start and move through your first session:

1. Have a list of your participants' names (and contact details – phone and/or email).

2. Send out a reminder email about the call.

3. Know your material inside and out.

4. Have a backup bridge line or system.

5. Make sure the recording is on.

6. Make sure you are on the line a few minutes early to troubleshoot with participants.

7. Make sure you start and end on time.

8. Review what you just did.

9. Ask group members to consider and/or share the main points of their learning and the takeaway/end result from the session.

10. Send out a follow-up email.

## HABITS TO CULTIVATE AND HABITS TO AVOID

*"Nothing is stronger than habit." – Ovid*

Habits are things we do consciously and unconsciously—we do them regularly, and over time, they simply become part of the way we do things. While we may think of habits as negative things, habits can also lead to mastery. Malcolm Gladwell speaks of the "10,000-Hour Rule,"[95] which states that mastery comes when you are able to complete more than 10,000 hours working at a task.

That 10,000-hour figure is currently being disputed and being replaced by what is called "deliberate practice."

Here's what Geoff Colvin has written about deliberate practice:

"Deliberate practice is characterized by several elements, each worth examining. It is activity designed specifically to improve performance, often with a teacher's help; it can be repeated a lot; feedback on results is continuously available; it's highly demanding mentally, whether the activity is purely intellectual, such as chess or business-related activities, or heavily physical, such as sports; and it isn't much fun."[96]

Just as drills and spurts can help a tennis player improve their performance, masterful virtual facilitators become better through practice and feedback loops. What are the drills that would be useful for you to go through?

Neuroscience is also pointing to the fact that changes can happen at a faster pace than was previously believed. Take a look at the Sprints Text Box to see how this is being translated at a virtual program level.

## Sprints

In today's business context, we don't always have the luxury of being able to spend all the time we want on certain activities. As such, it can be important to be able to create pockets or windows when we are able to focus deeply and intensively on business challenges. Sprints occur during focused bursts of work time. Whether it's a team that gathers for a series of two-hour meetings for five consecutive days to work together on a problem, or a set of colleagues who join forces to co-design a project, the time pressure invoked through sprints can help to focus and foster innovation and productivity. Organizations such as Google are leveraging the power of sprints to speed up the prototyping process. Consider how you can create virtual spaces that incorporate sprints in your facilitation.

You may want to consider the challenge your group members are facing at the moment, and how intensive bursts of focused energy might support them. Questions to consider when looking at focused virtual events include:

- What is the focus bringing people together?
- What's the purpose?
- What length of time may help people focus and work/write intensively? Would a five-minute warm-up give rise to a 10 or 15-minute sprint? What would a 45 or 90-minute focused activity look like?

Key in facilitating a sprint is to make sure people come to the call with a project they want to take action on. Set a timer and provide people with a question or activity which will give them a focus. Work together real-time via the phone or video-streaming. When you are done (whenever the timer goes off!) check in and have everyone share their achievements. This may be a great virtual motivator for projects that are in a slump and/or might need a bit of a kick start.

Case in point: The initial draft of this manuscript was written as part of an annual one-month focused campaign called NANOWRIMO—National Novel Writing Month. During NANOWRIMO I experienced the value of intensive bursts of focus, while connecting virtually with others. These sprints of intense writing were a collaborative way to come through and focus deeply. It was amazing how these short bursts created new insights and new context.

For the last year, I have been leading virtual sprints and hacks for program designers (coaches, trainers, leaders) who want to design and move their program ideas forward in a compressed way. Sprints and hacks range from 45 minutes to several hours, and are characterized by bursts of intense focus and output.

The following includes some of the everyday habits you will want to cultivate in creating engaging and effective virtual learning environments. On the right, you will find several habits to avoid.

| HABITS TO CULTIVATE AS A VIRTUAL CONVERSATIONALIST | HABITS TO AVOID |
|---|---|
| Calling on people by name. | Using word fillers—ums and ahs. |
| Reviewing feedback and making tweaks each and every time you offer a program. | Not having a plan for the call. |
| Doing a walk-through of the day/session/flow even if you have run the program before. | Not thinking about the key points (often 3 max) for the start, middle, and end. |
| Visualizing the roadmap of your call—noting the start, end and key points you want to reinforce. | Being late for calls. |
| | Trying to fit too much in. |
| Checking that your recording is really working. | Doing things alone. |
| | Not asking for feedback. |
| Getting on the line at least 10 minutes in advance. | Assuming everyone is okay—and okay with you. |
| | Talking too much. |
| Using a blend of media, even ones that you are not comfortable with. | Not listening enough. |

There are a couple of key practices you will want to cultivate as a virtual conversationalist. Consider these:

## THE MORNING OF:

- ☐ Check your connection.
- ☐ Check your batteries.
- ☐ Do you have all the materials available?
- ☐ Is the presentation showing on your screen?
- ☐ What do you notice about your setup?
- ☐ Schedule?
- ☐ Last minute changes?

## JUST BEFORE THE CALL:

- ☐ Make sure you have everything on hand.
- ☐ Grab an extra drink.
- ☐ Extra pen, cord and battery are good?
- ☐ Phone on mute.
- ☐ Review participant list.
- ☐ Consider how you will start the call.
- ☐ What main points are key to cover?
- ☐ What tone is needed?
- ☐ What presence is required for this call?

## JUST AFTER THE CALL:

- ☐ Follow up with the participants.
- ☐ What have you promised to send?
- ☐ Note for yourself what worked and what didn't.
- ☐ Note any changes needed (materials, slides, platform).
- ☐ What issues need follow-up?
- ☐ What core themes are important to note and carry forward for the next call?

## MOVING THE NEEDLE ON ENGAGEMENT – SIX AREAS TO CONSIDER IN ANY VIRTUAL PRESENTATION

While this chapter is not a replacement for more in-depth work around presentation skills, here are six areas to keep in mind.

1. **First impressions are key!** You have a limited time window to get their attention. What do you want to convey? Write down the 3-5 adjectives you want people to use to describe your presentation.

2. **Start and end:** People remember the start and end of a thing. Ask yourself:
   - What are you planning for your start?
   - How will you hook the audience?
   - What key points do you want to review/reinforce?
   - What are their next steps?
   - What's the summary or closure you want in the call?

3. **Activities for engagement:** What are the engagement activities (small group, dialogue, reflection etc)? When are these happening? Consider more regular interaction and pace changes help to boost engagement. A change of pace every 7-10 minutes (or sooner for some virtual programs) can be a marker.

4. **Hearing more than just your voice:** Having multiple voices can also create engagement. What strategies can you use around this? Can you get team members to read things out, or is there a TED Talk or other external media that would support this topic?

5. **Amount of peer interaction:** We don't always leave a lot of time to hear from our peers. What can you do to boost peer interaction? Consider: breakouts, chats, polls.

6. **Application to work/life:** Providing an opportunity for participants to regularly think about the WIIFM and *How can I use this?* also boosts engagement. What will you do to support

thinking about their application of the conversation to work? Life? Is there a one-page plan you want people to use and track throughout your work together?

Consider how you are going to approach these crucial areas—you may also want to download this worksheet at EffectiveVirtualConversations.com.

## Your Virtual Facilitation Toolkit

Items you will want to include in your virtual conversation/ facilitation toolbox:

- Microphone – Your microphone is your ally and should be a key consideration. Some laptops have amazing microphones with noise cancellation technology, while others pick up all the background noise. What do you notice about your sound quality?

- Headset – From a full headset to smaller ear buds, this will either minimize background noise that a computer would pick up (ear buds) and/or enhance the call quality. Consider if you want a wireless or wired headset. A wireless headset will allow you more freedom to move around.

- Recording options – With client permission, it will be important to record your calls in case group members are not able to attend. The caveat here is to encourage participants not to fall into the culture of "I'll catch the recording later," as it is more common that they may not listen to the recording.

- Applications – For those that spend an inordinate amount of time on the phone, it can be useful to invest in a device that you know can keep you connected. There are a myriad of apps that you may find useful for either Android or Apple devices including:

Mind Mapping software – check out MindJet, MindMeister, Coggle

Virtual meeting platforms – Zoom (*their mobile app connects you to the platform so you can take it on the go)

Skype

FreeConferencing.com (phone-based services with screen sharing plug-ins)

- Phones can also usually act as a hotspot in the event that your network goes down. I know for me, it's my backup option, which gives me confidence that I have a backup.

## PREPARING FOR YOUR FIRST EVENT

KNOW YOUR MATERIAL:

1. Do a run through – From start to finish make sure you know the transitions and are aware of the time frames. What are the areas that need to be expanded? Which need to be contracted?

2. Speak it out – Taking time to actually speak through what you plan to say can be an important step for getting the program into your bones. If there is no script because it will be a facilitated session, make sure you are talking through your instructions and noticing the flow.

3. Shadow another session – it can be useful to shadow another virtual facilitator and watch how they do things. You will probably want to note things like:
   - How do they open the session?
   - What do they do at the start to welcome people?
   - How do they transition from one setting to another?

- What do they do to close off the morning or transition in to breaks?
- What do you notice about how they interact and connect with each group member?
- What do you notice about the energy levels and engagement levels throughout the program?
- What are the favorite tools they used? Why? What did you notice was especially effective?
- What do you notice about pre-work and post-work opportunities?

4. Consider how you will use the key skills of facilitators. As you reflect on these skill areas:

- What do you notice about your strengths?
- How can you leverage these?
- What skills need development?
- Who can support you?

What areas are going to need further attention?

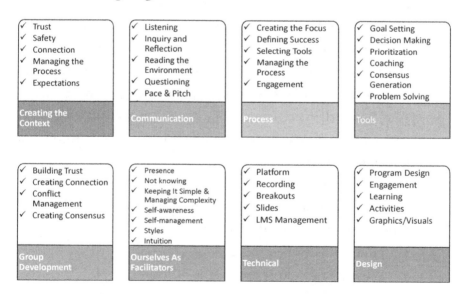

# WORK WITH A MENTOR

Having a mentor can be really useful as you grow into new areas. Having someone willing and available to share their insights and abilities as well as their best practices and things that did not work can be a very useful approach. Consider who might be a mentor for you and how they can support you. What type of support do you want? It could be a sounding board, a person to bounce ideas off of, a person who you learn from, a person who gives you feedback.

If you are able to work with a mentor or more seasoned facilitator, you may want to ask them these questions:

- What has helped you be successful?
- What tips do you have for multitasking?
- What suggestions do you have when things go off the rails? What techniques do you use to bring them back on course?
- What five items would you encourage me to have in my toolkit?
- What one word of advice do you have for someone new?
- What is the most important lesson you have learned in your work?

# GET FEEDBACK

Feedback from your group is essential to facilitator growth and mastery. You may invite feedback from peers and/or group members in the areas including:

- I appreciated…
- One of the strengths of the session today was…or one of your strengths as a facilitator today was….
- I would like to see _____ next time.

These questions provide both a positive/appreciative and constructive approach to feedback.

Take time to reflect on the trends you are noticing as you go. You might look at questions such as, *Where do people engage? Where do they shut down? What is their appetite for the platform? What are the areas that are problematic?*

Note program changes for next time. There will always be an opportunity to make changes along the way, so what are the three things you will change next time? Write these down, perhaps on a sticky note that you can place at the front of your file in order to remember them the next time you review.

### Four Tips for Fluid Speaking

One area that has tremendous impact for virtual facilitators *is how* we speak. Our voice is our instrument. Consider these tips next time you are scheduled to deliver a presentation, give a webinar, or lead a class:

**Practice, practice, practice** – After all, practice makes perfect. Run through your presentation several times, speaking it out loud as opposed to only reading it through.

**Visualize yourself giving the presentation** – Visualization from start to finish has been shown to be an important strategy for professional athletes. Why not try it out before your next big presentation? Imagine yourself giving the presentation. Picture your location, as well as the audience reaction. Consider where you want to put the most emphasis, and think about the close.

**Consider what can be expanded/compressed** – The "accordion" effect can be a great strategy for ensuring flow, and to hold off panic when things do not go as planned.

**Really hone your start (and end)** – The start of a presentation can be the most stressful for many of us. Unfortunately, these are also the first few, crucial moments for connecting with your audience. Consider your start and how you will engage them—is there a question you will pose? A story you will share? Something else? Hone your start and end.

Consider putting a focus in these areas in preparation for your upcoming presentation and let us know what impact it has for you.

## I GUESS I'M STUCK WITH YOU...

As a virtual facilitator, some unpleasant situations are sure to arise that you don't know how to deal with. At some point, you are bound to experience:

- Content you don't like or even agree with
- A co-facilitator you don't get along with
- An experience or group that is not going well

When these things happen—and they will—it is important to find ways to put the groups' needs before your own to get things back on track. Some tricks you can try include:

- **Check your mindset.** What is going to turn this around for you and the group? What has gotten triggered for you? How are the assumptions you are holding influencing your behavior and results?
- **Get grounded.** What's going to allow you to move forward powerfully and positively? What is the impression you want to leave people with? Regardless of the experience, it is important to put it in perspective. What is going to allow you to proceed with confidence? Who can you look to for support?
- **From whose perspective is it not going well?** Are you the only person aware of the problem you're experiencing? Remember, the most important perspective is that of the learner. Ask them how

231

it is going. What are their individual goals for the rest of the experience? What changes would they like to see?

- **Take a break!** When we get triggered, it releases hormones that can take 15-20 minutes to return to homeostasis. If possible, take a break, or move people into breakouts for some group work. Take a few moments to get up, move around and regroup. Take a mini-walk to clear your mind.

- **Manage the inner critic.** Those critical inner voices tend to show up and play havoc when we are not confident with the material, our abilities or the group we are working with. A dose of positive self-talk can be useful, as can asking for feedback from the group in terms of what materials/concepts they are connecting with and/or what they are going to be able to apply in their work. What are the affirmations you want to create?

## BRAIN-BASED TIP – PRIMING

One effective way to set people up for success is *priming*, or creating a platform on which they can make mental models. Different opportunities exist for laying the groundwork in these areas including:

- Getting people to complete pre-work—perhaps viewing a video or reading a short article.
- Undertaking a self-assessment to consider where their skills are and what they want to be focusing on in your work. This can be revisited mid-point and at the end of the program to support learning.
- Gaining clarity on the goals of the program.

There are also several questions we can ask at the start of a program to get people thinking about their levels of engagement. These include Peter Block's questions:

- How engaged do you plan to be in this conversation?
- How much risk do you want to take?

When working with adults we come up against a wide variety of issues we may not see when working with children. As adults, we may perceive a number of risks to our image which get in the way of our active participation, and impact our ability to speak up. These are important to keep in mind and consider how you can minimize these in virtual conversations. Edmonston indicates that there are four risks that impact psychological safety in work teams:[97]

- Being seen as ignorant
- Being seen as incompetent
- Being seen as negative
- Being seen as disruptive

What can you do to mitigate against these risks? Mitigation does not mean totally removing them, but it does mean minimizing them. What can you do to create a more engaging, "safer" environment for virtual conversation?

## KEEPING YOURSELF FOCUSED AS A REMOTE WORKER

Chances are if you are leading virtual training it is likely that at times you are working remotely as well. One of the greatest challenges when working remote can be the number of distractions. Here are four ways to minimize distractions when working remotely:[98]

1. **Clear space for where you are going to work**. Whether our workspace is a small table that folds back into the wall when we are done, or we have dedicated office space, clearing the clutter can be an important step in creating space to focus and be productive. Consider where you work—what needs to be cleared? Spend 15 minutes this week clearing yourself more space.

2. **Make sure you have what you need in order to do your work.** Small issues can become big issues when working remotely. An old laptop that crashes regularly, taking with it your hard work, becomes a liability. Slow internet speeds can also take a toll. While these issues might be a minor pain once or twice a month, if you need to work remotely several days a week, the cost adds up. Consider what you might be tolerating in terms of equipment/resources that just aren't cutting it. What's the cost of replacing them? What's the cost if you don't?

3. **Consider when you are at your peak for different types of work.** Some of us like getting thoughts down on paper first thing in the morning, while others like to tackle calls while they're feeling fresh. Consider your style and preferences in terms of when you will most effectively get different tasks accomplished, and schedule them in.

4. **Create focus.** We can get distracted when we don't allow ourselves time for a break, or when we don't allow ourselves the space we need to get into the flow of one activity at a time. Consider using the Pomodoro approach, where you set a timer for a set amount of time (i.e., 25 minutes) and work until the alarm goes off. Other time-management gurus recommend a 10-minute break every 50 minutes. What is going to keep you focused and at your prime in terms of productivity?

Even with the best planning, real life can intrude into our professional lives. Consider the recent viral sensation of the political expert who was in the middle of a BBC interview when his young children popped into the room—and onto the screen—hoping to join the conversation. Sometimes we have to make the best of a bad situation and keep going. Who knows, it might even make us famous!

### Practitioner's Tip - Getting into the Dark Corners:
### Being Vulnerable

As Brene Brown writes in her book *Daring Greatly,* "To reignite creativity, innovation, and learning, leaders must rehumanize education and work. This means understanding how scarcity is affecting the way we lead and work, learning how to engage with vulnerability, and recognizing and combating shame. Make no mistake: honest conversations about vulnerability and shame are disruptive. The reason that we're not having these conversations in our organizations is that they shine light in dark corners."[99]

It is not every day that we have the safety or invitation to shine the light in the dark spaces. More often than not, teams I work with would rather sweep things under the carpet than bring them out into the light. Raising the issues that are taboo, surfacing the difficult conversations are areas that team coaches tackle in service to those teams that really do want to move forward. If the dark corners continue to be skirted, forward movement simply is not possible. Instead, circling occurs. Part of the role of the virtual facilitator or conversationalist is to create the space of safety for the dark corners to be named and explored. This requires deep levels of trust and a belief that the people we are working with are resilient, capable, and whole. Our vulnerability opens the doorway for others to be vulnerable and speak their truth. Sharing our own vulnerability is an important part of boosting trust.

## CHECK IN WITH JANE – BLAST OFF

Jane has been tasked in leading a special session for new virtual facilitators at the organization. Part of her mandate is to help them develop. She decides that she is going to highlight these main points for her own preparation:

235

- The best practices of PEBBLLES ETC
- Reminder of less is more and the 2:1 ratio
- In thinking about design, remembering the four principles of Process, Engagement, Variety and Pace

As she considers her group, she is going to keep in mind:

- Getting to know the group members to ensure that proper platforms are chosen
- What pre- and post-program touchpoints she wants to plan with the group
- How she is going to remain open to change and being vulnerable

*What else do you think Jane should take note of?*

### END OF CHAPTER QUESTIONS

What are the key activities you want to undertake in terms of preparing for blast off?

What are you finding challenging? What resources or people will help you with this?

What is the one thing that will help you be successful?

What haven't you thought of yet?

Take note of any action steps from this chapter in your Action Plan Tracker.

## CHAPTER 7

# ACTIVITIES AND ENGAGEMENT IN THE VIRTUAL SPACE

*"Having a robust toolkit can help us avoid the Death by Conference Call mindset."*

*– Jennifer Britton*

## THE VIRTUAL FACILITATOR'S TOOLKIT

The tools of the trade are a facilitator's greatest resource. Whether we are leading a virtual team meeting, a webinar or a conference call, it can be very helpful to have some "back pocket" tools to use in our work. In this chapter, we'll take an in-depth look at a variety of facilitation tools and skills, as well as considerations for bringing different tools into your work. We will explore:

- Considerations for selecting or creating activities
- Twenty-four different tools for working in the virtual space

This chapter also connects with Chapter 4 on the Range of Different Approaches, and also Chapter 5 on Design.

Just as we have a range of approaches of how we might work with groups in the space of virtual conversations, no book on this topic would be complete without a list of different ways to engage and interact with your group or team members. This list is not comprehensive but should get your juices flowing around different things you may want to incorporate in your work.

Take a look at the Wordle and note the two dozen different tools listed here:

| Polls | Breakouts |
|-------|-----------|
| Chats | Emojis |
| Questions | Pre work |
| Paired partners | Self-assessments |
| Photographs | Maps |
| Drawing | Packs mailed out to participants |
| Cards | Bring your own…. |
| Puzzle ticklers | Fill in the blank |
| Scenarios | Animation |
| Videos | TED talks |
| Round robins | Action plans |
| Debriefs | Storylines |

# CONSIDERATIONS IN SELECTING OR CREATING ACTIVITIES

Being intentional with what you choose to bring into a virtual conversation maximizes the time you have together. Consider the following when you go to select or create activities to include:

### What's the purpose of the activity?

It is always important to lead from thinking about the purpose for the activity. Is it to reinforce what was covered already, support goal setting and achievement, explore new perspectives, or deepen awareness around strengths? The purpose will shape how you use different tools.

### The 2:1 Ratio

In any activity, it is important to remember to leave as much time for dialogue *about* the activity. Our group members are usually eager to connect and be in dialogue with each other. In working with more than one person we have the opportunity to leverage the peer learning process. Leave at least the same amount of time—and up to twice the amount— for discussion and dialogue or debrief when you are including activities. It's not just about doing something, it's also about discussing it. The experiential frame of questions of *What? So What? Now What?* can be a useful framework in taking people through a facilitated process.

### It's also about the *and*

Part of the process of virtual facilitation is that it's about the *and*. It's about having structure *and* space, focus *and* expanse, width *and* breadth. When we step into a dichotomy of either/or thinking in a group, we lose the ability to create the space for some new possibilities. What can you do to consider the *and* in your next program design and/or conversation?

### What if?

Part of the space of inquiry and possibility is opening up the space for dialogue around the question, *What if?* What if you won the lotto? What if you had that extra set of hands as a leader or single parent? What if… When we ask the question *What if?* it can take us out of our current mindset, opening the door to a realm of possibility we might not know existed.

## Looking at motivation

In my work as a coach I spend a lot of time supporting individuals, teams, and groups throughout the change process. Motivation is a critical part of this equation in terms of looking at where our locus of control and motivation is. Is it internal or external? In virtual programs tapping into people's motivation helps with engagement. It also helps people move through the ups and downs of change. Understanding our motivation (i.e., why I am doing this) helps us to remember what's important.

Here are some interesting statistics from HRZone around engagement and motivation:[100]

Only **60%** of employees have a clear understanding of their role and purpose. One essential factor for an engaged workforce is knowing what is expected and that they are on the path to achieving it. **40%** of people don't have an answer to this basic question.

**57%** of people have autonomy over only the small things in their job or none at all. Autonomy is a huge factor in having a sense of control over work and helping to provide meaning.

## Looking at what's fun and easy

In creating an enabling environment for change and growth, it can be provocative to ask the question *What's going to be fun and easy?* It is often felt by many that in order to effect change, it needs to be difficult and serious. When things are fun and easy, we may be more apt to continue doing them. Consider integrating the question of what is fun and easy into your next conversation. What's the impact?

## Fueling the small wins

We know that the development of habits take anywhere from 21 to 66 days. What is possible for the people you are in conversation with to create some small wins? Creating momentum around small steps and early successes helps to boost confidence, and becomes a feedback loop in and of itself. Questions to ask are *What are the immediate wins? or What are the low hanging fruits?* to fuel this area.

## Making it kinesthetic

There are a number of ways that we can make virtual learning more kinesthetic. Moving it into our bodies is an important process. Consider how you can get people interacting with their screens, noting things and/ or moving around (safely!) in the calls you have with them.

## Making connections visually

A large part of the learning cycle is getting people to make connections. In the virtual domain, anything we can do to support making things more visual can boost connection, trust, and focus.

Some possible ways to do this include:

- Selecting platforms that are more visually oriented where people can see each other, such as Skype or Zoom.
- In a virtual program, creating connections visually could include mapping things or drawing out a roadmap.
- Visually creating connections could also involve constellation work, which gets you to map a series of relationships. The benefit of giving people time to do this is that it creates a visual anchor and clarity around next steps.
- What are the opportunities in upcoming virtual events for you to create connections? What approaches do you want to use to make it more visible?

## Silence is golden

Silence is often short-changed in the virtual domain. It is very important to create pause points for you and the participants along the way. Rather than just letting silence hang, provide group members with instructions like: *For the next minute, I want you to write out your response to this question.* Having a timer handy, which can provide a nice tone at the end, provides the space for more reflective practice.

Some common reflection questions might include:

- At the start – *What's important? What's your focus? What do you want to get out of the experience?*
- At the end – *What are you leaving with? What are your next steps?*
- Focusing questions – *What's important? What's become clear for you? What aren't you considering? What assumptions are you making? What else?*

## AVOIDING THE PITFALLS

To avoid common pitfalls around exercises, consider:

- **What are the style preferences?** Different groups have different appetites. What do you notice about what makes the group you are working with shut down or tune out? How innovative are they? How much are they willing to take a risk in trying things out? Consider your group members.
- **What constraints do participants have?** For example, streaming may not be possible due to lack of access to a webcam, or broadband issues may force them to use the phone only.
- **Sequencing** – How do activities build upon one another from lower risk to higher risk?
- **Participant behaviors** (refer to Chapter 8)
- **Making sure everyone is set up for success** – are you giving people enough time and instructions to set things up prior to the call? Are there any pre-reads required? What follow-up is needed?
- **What's a motivator for your group members?** We are motivated

by both external and internal factors. What are the motivators for your learners? Is it achievement, status, etc?

## TWENTY-FOUR DIFFERENT WAYS TO ENGAGE YOUR GROUP

Going back to our Wordle at the start of the chapter, let us take a deeper exploration of two dozen different ways to engage with your group.

| 1. Polls | Polls are a great way to interact with a group. In platforms like WebEx, you will need to prepare for polls, but this is a great engagement tool. You can also send out polls through Twitter or Facebook.<br><br>Here are some possible ways to use polls:<br><br>• To test knowledge and what people have absorbed. It could be a multiple choice format. For example, after showing four options, ask group members to flag which ones are true: A, B and C OR A and C only.<br><br>• To solicit input, i.e., *What do you prefer?*<br><br>• To gauge agreement, i.e., *How much do you agree (strongly, somewhat, neutral, disagree, strongly disagree)?*<br><br>• To get feedback. You can also get people to choose an emoji that represents how they feel as they are going off to lunch.<br><br>• To consider what's next, i.e., *What do you think will be the outcome (a, b, c, d, etc.)?* |
| 2. Breakouts | Refer to the section on breakouts in Chapter 4 under Category #9 – Peer Partners. |

| 3. Chats | If a chat function is available, get in the habit of varying verbal responses with chat. In larger groups, chat may be the only mechanism to get interaction. |
|---|---|
| | Things to keep in mind when using chat are: |
| | • Being specific with the question you are asking. |
| | • Leaving time for people to pause and type. |
| | • Sprinkling chat opportunities throughout the virtual event, especially if this is the only way to engage people. |
| | • Consider a new chat question every 5-10 minutes to break up the pace. |
| 4. Emojis | Use emojis to get people to provide insights about what they like and how they are feeling at strategic times during your session. People can add emojis to the chat before lunch, after lunch or during a break. You may want to check back in with people putting up their emoji on the white board. Review Tool #9 later in this chapter for five ways to use emojis for feedback and engagement. |
| 5. Questions | Questions form the backbone of any facilitation experience. Take note of all of the different questions sprinkled throughout this book. |
| 6. Pre-work | What text resources, articles or videos could people benefit from watching or engaging in pre-session? |
| 7. Paired partners | Refer to discussion in Chapter 3 on using paired partners in breakouts, peer partners etc. |

| 8. Self-assessments or personal inventories | What self-assessment could you get for people to take stock of where they are at? There are several personal inventories in this book, for example, Virtual Team Leadership in Chapter 10, or the Virtual Skills needed in Chapter 3. For programs that run longer, it can be useful to incorporate a self-assessment at the start and end of a program to provide a baseline and checkpoint around what is learned and what changes during the course of your work. |
|---|---|
| 9. Photographs | We connect with photos in a different way than text. Maintaining a respect for copyright, what are the ways you can incorporate photographs?<br><br>In the **40 Ways to Work with Visual Cards** e-manual at ConversationSparker.com, I explore a range of ways including using them for strategic planning sessions, to sessions around innovation, to using photographs in designing vision. |
| 10. Maps | As a session start-up, have people identify or draw on the map where they are calling in from. You can also use the visual representation of a roadmap in having people specify their next steps. |
| 11. Drawing | Get people to draw things out. This could include anything from process flows to a visual roadmap. One of my favorite activities in hosting virtual coaching groups is having group members create a logo during our call that represents what they bring to our group process. The sharing of these logos across the group creates connection and synergy. |

| 12. Packs mailed out to participant | Are there physical items you want participants to have on hand to facilitate your session and engagement together?<br><br>A participant kit might include:<br><br>• Post-it notes of varying sizes<br>• Markers<br>• A timer<br>• A notebook or journal<br>• Visual card decks you may be using<br>• Any special maps or things they will need.<br><br>Consider how you can also send out materials for different activities in soft copy i.e., Skills Wheels. |
|---|---|
| 13. Cards | Visual cards are a powerful conversation "sparker" or prompter. Refer to Tool #1, which follows in this section on how to incorporate visual cards in your work. |
| 14. Bring your own.... | What can people bring to the session? A great introductory activity can be to have people bring something that represents their geographic location. Depending on the time of year I might bring a maple leaf (not only on our flag in Canada, but abundantly found outside the windows of my offices), or a Blue Jays baseball token, or... |
| 15. Puzzle ticklers | My son reminded me of how important it is to have something in your back pocket for all ages, not just adults. Word puzzles are a great way to get the brain stimulated and flowing, especially mid-afternoon, after a big meal or when energy is waning. What other activities do you have in your back pocket? |
| 16. Fill in the blank | A fill in the blank can be really easy to make and allow people to comment on in a virtual learning event. Have them fill in the blank either as a review of what you have covered or as an energizer. |

| | |
|---|---|
| 17. Scenarios | Scenario-based learning can be really valuable for exploring complex topics. Animations also bring complex topics to life. It can be useful to keep the following in mind:<br><br>• We learn through examples. Scenarios and animations bring things to life.<br><br>• We learn through dialogue. Scenarios provide learners with an application experience and opportunity.<br><br>Scenarios provide us with an opportunity to make the learning real. *What would I do?* It also allows us to reflect and share. *What have I done in the past? What has worked and what hasn't?*<br><br>See Tool #11, which follows on scenario-based learning. |
| 18. Anima-tions | Animations are another great way to bring conversations to life and skills to the forefront. Rather than shooting video with real people, animations can give a shape and a voice to the conversation. Like scenario-based learning, animations are best used with complex topics when those topics need to be modelled or demonstrated. |
| 19. Videos | Videos are a great way to:<br><br>• Demonstrate core skills. With video you can show a process from start to end and then break it down. You can also illustrate different skill levels (beginner to mastery).<br><br>• Reinforce what was learned in the virtual classroom as a follow-up.<br><br>• Bring different voices into the conversation—this might include subject matter experts or peers. |

| 20. TED Talks | TED Talks come in all shapes and sizes. From MEdX in the medical field, to EdX in the primary and secondary school system, TED Talks provide crisp soundbytes of learning. What TED Talks would be good to have people watch prior to your conversation? What TED Talks might be great follow-up? |
|---|---|
| 21. Round robin | Going around the room can create a sense of connection for group members. At the same time, hearing from everyone can take a long time when group size is large. Consider varying round robins with breakouts. |

Tips for making round robins work:

- Have a question that everyone can rally around.
- Give a specific amount of time that people should be talking for.
- Notice the amount of engagement and when people start to disengage.
- Make sure that you hear from everyone.
- Provide people with the opportunity to pass if they need more time to process or consider their response.
- For more introverted groups, give them a moment to pause and note their response for themselves before speaking.
- Change up the order in which people respond. In many calls I facilitate, I ask participants to draw out a table if we can't see each other. The *Virtual Table* provides us with a map of "where everyone is" and gives a sense of who is where. That way it makes it easier to move from start to finish (i.e., Sujit to Susan) and then reverse order (i.e., Susan to Sujit). It helps to alert people to who is next. It's also important to note that people should feel comfortable in "passing" if they don't have anything they want to offer. This is where having a virtual table can be useful so you remember the flow and can adjust it. See Tool #1 – Working with Visuals.

| 22. Action Plans | Given the usual "solo" nature of virtual calls, it is likely that each person will be developing their own action plan as a result of the conversation. You may want to have a one or two pager sent out in advance for people to take notes on, or use for action planning. For some programs, you may have a cumulative action plan. As a coach, I usually provide everyone with a template of a ***One-Page Plan*** for people to complete and fill out before we meet again. This process stemmed from my work as a virtual team leader in finding the value of knowing on a quarterly basis what my team members were focusing on, their key milestones, and resources needed.<br><br>**Download a One-Page plan at our site**. |
|---|---|
| 23. Debriefs | The art of the question frames a debrief. As indicated in Chapter 2, many debriefs follow the experiential education process, getting people to reflect on and share their feedback around:<br><br>**What?**<br><br>&bull; What did you do?<br>&bull; What did you observe or think about during the exercise?<br>&bull; What feelings did you have during the exercise?<br><br>**So What?**<br><br>&bull; So what did you learn or have reinforced?<br>&bull; What are the implications of this exercise for you?<br>&bull; How does this exercise relate to your "real world"?<br><br>**Now What?**<br><br>&bull; How do you want to do things differently in the future?<br>&bull; How can you extend the learning you had?<br>&bull; What steps can you take to apply what you've learned? |

| 24. Story-Boards | Another way to work with vision is to get people to create a story or story board of where they are going. Provide teams or individuals with instructions to bring materials to the session so it can be worked on real-time. Materials could include old magazines, markers, calendars, or quotes. You may provide one or two prompting questions, but overall, leave people to create their own story. As an example: *Using the easel provided, draw out the story of your team moving forward in the next year.*<br><br>If you are working with a team, have them create a shared team storyboard on a shared screen where they each contribute words, icons or photos. You may only need 15-20 minutes to undertake this activity. |
| --- | --- |

## LEVERAGING THE PEER PROCESS

In Chapter 4, we explored how peer learning is a powerful part of the learning and conversation space. Wherever possible, we want to create the conditions for great dialogue. There are many formats that lend themselves to a peer process including:

- **Masterminding** In masterminding there is an opportunity to focus and get feedback from peers on key topics that could include things such as growing your business. Mastermind groups may meet weekly, biweekly, or monthly at a fixed time. Key to the process is getting feedback on the issue that has been brought to the table.
- **The Quakers Clearness Committee** Historically, the Quaker religion has had a "Clearness Committee" whose role is not to advise others in a group, but to ask them questions. The root of group coaching has group members interacting in this way, by asking questions to help create awareness, focus, insights and action.
- **Feedforward** Marshall Goldsmith created this dialogue process that is best used when you have a group, and each group member

is looking for some ideas or options to explore regarding their biggest business challenges. The first step is to get each person to think about an issue they would like to explore. Next, they share their idea with one other person who immediately shares the first idea that comes to their mind as a possible solution. There is no dialogue, rather the person seeking input notes the idea and thanks the other person. The roles then reverse and the second person shares their idea. Once the initial round is complete, the pair moves on to connect with a new person, and the rounds continue. This is a very quick activity allowing for many new insights around issues. For more ideas on this process, please visit MarshallGoldsmith.com.

## ENGAGING ACTIVITIES – BACK POCKET TOOLS

In addition to the activities already listed, I will now share more detailed instructions for eleven different tools you may want to use as a virtual conversationalist. These have been chosen because they are applicable across the different disciplines, and can be used whether you are a facilitator, coach, mentor, educator or peer. They are:

1. Working with Visual Cards
2. Force Field Analysis
3. Dotmocracy
4. Appreciations and Acknowledgements
5. Vision
6. Journaling
7. Activities to get people moving (virtually!)
8. Strategic Planning Tools – SWOT and SOAR
9. Emojis
10. The Five Whys
11. Scenario-Based Learning

## TOOL #1 – WORKING WITH VISUAL CARDS

**Focus:** Opening, goal-setting, finding connection, strategic planning, innovation

Visual cards provide us with an opportunity to create meaning in a different way than the spoken word. It is commonly stated that your brain processes visuals 60,000 times faster than words. They are a wonderful tool if you are working with people from different language backgrounds.

I use several visual card decks to get people engaged in conversation. Some are designed to help people find connections, others to identify vision and learning, and there are many other varieties. Some of the decks can be used digitally, or you can even create your own. Different decks to check out include:

- The Visual Explorer Deck from the Center for Creative Leadership
- The JICT Deck
- Points of View – The Coaching Game
- My own deck – Conversation Sparker Cards

**Set up:**

There are many different ways you can use visual cards – from working with vision, to strategic planning, and helping a group come to consensus. In the following text box, you will find instructions for an exercise to explore synergies across a group or team.

In general, when working with visual cards:

- Consider a question that will frame people's selection and exploration of the cards. For example, "Select a photo that represents your vision for this team."
- Use the card as a prompter or "Sparker" to get the conversation going.
- Give people time to reflect on and look more deeply at the card.

You may want to prompt them with questions like:
  o  What does the photo represent for you?
  o  What is in focus?
  o  What is dominant?
  o  What feelings does it cultivate? (or what does it evoke?)

- Have four times as many cards as participants so you have enough to draw upon.

- Provide people with an opportunity to go into breakouts and discuss this further. There is often new learning created when we have the chance to articulate our choices and/or hear insights shared by others.

### Working with Visual Cards: Synergies

In 2015 I created a digital e-manual called the *40 Ways to Work with Visual Cards*. Here is one of those 40 Ways, called "Synergies," which is ideal in helping teams or groups find connection.

**Introduction:** It can be important to find synergies amongst group members early on. You'll need a series of photographs for each person to look at. You can post these on a screen share (using something like Zoom—a great virtual meeting resource) or send out a series of them as a PDF. Make sure you have copyright access to the photos! You can purchase stock images at sites like Adobe Stock or iStockphoto.

> Synergy is the highest untapped activity of life. It creates new untapped alternatives; it values and exploits the....differences between people.
> - Stephen Covey

Invite each group member to select a photo that represents what they bring to the group. As they share their choice and explanation one by one, take note of the synergies that emerge. Have some dialogue around

253

what you notice are common themes and differences. How can you leverage these synergies as a team?

**Time Required: 15 – 30 minutes**

**Set up:**

Share the following with the group:

Whether we call it leverage or synergy, combining forces allows us to create more with what we have.

> Dictionary.com calls synergy, "the interaction of elements that when combined produce a total effect that is greater than the sum of the individual elements, contributions, etc." (www. dictionary.reference.com/browse/synergy)

Lay out a series of photo cards, approximately four cards for every participant.

**Instructions**

1. Ask participants to think of a current situation they are facing and would like to explore. This will be the frame through which they look at synergy. If you are working with a team, they are often focused on one collective issue. If you're working with a group, each person may have different focus areas.

2. Have them select a photo that represents what they see as the *synergy of what they can create together*.

3. Provide these instructions: As you look more closely at the photo, consider some of the "Sparker" questions such as: *What's possible? What is additive? What gets maximized?*

You will also want to note: Synergy is important for teams as it allows teams to create more than the sum of the individual parts.

Synergy also helps with connection, leading to trust and safety within a team.

After everyone has shared, facilitate discussion across the group or team (in large group plenary or smaller breakouts) around:

- What is the synergy/connection between the things you have all chosen?
- What new solutions do they offer?
- What else is possible?
- What are the differences?

Invite group/team members to note their next steps.

## TOOL #2 – FORCE FIELD ANALYSIS

**Focus:** Change, Planning, Strategic Connection

The Force Field Analysis is a tool from Kurt Lewin, which allows a person or group to explore the forces that are driving change and those that are getting in the way.

In facilitating this you will want approximately 15-30 minutes to identify the change, and then explore the enabling and restraining factors.

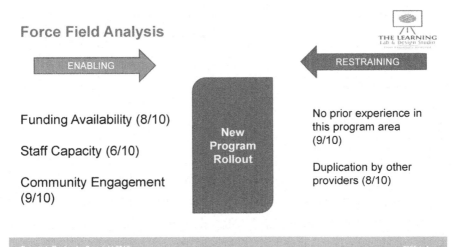

255

**Set up:**

On a whiteboard, label a box in the middle *Future State* (or *The Change We Are Moving Towards*).

Label the left side *Forces Moving Us Forward* (or *Enabling Forces*, or a green arrow).

Label the right side *Forces Holding Us Back* (or *Restraining Forces*, or a red arrow).

Get each person to use their pen to annotate what they see as forces that are driving change towards the future and those factors or forces that are holding things back and/or restraining the change.

If group size is large, this can be done verbally, in smaller breakout groups. It can also be done individually on a worksheet if you are working with a group that has diverse change factors.

I have included an example from some of the work I have done virtually. In the example shown, we were looking at the forces affecting a new program roll out. As you can see, the group identified many factors helping the rollout. Each factor was given a weight from 0-10 in terms of strength.

The next step was to move to the restraining factors—identifying and weighting them. Notice how strong some factors are as opposed to others.

## TOOL #3 – DOTMOCRACY

**Focus:** Setting the context of the work, consensus generation, prioritizing, identifying focus areas

Virtual groups may be really good at getting into the conversation, but may struggle with what is truly a priority for the group or team. This is where the use of voting and colored dots or checkmarks come in.

Dotmocracy is a wonderful tool for prioritizing, coming to consensus or setting the context of the work.

**Set up:**

Get the group to brainstorm all of their ideas. List these on a white board, just as you might list them on a flipchart.

Once all of the ideas are captured, get each person to dot or check their top one or two preferences. If you want to synthesize a long list, each person may only get one or two votes (or dots or checks to use).

Once everyone has placed their dot or checkmark, note what items have come out as priorities.

This will enable the group to visually see where the primary interest is. This works especially well virtually because names are not usually associated with the ideas, so people can feel comfortable voicing their priorities. At the same time, it is important to watch for groupthink, where members in a group all start thinking the same way and influence each other. My experience has been that this approach in the virtual realm quickly surfaces needs and priorities from across the group.

**Applications:**

This can be used to prioritize goals or what areas are going to be included or focused on in a program. This is a quick way to support prioritization in a participatory fashion, getting everyone's voice heard.


TOOL #4 – APPRECIATIONS AND ACKNOWLEDGEMENTS

**Focus:** To create a pause point for group members to take stock of what they are learning and also to provide feedback and acknowledgements to other group members. This is a great activity to include at the mid-point for groups that meet over a longer period, or for shorter-term groups at the end of the session.

Holding an appreciation session prior to the end of a program can be a significant way to close off. Facilitate this by having each person share one thing they appreciate about another group member, or all the group members.

**Set up:**

In creating space for this activity, you will want to consider the following:

- The number of group members. This activity is beneficial for smaller groups. In larger groups, there may only be time for one statement.
- The level of trust in the group. Some level of trust is required.
- How people can see each other. The ability of people to see each other may help to make this flow.

**Instructions:**

Introduce the activity and share why acknowledgements and appreciations are important. Provide instructions and a timeframe for this activity. For example:

*You are going to have ten minutes to complete this activity. The intention is for you to be able to share your acknowledgement with two other group members. As you move to breakout, one at a time, share your responses to:*

- I appreciate…
- I see one of your strengths as…
- If I got to work with you again, I would like…

Set up breakouts for triads. Give them the allocated time to connect.

TOOL #5 – VISION

**Focus:** To create a shared vision of where you are going.

Vision is an important area of focus for groups and essential factor for high performing teams. Vision work can be done collectively in a team, or with an individual focus as a group.

There are several ways to work with vision including:

- Creating a vision board
- Having a team create a storyboard of where they want to be in a year, or five years
- Doing a visualization where you take people through a series of questions
- Having people reflect on vision questions and note their responses real-time

**Set up:**

One way to support the creation of vision in groups is to provide a series of questions related to vision. I have included here questions I use in the virtual retreat work that I undertake with business owners and coaches. I usually pose one question at a time, leaving a pause of three to five minutes between each question, allowing people time to reflect and write. You can also send these questions out as a PDF, providing the space for each person to work through them at their own pace. Just as we would in an in-person environment, allot sufficient time.

Potential vision questions include:

*Consider that it is one year/five years/ten years from now…*

- What do you want your business/your work/your life to look like?
- What major goals have you accomplished?
- What are your total sales? What is your total revenue?
- What's the major mix of your lines of business?
- What impact has your business or work had?
- What are people saying about you? Your company/work?

- What successes have you had?
- What challenges have you overcome?
- What has been your biggest achievement this year? How can you expand on this?
- Who is on your team? What changes does your team need?
- What's working really well? What do you need to let go of?

These questions can provide material for multiple virtual conversations and/or action plans.

## TOOL #6 – JOURNALING

**Focus:** Gaining awareness, expanding insights

In the virtual world, group and team members can benefit from reflective practice (space and time for pauses) during the calls and in between the calls. Journaling can be done "old school"—i.e., in a notebook or journal—or online using tools such as Journal Engine. The benefit of going back to paper and pen is that our brain processes learning differently when written versus when it is typed.

**Set up:**

Provide group members with a question that they will write and reflect on that week (or daily). Focus areas for journaling could include:

- Around a practice – For example, journal prompt on what are they noticing when they are being more proactive in having difficult conversations, or more consistent with their follow-up, etc.
- Around what happened – Capturing key events during their day.
- Around key learning – For those in new roles the first few weeks and months are often an upward slope of learning.
- Around feelings
- Around key relationships
- Reflections from the day or from meetings

- Noting action taken
- Insights gained from their learning
- Around gratitude – A very common activity that has come out of the positive psychology movement is known as a *Gratitude Journal*. In it, people note the three things they are grateful for each day. This has been seen to have an impact on resilience.
- Decisions they have made and what they learned through the process
- Tolerations
- Perspectives

**Resources for journaling:**

Today there are a number of online journaling tools. In writing *From One to Many: Best Practices for Team and Group Coaching*, I spotlighted two journal resources: Journal Engine, and also Lynda Monk of CreativeWellnessWorks.com.

Julia Cameron's *The Artist's Way* also includes additional tips on how to make journaling and writing a regular practice.

TOOL #7 – ACTIVITIES TO GET PEOPLE MOVING

**Focus:** Interactivity, energizer

In a virtual call, it may be perceived that people need to do everything sitting down. It is critical to get people moving to boost engagement, not only for learning, but for health reasons. Sitting for extended periods of time can be detrimental in more ways than one!

Remember that several of your group members may be kinesthetic learners and learn by doing. As such, you may want to get people moving on activities during the call, such as doing planning real-time, or undertaking activities real-time from their location. Quick activities to get people moving could include:

- A scavenger hunt
- Wheel of Life
- Whiteboard/MindMapping
- Stretches
- Creating an activity using Post-its and having them lay it out and post it up in their office. As the facilitator, you can read out the questions and have each person write them out.

Just do it! One of my favorite activities in the virtual realm is to get people to do things real-time. For example, when I led virtual retreats focusing on getting organized, I gave people 15-30 minutes to clear the clutter off their desk, or held 45-minute business planning sprints with solopreneur/business owners where they created their first draft of their annual plan.

*What are the activities you can use to get people moving?*

## TOOL #8 – STRATEGIC PLANNING TOOLS: THE SWOT AND SOAR

**Focus:** Planning Tools

Many of us are familiar with the SWOT—a foundational, strategic planning tool that can be used at an offsite, or even in the context of a team meeting. At the top, we have two quadrants—S for Strengths (those internal skills, strengths and talents that exist in the team or organization), and W for Weaknesses (those internal weak areas that might get the team, or organization, into trouble). These two things comprise *the internal* environment. The bottom part of the matrix gets you to list, and explore, *the external* environment. O represents Opportunities, which are external factors that are working in the team or organization's favor, while T represents the Threats that might derail the business or team.

# SWOT

## Strengths, Weaknesses, Opportunities, and Threats

| STRENGTHS | WEAKNESSES |
|---|---|
| What are my greatest assets, gifts, and strengths? | What weaknesses do I have that need to be addressed? |
|  |  |
| **OPPORTUNITIES** | **THREATS/OBSTACLES** |
| What resources, people or situations can help me move forward? | What situations if left unattended would derail my plans? |
|  |  |

**Set up:**

If you are considering using this as a tool, provide the group with a blank matrix (like the one you see here). Have the large group (or a subset of the group) brainstorm and list out the internal Strengths and Weaknesses of the team (or organization).

Next, have the team identify things in the external environment that may be Opportunities (new collaborations, new client bases, technology) or Threats (new taxes, etc).

If you have enough time in the discussion, use a whiteboard to annotate responses. If there is not sufficient time, break into smaller breakout groups, and assign each group one or two areas to explore more deeply and then share in the large group. They will return to the large group to present back, and the larger group members can add any additional insights to create a master list. This whole process can take 20 – 60 minutes or more.

## THE SOAR – FROM THE APPRECIATIVE STANDPOINT

The SOAR is an alternative to the SWOT that has emerged out of the Appreciative Inquiry space, which places an emphasis on strengths and appreciation. SOAR stands for Strengths and Opportunities (as the S and O do in the SWOT) as well as Aspirations and Results.

Stavros and Hinrichs (2009) provide these questions for exploring the different stages of the SOAR:[101]

Strengths: *What can we build on?*
Opportunities: *What are our stakeholders asking us for?*
Aspirations: *What do we care deeply about?*
Results: *How do we know we are succeeding?*

As with the SWOT, this can be completed together as a large group, or you can have smaller groups break out to discuss, presenting back to the larger plenary to create a master list. Your choice may also be dependent on whether you have breakout capability or not.

TOOL #9 – EMOJIS

**Focus:** Evaluation, Feedback, Learning Pause

Emojis are not only fun (or silly to some)—they can also be used as a great "pulse check" and tool for learning and evaluation. There are several ways to use emojis:

- As a check-in at the start of the call. Have people select and share the emoji that represents them as they start the call.
- Mid-point. Do a check-in to see how people are feeling about their learning by having people share the emoji that represents how they are feeling or what they are learning.
- At the end of the session. Have people choose an emoji that represents their overall learning experience with you that day.
- Two other ways we can incorporate emojis are:

   A. In communication skills training if you are using scenarios, get people to select emojis that represent each character's mindset after showing a difficult conversation.

   B. In leadership skills training for virtual leaders, have group members listen to a voice-only call between a leader and their team members. Get people to select an emoji to represent how they think the two parties are feeling. Then show them a video recording of the same conversation where you can see the participants' faces. How accurate were they?

TOOL #10 – THE FIVE **WHYS**

**Focus:** Getting to root cause, or exploring an issue in all its layers

Popularized by today's focus on Agile (a methodology that is grounded in ongoing experimentation, and rapid refinement), the *Five Whys* tool provides group members with the opportunity to unpeel multiple layers of an issue they are considering.

**Set up:**

Identify the focus of the question you want to explore. Proceed with drilling down into the issue by asking a series of *Why?* questions five times.

For example, if I am working with a set of new leaders we might incorporate the Five *Whys* as:

Question: What is the most important business issue for you right now?

Answer: Growing sales in the nearest town.

Question: Why?

Answer: There has been a significant change on this line of business.

Question: Why?

Answer: We've noticed a significant drop which impacts 50% of our revenue.

Question: Why?

Answer: Our routing of deliveries have changed due to infrastructure work, impacting our speed to market.

Question: Why?

Answer: We have been dependent on one way to deliver the product and this is now leading us to think about a virtual/electronic delivery.

Question: Why?

Answer: We are not just seeing this in the next town but in many locations. And as I am looking at this right now I am realizing it is important to prioritize this issue within the team for our next meeting. We need to check in on the timeline for the availability of this digital product.

The Five *Whys* helps us to connect more deeply to the root of any issue. Notice how in this example, the conversation quickly switches from looking at one specific issue to moving to the root of a much larger issue, which can then be followed up on.

## TOOL #11 – SCENARIOS AND SCENARIO-BASED LEARNING

**Focus:** Exploration of complex topics like decision making, skill application, and critical thinking

In the virtual realm, scenario-based work is another area of rich learning. For topics that are complex, such as leadership or coaching skills development, scenarios provide us with a common platform in which to enter and talk about possibilities. Scenario-based learning is often best for exploring complex topics requiring the use of critical thinking and decision making. When working around topics like leadership or coaching skills development, it can be very useful to have group members apply their conceptual learning to scenarios they may encounter. In the virtual realm, providing case studies and scenarios helps to create a common platform for people to speak from.

Here's one definition of scenario-based learning: "Scenario-based learning (SBL) uses interactive scenarios to support active learning strategies such as problem-based or case-based learning. It normally involves students working their way through a storyline, usually based around an ill-structured or complex problem, which they are required to solve."[102]

Examples of scenario-based learning could include scenarios developed for new leaders to explore the area of collaboration, problem solving and/or how they want to adjust their leadership style. Breakouts provide the space for deeper dialogue and sharing of perspectives and development of a team approach. The scenarios provide an opportunity for immediate application of new tools and templates and realistic role plays. Unlike one-off role plays, scenarios are often a series of different pieces of information with the learning built into stages.

In the virtual realm, large groups and breakouts will usually dominate the conversation. When using these, note the importance of keeping the same group of learners together throughout the entire scenario to develop that sense of "team" and "shared understanding".

Scenario-based learning is often the foundation of e-learning programs. It is great for engagement and attention, inviting people to interact. It also really helps with learning and skill development.

**Practitioner's Tip: Cool Idea to Explore – Graphic Facilitation**

As the field of facilitation continues to expand, graphic facilitators bring a visual element to everyday conversations. Graphic facilitators map or draw out what the conversation is. We can bring this element into our virtual calls easily by using tools such as Skype and Zoom for video conferencing. Years ago, I was joined by a wonderful graphic facilitator, Julie Gieseke of MapTheMind. org, who brought to life the conversations we had in the Group Coaching Essentials program. The visual capturing took the learning to another level.

Imagine being on a phone call where you can't see each other, but after the call, having a visual map of your conversation. Here is an example:

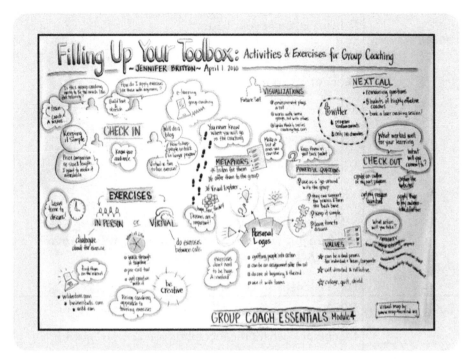

## ADDITIONAL IDEAS FOR YOUR TOOLKIT

Masterful virtual facilitators can never have enough resources. Throughout this book, I've illustrated several other tools including:

**Wordle** – Word clouds are a great way to bring to life many pieces of information. Notice the impact of the visual compared to the listing of 24 activities. Which had more impact for you?

**Icons** – Icons continue to replace a lot of text and are transferable across cultures and language. Take note of the use of Icons in the To-Do List download, which accompanies this book.

**In addition to the activities we've covered here, here's a quick list of some other key virtual topic areas and activities you might use:**

| INTRO-DUCTION | When are you at your best? |
|---|---|
| | White board Post-its |
| | Series of questions |
| | Map introduction |
| | Self assessment |
| | Virtual table |
| | Mapping = Where are you? |
| | Select the photo that represents: ***What's the energy you are bringing into this conversation?*** Or, ***What you are uniquely bringing to this conversation?*** |
| | Personal logos and other activities which will keep it alive. |
| CLOSURE | What are you going to take forward from our experience? |
| | Metaphor – what's the metaphor you are leaving with? |
| | Walk through – walk through key points of your journey. |
| | Next steps |
| | The one thing – what is the one thing you are leaving with? |
| | End summary |
| | One-page summary of everything you have learned or one page MindMap of key learning items |
| | One-Page Plan or action plan built up |
| | Review self assessment |
| | Head, heart, and hands |
| | Structures: to remind us of what is important to us and what commitments we have made. Could be an audio or a video montage of your main points |

| STRATEGIC PLANNING | Strategic Issues Mapping |
| --- | --- |
| | SWOT |
| | SOAR |
| | Prioritization question |
| | Start, Stop, Do |
| | Red light/green light |
| MAKING CONNECTIONS | Mapping it |
| | Road map |
| | Constellation work |
| | Metaphors |
| | Story chain – A fun way to get creative juices flowing with a group or team that may know each other. Have someone start the story by contributing a sentence such as, *It was a dark and stormy night...* Each person then contributes one sentence to the story. |
| ENERGIZER | Little known fact about me |
| | Find the connection |
| | Top five ideas covered so far |
| | Application of skills real-time (i.e., Just do it!) |
| | Funniest moment |
| | A through Z |
| | What's your shoe – what do you want |
| | Photo – What's a counterpoint to you? |
| DECISION MAKING | Dots |
| | Cost Benefit Analysis |
| | Red Light, Yellow Light, Green Light |

| CREATING FOCUS | Unstructured writing |
| | MindMapping |
| GOAL SETTING | One-Page Action Plan |
| STRATEGIC PLANNING | SWOT |
| | SOAR |
| | Strategic Issues Mapping |
| PRIORI-TIZATION | Dots |
| | Priority Frameworks |
| CHANGE MANAGEMENT | Force Field Analysis |
| | Moving through change – visual decks |

RESOURCES FOR FOLLOW-UP:

There are many resources you may want to follow up with in building your own toolkit including:

1. Wilderdom.com
2. Business Balls.com
3. MindTools.com
4. Appreciative Inquiry
5. World Café
6. Open Space Technology
7. In late 2016/early 2017 I did a series on "The A-Z of Team Development Activities" at our Blog, PotentialsRealized.com. Check these posts, which also include video and audio posts at: www.potentialsrealized.com/teams-365-blog.

# CHECK IN WITH JANE – BUILDING THE TOOLKIT FOR VIRTUAL WORK

Jane has been tasked to do a one-day executive retreat with a focus on strategic planning, visioning, and action planning. The executives will be calling in from all over the world. She turns to her toolbox and decides that four of the main activities she is going to incorporate are:

- The SWOT
- Visioning
- Action Planning
- Working with Visual Cards

She also decides that she is going to use colored dots (Dotmocracy) to get the executives to highlight their most urgent priorities. She has also left a two-hour block of open space. Based on their prioritization during the session, the group will design and scope that real-time.

## END OF CHAPTER QUESTIONS

What resources do you want to check out?

Who can be a support for you?

Is there any additional training you want to undertake?

Make a note of your action steps from this chapter in your Action Plan Tracker.

CHAPTER 8

# WHEN THINGS GO WRONG: TRICKY ISSUES, DEALING WITH CONFLICT, DIFFICULT PARTICIPANTS

*"Embrace the Chaos"*

*– Deborah Barndt*

The road to a great conversation isn't always smooth. This chapter explores:

- Pitfalls for virtual conversations
- Tricky issues
- Dealing with conflict
- Difficult participants

We'll take a closer look at some of the most common tricky issues faced in virtual conversations—the things that can go wrong. We'll also explore strategies to mitigate against tricky issues or address them if they emerge.

The quotation at the beginning of this chapter comes from one of the professors who supervised me during my grad studies more than two decades ago. As I started my work as a critical educator, community mobilizer and virtual leader, she encouraged me to "embrace the chaos." This phrase stuck with me, given how it captures the essence of how we need to flow in our work. It is also a mantra I continue to share with others in my facilitation skills training and work with virtual leaders. As much as we can pre-plan in our work, there is always going to be something different and unexpected that emerges.

There are many layers to virtual facilitation, and part of what we may need to do is embrace the chaos rather than try to fight it. As we approach the topic of tricky issues, keep in mind your perspective around what "tricky issues" mean, how you want to mitigate against them, how you want to address them if they do occur, and what resources, including your groups, you have on hand.

## PITFALLS FOR VIRTUAL LEARNING – TRICKY ISSUES

There are several pitfalls when we come to virtual conversation and learning including:

- Technology issues
- Facilitation issues
- Group member issues

Tricky issues usually emerge when people do not feel connected, safe, or heard. Throughout this book, we have explored different ways for people to feel connected with each other, and how to create safety. A reminder of several key things:

- Connect people early on with their WIIFM (*What's in it for me?*)

and what they want to get out of the call.

- Create shared agreements of how you as a group want to operate. This also connects with the discussion around creating shared agreements on topics such as confidentiality (what is said on the line, stays on the line), respecting differences, being present during the call, making requests so you get what you need, and asking questions.
- Create shared expectations about the call and outcomes.
- Address tricky issues as they emerge. Don't sweep them under the rug.
- Address tricky issues respectfully. In working with adults, many of these issues may be addressed "offline."
- Ensure you are creating a safe environment for everyone.

## TEN COMMON PITFALLS IN VIRTUAL FACILITATION WORK[103]

In facilitating virtually there are some common areas many virtual facilitators may experience pitfalls. These include:

### PITFALL #1 – TECHNOLOGY DOESN'T WORK

Knowing your platforms is critical. Through practice and experience you will be able to figure out some of the immediate steps when technology doesn't work.

**Solution:** When breakouts don't happen as planned, you might need to adjust on the fly and change the activity into a chat, voice, or whiteboard activity.

Having a backup is key, and allowing yourself enough time at the start of the virtual event to know that things are working okay is also another way to mitigate against this common pitfall. Just as you want to show up in the room a few minutes in advance of an in-person event, build yourself a buffer so you arrive in the meeting space well in advance of your participants.

## PITFALL #2 – YOU LOST YOUR PRESENTATION OR CAN'T UPLOAD IT

**Solution:** If you are relying on slides, make sure you have some backups. This might include:

A PDF copy of the slides you have on hand, which you can send out by email to participants during the call.

A shared site where participants can download the slides. This requires less immediate effort on your part if you are the only one leading the call, so it is usually less disruptive.

Make sure you think about this in advance.

## PITFALL #3 – YOUR GROUP CAN'T HEAR YOU

**Solution:** Occasionally this crops up. You may need just to log in again. Some platforms allow you to do an audio test prior to the session, so you are confident you can be heard. If only one or two participants can't hear you, then it is likely their connection and not yours. Before you log off to reconnect (which may disrupt the system), check on how many people can't hear you.

## PITFALL #4 – ONE PARTICIPANT CAN'T GET ON THE PLATFORM

Virtual events can be intimidating to certain learners and staff members. Spend time with your team/event participants in advance setting them up for success.

**Solution:** Give participants the opportunity to log on and test the systems prior to the event. Be specific on what time you want everyone on the line. For example, if a call starts at 9 a.m., encourage them to be on the line at 8:45.

It can also be useful to develop a troubleshooting guide people can refer to (i.e., if *this* happens, try *this*...) or provide a video tutorial for common blips and challenges.

It is important to keep the program moving, so always have a backup person who can help a struggling individual rather than leaving them to figure it out for themselves.

Finally, figure out if there is an alternative way for people to join. For example, if they are having problems with their broadband, can they call in instead? What supports would they need in advance to benefit from this?

## PITFALL #5 – THE RECORDING DOES NOT WORK

Sometimes, group members will not be able to attend calls and will want to catch up by listening to a recording. Sometimes this does not work.

**Solution:** Make a habit of checking and knowing that your recording is working. If you run a similar program over time, it can be useful to have a recording for classes recorded each time. If the system's recording facility does not work, what can you put in place? My usual backup is often going to OneNote, which can usually record the audio component of my call. I always have a spare laptop on hand to do this so that it is not recording from the system.

## PITFALL #6 – TECHNOLOGY BREAKS DOWN

Technology glitches are one of the most common tricky issues facilitators can face.

**Solution:** Always have a backup—or multiple backups—to guard against this. Check out the services you are using and have a backup.

Make sure your connection works from your landline and mobile (and VoIP). Sometimes there can be a difference as to what you can access and where. Know how to complete quick items like record, mute, unmute, raise hands, chat or work a white board. Practice is usually the only way to master these.

## PITFALL #7 – NO ONE, OR LESS PEOPLE THAN REGISTERED, SHOWS UP

Rescheduling can become a slippery slope. Whether you have four people on the call or 40, consider how your virtual program (or components of it) can be packaged for future benefit. How will you record the call? What changes might need to be made to the process and approach? It is likely that people will be running late.

**Solution:** A best practice is always to start and end on time, given that people are likely to be calling in at different times of their days. As a facilitation team, consider how you are handling missed attendees and last-minute cancellations.

## PITFALL #8 – LOW ENERGY

Virtual programs can be challenging for new facilitators in terms of the energy and feedback you receive.

**Solution**: If you are using a phone-based system only, other than enabling people to raise their hands in response or signal their agreement on their keypad, it may feel like you are talking into a black hole. Your energy is imperative in keeping the flow going. Remember that it is critical to engage your group members every 5-7 minutes. Without involvement and engagement, it is challenging for anyone to continue to focus, let alone participate.

## PITFALL # 9 – LACK OF CONNECTION FELT BY THE GROUP

It is surprising how facilitators overlook how important it is to build connection amongst group members. Connection is an essential ingredient for virtual programming, and is an important foundation even with a teleseminar or teleclass, which may be more content focused. Engagement levels will be impacted if group members do not feel connected with the host and/or others.

**Solution:** Consider how you can build connection (as appropriate) amongst group members. If it is an extended program, are you giving air time for everyone to speak? Are you encouraging people to share a bio/photo at the start of the program? For one-off engagements, are you posing questions to the group that they can respond to verbally, by email/chat or by using their key pad? If you are hosting a longer program, are you creating "learning partners" or buddies?

## PITFALL #10 – THE MULTITASKING MINDSET

The multitasking mindset can be commonplace for many of us. What can you do to capture people's attention and keep it focused?

**Solution:** Consider these questions.

- Are you making a request for people to disconnect from other technologies?
- Are you changing the pace frequently (i.e., every 5-7 or 10 minutes)?
- Are you creating opportunities for individuals to pause and engage at their desk?
- What engagement strategies are you employing?

# CALL MANAGEMENT ISSUES—PERCEIVED TIME SUCKERS

Call management issues can also lead to tricky issues. For some group members addressing these areas may be perceived as "time suckers" which may lead to disengagement and people moving to multitasking. In keeping things moving in the virtual domain, you will want to watch for these time suckers:

### TOO MUCH TIME IN INTRODUCTIONS OR CHECK-INS

A critical skill for keeping the flow of each conversation is to introduce the skill of *bottom lining* or *laser speak*. This is a coaching term for getting people to speak to the core of the issue. Let group members know how much time they will have to speak to set them up for success. Also, pose specific questions (one or two) for what they should share. If "over talking" or "hogging air time" is really an issue, it may be useful to do some skill drills around brevity in speaking—a core competency for many leaders today.

Consider how you can also elicit input from others, which might include using the chat function. For smaller calls, the chat function can be an invaluable tool. You may also get people to use any annotation tools that are available to get their input. With larger groups, using chat can create a little chaos given that comments may be "whizzing by" where engagement is most important. Be prepared with some humor!

### TAKING TOO MUCH TIME TO HEAR FROM EVERYONE

It is important for people to recognize that the call is probably one part of the entire learning process. It's very easy to get bogged down in check-ins at the start of the call. While I am a believer that the check-in is a critical part of the peer learning process, if it goes on too long, you run the risk of losing everyone's attention.

It's also important to get feedback throughout the call, especially if you can't see everyone. Taking the pulse from across the group is important, so you might:

- Use hand raises to the question "Who got something useful from that?"
- Have everyone pick an emoji that shows how they are feeling.
- Only take a few examples.
- Acknowledge the range.
- Use breakouts liberally!

## NAVIGATING THE SYSTEM

A lot of questions about how the system works can be a time sucker for participants who are well-versed in the systems and platforms you are using. Prior to the start of the session, provide group members with links to how the system works (tutorials or FAQ) or create a tutorial on how to connect. Meet on the platform you are using to host the call for your pre-calls so you know it works for everyone. Providing a video tutorial for group members can be a useful approach to help people understand how to access the calls.

Refer to Chapter 3 for more information on what to include in your Frequently Asked Questions.

## OVERVIEW OF THE COURSE

One of the benefits of having a pre-call with each person (where feasible) is that it provides an opportunity for people to ask questions about the overview of the course and any technical questions they may have. Point them toward the system's FAQ and tutorials, which can walk them through the main functions and answer any questions they may have.

One area that is not a time sucker and should not be skimped on is the co-design of the Ways of Working or group agreements. This creates the context, norms, and boundaries of the conversation. It's a critical part of creating a safe space for conversation and engagement. In *Smarter Faster Better,* Charles Duhigg shares research from the Google experience, which found that one of the greatest contributors to creating safety was shared agreements.

## Practitioner's Tip – TIME

Time and pace is an important factor in creating engaging and effective virtual conversations.

It is important to keep the flow of things going in the virtual domain. Keep in mind these items:

- Creating engagement touchpoints where people are encouraged to pause, reflect, or change pace every 5-10 minutes is critical to ensure there is connection and avoid the multitasking mindset. *What engagement touchpoints do you want to include?*

- Check-ins at the start and check-outs at the end of the call provide important "priming" and feedback loops. These check-in and check-out bookends are usually 5-15 minutes each. Feedback at the end of each call might involve asking questions such as, "What worked well?" "What are you taking away?" "What should we do differently next time?" *What will the check-in and check-out of each call look like for you?*

- Keep the calls moving. It's important to be aware of the natural ebbs and flows during the day. Some facilitators will opt to take a break every 50 minutes whereas, others may keep going for 1.5 hours while ensuring that there is quite a bit of interactivity through breakouts, polls, and live audio input. *What will you do to keep calls moving?*

- It is especially important to note the dips and energies mid-morning, at lunch, just after lunch and towards the middle of the afternoon. In the virtual space note that not everyone may be at the same time of day. *What changes in your design do you want to make in order to address or acknowledge these ebbs and flows?*

Question to consider: **What is important for you to note around time and pacing?**

# OTHER TRICKY ISSUES

In addition to the pitfalls mentioned earlier, there are a couple of other tricky issues virtual facilitators can experience.

## LOW EVALUATION SCORES

These can signal several things including:

- a lack of engagement on the part of the participants
- problems with how the program, or calls, are structured
- mismatch between what the facilitator is bringing and what the call needs
- not having clarified what the takeaways or success factors might be
- a lack of comfort on the part of the group members with the technology

Low evaluations scores are an important flag, so instead of making anyone "wrong," it is important to explore what might be happening.

**What to do:**

- Take a look at the evaluation and feedback you have received. What are the trends?
- Reach out to your mentor to find out what suggestions they have and/or ask if they are willing to listen to the recording with you.
- Reach out to group members to get further feedback if you are

able. If this is an ongoing group, in your next call get them to identify what they would like from you in the call.

- Make sure you have participants start with their WIIFM and what their success factors are. Have them share this at the start of the call, and revisit it at the end of the call so that you can get real-time feedback.

## DIFFERENT LANGUAGES AT PLAY

Another common virtual tricky issue is working with group members with different first languages. This is likely, and in global organizations there is usually an established "working language of business."

**What to do:**

- Speak slowly (not necessarily louder).
- Use more written instructions and make these visible during the call.
- Notice how complicated your word choice is. Watch for slang language or lingo.
- Check in for understanding regularly. Make sure the message is being received as intended.
- Consider if there will be value in some individual touchpoints between group calls with each person to answer any questions they may have.

## OVERCOMING A BAD SESSION

At some point in your career you will have a session that "goes south" or is bad for one, or more, reasons.

**What to do:**

- Take ownership. Take responsibility for what didn't work well. As a facilitator, we are responsible for what happens in our "room," even if that room is virtual.

- What would mitigate against this happening again? What do you need to put in place?
- Look at what skills you may need to develop.
- Look at what additional supports might be beneficial to you.
- If the program has been designed for the in-person realm and is now being rolled out virtually, what changes need to be made? Identify what exactly is not working and make the changes accordingly.

Getting back on the horse is critical—I say this as someone who was six years old when I was bucked off a horse at a summer camp, not just once, but multiple times. I remember how the counselor encouraged me to get back on the horse and work through my fears. Decades later I realize that this taught me a lot about resilience—trying it again, and then being able to make a decision not out of fear, but out of at least having tried.

## DIFFICULT CONVERSATIONS VIRTUAL FACILITATORS NEED TO HAVE[104]

Not every conversation is a cheerful one. As virtual facilitators, there are a number of issues and questions we need to pose in a group or team, and sometimes we are the ones who surface the elephant in the room. In the virtual space, it is important to address tricky issues early on. Note that many of these conversations may take place "offline" rather than during the call. We always want to be respectful of our group members and not call them out in front of others, however, we also have a responsibility to ensure a safe environment in any virtual call. It will be important to note how to mute or block someone who becomes offensive.

There are several difficult conversations virtual facilitators may need to have, including:

## WITH THE GROUP OR TEAM MEMBER WHO CONSISTENTLY DOES NOT TAKE ACTION AROUND WHAT THEY HAVE COMMITTED TO

It is easy for coaches to fall into the habit of overlooking a group member who isn't following through on their commitments. Consider how it might be more in-service to have a coaching conversation with the group or team member who is constantly letting things slide. You might consider asking them:

- What took precedence this week for you in respect to the commitments you had made?
- What was important about doing that versus what you had committed to?
- How is this pushing aside your own commitments showing up in other areas?
- What value did the actions you ultimately took have?
- What would you do in the future if you faced this choice?
- In our context what changes do you want to make around the commitments you make?
- Do I/do we have the opportunity to check in on how committed you really are on your commitments each week, in service to what you've said you want to get out of the work we're doing? (Note this question is a little long—not the short, snappy 5-7 words we often aim for in coaching questions!)

## SURFACING THE TABOO ISSUES TEAMS HAVE

Maybe there are things that are not talked about in the team. This might be an unspoken truth, the issue that is being swept under the carpet or something else. What's taboo for the team or group you are working with? What would be the value of asking them that question?

## SUPPORTING A TEAM THROUGH CONFLICT WHEN THE TEAM IS CONFLICT-AVOIDANT

This is not only a difficult conversation, but also a tricky one. It's important that we provide teams and other clients we work with with tools, skills, and approaches to navigate conflict. This may involve some "teaching" or the introduction of a model they can all have a conversation from.

What do you notice about conflict and the way the group and/or team members you are supporting approaches conflict?

## WITH THE GROUP MEMBER WHO CONSTANTLY HOGS OR DOMINATES THE CONVERSATION

For some coaches, supporting the dominant group member who may "hog" the space or bulldoze others may be challenging. Each of us will probably find different types of group members more challenging to work with than others. In the many years I've supported coaches it is often the Challenger, or dominant group member, who coaches note would be the challenging one for them to support.

## WITH THE GROUP MEMBER WHO IS NOT ENGAGED

In coaching, coachability should always be at the forefront. Is this person ready and interested in being coached? Give group members an opportunity to explore what role they are playing in the group and how that is impacting others.

*What do you see as the most difficult conversations for yourself?*

# DEALING WITH CONFLICT

Conflict is a common occurrence in any group development or team development process. As explored earlier, it's a natural part of the evolution of a team or a group. Conflict does emerge in the virtual space and can take a variety of forms. It can be very explicit with people voicing concerns or being verbally conflictual. For other group members, it might take the form of withdrawal—people not showing up or double-booking themselves multiple times.

Three things to keep in mind when dealing with conflict:

1. Levels of trust and connection
2. It's about behavior, not personality
3. Everyone has a different perspective around what is at stake

Everyone will probably have a different approach to conflict. Some group or team members may be more conflict-averse, preferring to sweep things under the carpet, compared to a team member who embraces conflict and enjoys competition. Helping team members understand their typical approach to conflict can be very useful. The Thomas-Kilmann Index (TKI) is one assessment which does this.

Finding the common ground of everyone's experience and perspective is critical in dealing with conflict. Finding the *2%* of agreement or alignment can make the difference between deadlock and a way forward.

Conflict naturally emerges within groups, particularly in the Storming stage. It becomes dysfunctional when people do not feel equipped to navigate conflict, or do not feel "safe" to raise issues, which are in opposition. The establishment of ground rules or Ways of Working early on makes it possible for groups to have alignment and a shared approach to how to proceed with difficult issues. If your group or team is not static and is changing all the time, you will need to co-create the agreements with them regularly.

In approaching conflict, take note of why conflict is surfacing and what the issues underneath it are. Try to unpack with the group what's at the core. As we know conflict can stem from many places—lack of resourcing, perceived inequity, personality differences or lack of information. Blame and finger pointing can become commonplace in conflict situations, rather than getting to root cause. In past work around conflict, one of my co-facilitators has suggested the question, *What is the request behind your complaint?* to those who find themselves in the framework of blame. This is a powerful question as it shifts responsibility to the person making the complaint, inviting them to come up with their own solution.

## WHEN CONFLICT DOES HAPPEN – FOUR KEYS TO NAVIGATING CONFLICT

It is likely that conflict will occur, either early in the Storming stage of group development, or if learning and engagement needs are not being met. In navigating conflict, it can be important to keep these four keys in mind.

1. **Be proactive and address conflict early on.** While this is easier said than done, many view navigating conflict as very challenging in part because issues may have escalated even more than at the start.

2. **Find the common ground.** Finding similar vantage points or even "slivers" where you can see "eye to eye" is a starting point in navigating conflict. These mini-windows are opportunities to open dialogue and mutual problem solving, rather than raising walls.

3. **Recognize that conflict can be a healthy thing when we have the tools to navigate it.** Where cultures do not recognize that conflict is a normal and natural part of human relationships, it may be minimized and swept under the rug, or it can be seen as "abnormal" and "vilified where something is wrong. What is the culture at your workplace around conflict?

4. **Invest in your skills in navigating conflict.** Conflict management is not always well-modelled in our work places and families. If this has been the case with you, it can be useful to invest in some professional development and/or mentoring so you have more

phrases and even a model or process to follow. Where is conflict management well modeled? What tools and resources are people using?

5. Navigating differences is an important skill set for today's global environment. *What actions do you want to take towards building your skills and capacity?*[105]

## DEALING WITH DIFFERENT PERSONALITIES IN A GROUP

Part of what keeps virtual facilitation fresh is the variety of people who show up in your virtual room. This translates to having many different personalities in a group, some of which might feel like a difficult issue. In this section, we are going to explore several of the typical personalities that might emerge.

Ravensfeller, 2014

In supporting difficult participants, it is important to keep in mind these principles:

1. The facilitator's role is to support the entire group
2. Always be respectful
3. Remind people of ground rules
4. Take it offline
5. Self-manage your emotions and triggers
6. A variety of perspectives will exist

As I have written in past articles:[106]

For each one of us, "difficult" looks a little different. It's also important to note that at times we may be someone else's "difficult participant."

The idea of working with difficult participants is a perspective. It is important to remember that tricky issues will emerge in a group or team coaching engagement when people *do not feel safe, valued, or heard.* This points to the importance of building trust and connection amongst your group members and spending time early on getting to know them. A best practice around group coaching and virtual work is to schedule a one-on-one, 15-minute call with each participant before the start of the program to learn more about them, what's brought them to the program and what they want to get out of their work.

As coaches and virtual leaders, there are several tenets we want to always remember in our work. Our clients are naturally creative, resourceful, and whole. As coaches, we trust in the ability of the clients themselves to be resourceful. Philosophically, they bring the expertise and capability needed. As facilitators, part of our role is to help group members connect with this wisdom, or access the wisdom themselves. Early in the coaching engagement it is important to ensure that all participants understand their role in coaching.

As a coach or group facilitator, it is important to keep in mind three other areas. First, it is important to *meet people where they are at.* Consider each person's motivation, how they prefer to communicate and be supported. At the same time, it's important to ensure that the "greater good" and overall group needs are being met. Part of the learning process in a group or team coaching engagement is the self-awareness we can gain around our impact on others. This also helps to shift what may be perceived as difficult behaviors. Finally, as coaches it is very important to explore with that person if they are coachable. Are they ready to take responsibility for their learning and action and change? If not, they may not be a good fit for the coaching process.

When working with a group or team, we are faced with a wide variety of personalities and personas, which does keep this work exciting. Throughout your journey of group and team work, you may meet some of these types of people:

| | |
|---|---|
| The Dominator | The Quiet One |
| The Shy One | The Challenger |
| The Center of Attention | The Unfocused One |
| The Joker | The Superachiever |
| The Devil's Advocate | The Know-It-All |
| The Argumentative One | The Avoider |

Keeping these three tenets in mind, let's take a quick look at some of these personas, which practitioners can find challenging:

## THE SHY ONE

In many groups we may have shy, withdrawn, or quiet participants. Engaging in the virtual space requires both verbal input and also initiative, especially when process is not focused on getting everyone to input or engage. It is important to recognize that not all participants process or engage in the same way. Those that are shy or quiet may benefit more from small group or paired work and individual reflection activities. Do not assume that quietness means lack of engagement. Include a variety of ways for participants to engage, reflect, and learn. Providing a few minutes for people to write things out before responding can create more safety for group members.

## THE CHALLENGER

The Challenger may wish to challenge everything you say. Depending on our role—for example, as a coach working in the virtual space—we need to continually reinforce that our role is not one of expert, but that they are. The same holds true when virtual leaders manage teams globally, a staff member may be the expert on the local level realities. This often switches the focus for the Challenger to move to the Know-It-All role.

## THE DOMINATOR

It is quite common to have one verbally dominant person in a group. They will often let you know this in a pre-call. That's a perfect opportunity to introduce the coaching skill of *intruding*, and letting them know that you will be jumping in and asking questions to help them get to the core of the story. Also, teach group members the skill of *bottom lining* or *laser speak* at the start and remind the group about this skill throughout your work. If someone continues to be dominant, it may be a good opportunity to break into smaller groups, whether you are in-person or virtual.

## THE UNFOCUSED ONE

The unfocused participant may show up as someone who is inattentive and "wandering off." In the virtual world, it is important to let people know where you are going. Provide an overview of the process and ask what they want to explore or get out of the conversation. What else will help them create focus?

Other times we may work with clients who just "don't know." Providing opportunities for them to become more focused include asking questions such as:

- What are your key goals?

- What do you need/want to do to get there?
- What do you want to get out of the conversation?
- What's really important?
- Where do you need to move the needle forward this week?

## THE SUPERACHIEVER

The Superachiever can pose a challenge for some coaches as their endless achievements may cause feelings of inadequacy in other group members. It is important to reinforce with your group that everyone will be moving at their own pace within a group coaching process, and that wins and successes happen at different stages for each person. Having the Superachiever share what they learned from their experience can spark and inspire others with new ideas and insights.

## THE CENTER OF ATTENTION

It can be common to have someone who wants to be the center of attention. There are several roles that you can invite them to participate in—time-keeper, flip-charter, note-taker. Some of these will "give them the spotlight" and fill the need to be seen. This is also a rich area for exploration in an individual coaching conversation with them. Coaching questions to ask them include:

- What's important about being seen?
- What impact does it have on others?

## THE JOKER

Humor can provide lightness in the coaching process. Again, it's a rich perspective to explore with the group. Where do they need to infuse some humor around the issues being explored? What needs lightening up? Sometimes, the Joker may take humor to the extreme. Be aware of the impact it is having on the group. Ask the Joker to consider how they might be affecting the group.

## THE DEVIL'S ADVOCATE

The Devil's Advocate can take us into the rich terrain of perspectives. Their voice is a great reminder that there are many different perspectives which exist in groups and in a team. What is the flipside? What important issues does the Devil's Advocate point to?

## THE ARGUMENTATIVE ONE

Some participants may want to argue for argument's sake. Questions to ask might include:

- What's at stake?
- What's the request behind your complaint?

## THE KNOW-IT-ALL

Coaching rests in the belief that our clients *do* know it all! In the virtual space, one person may know more about their reality than others in the group, team, or call. A central question to explore with the person who feels like they are the Know-It-All include:

- What is important for the rest of us to know or understand?
- What makes you unique?
- What do you have to offer?
- How can you share your expertise in a more positive fashion?

Now that we've met these different personalities, who is really going to be a challenge for you? Are they really that difficult? What's the perspective you want to hold? What can you do to support the unique needs of each one of your group members? What conversations are you looking forward to having?

In facilitation or coaching skills training, I usually ask people which personality styles they would find the hardest to deal with. These four usually are mentioned, so I wanted to go a little more into detail with each. Two are from the group we just explored, whereas two are new ones.

## THE CHALLENGER

The Challenger challenges everything, and this may include your meeting, who is at the table, and outcomes. In the virtual realm, the Challenger can quickly turn everyone off. Being clear prior to the start of the meeting with process—around outcomes and agenda items—is one of the ways to mitigate against this. In the virtual realm, clarity of communication and process is key.

The Challenger's vantage point is usually one of great value. Typically, there is always value, and something to be learned, from the perspective of the Challenger. What is the request behind the Challenger's complaint?

## THE AVOIDER

The Avoider may be a more passive group member who is disengaged and does not take responsibility for outcomes, participation or next steps. While we can only influence, as a facilitator our role is to make sure there is agreement around what next steps are, who is responsible and what is expected. It may be important to talk about *What happens if these are not followed through?* Let the group and/or systems in place also address the impact of the Avoider.

Creating opportunities for work and dialogue in smaller groups, such as virtual breakouts, often encourages and necessitates that the Avoider becomes a more actively engaged participant around the virtual table. What is behind this avoidance? Lack of knowledge? Skill? Understanding? Lack of confidence? If you are working with this person for a longer time, helping the person become aware of the impact they are having in the virtual space can be an important series of conversations to have.

## THE DOMINATOR

The Dominator wants to take charge and probably wants to be leading the meeting. They usually hog air time and dominate the call virtually through speaking, sounds (grunts), or even over-annotating with tools they have. Consider providing this person a structured role so they can positively channel their focus. Perhaps they become a time-keeper or minute-taker for the process.

## THE MULTITASKER

The Multitasker is a very common—and difficult—participant, who can be present in most virtual calls. Their multitasking may be visible through typing, background noise etc. Creating shared expectations as a group with respect to what focus and engagement is expected can provide encouragement. When you have rapport with group members, letting them know that you can see their multitasking online may prompt them.

- What will help this person focus?
- What do they need in order to stop multitasking?
- What are they aware of in terms of their impact?

While there are many more difficult issues, these are four common ones that show up in different virtual calls. As the facilitator, you play a key role in ensuring that it is a safe and positive learning environment for everyone, grounded in respect.

*What strategies do you want to employ? How are you also someone else's difficult participant?*

## ALLOWING FOR THE STRUGGLE AND UNCOMFORTABLENESS OF LEARNING

In stepping into the stance as a facilitator or coach, we are holding that the group we are working with is *naturally creative, resourceful, and whole.* The learning process is naturally mucky and uncomfortable. It has become common practice in many organizations today to jump in and "fix things." What is lost is the ability to learn from the process, the bumps and dips. As facilitators, it is important that we allow the learning process to take place. This may be something we "name" or reference at the start of our work, especially as in the virtual domain things can be more pronounced.

Trevor Bentley captures this well and writes in his book *Facilitation*, "Perhaps one of the most difficult things for a facilitator to do is to allow someone to struggle. To rescue people from the struggle immediately shuts off an opportunity for them to learn and grow. Supporting and encouraging them through the struggle is much more rewarding for everyone involved."

Note that allowing for the struggle and uncomfortableness of learning not only applies to group or team members. This also applies to us. Notice when you feel the churn of new learning. What do you need to do to ground yourself?

## CONCLUSION

As we wind down this chapter, it is important to note that virtual facilitation is not for the faint-hearted. Our skills in relationship building, addressing difficult issues, and creating and environment of trust, respect and safety are essential when we are faced with tricky issues. Tricky issues can emerge at any time for new and seasoned virtual facilitators and leaders. What is important is to mitigate, and be in dialogue, addressing issues before or as they emerge. Take some time before you move on to reflect on the end of chapter questions.

## END OF CHAPTER QUESTIONS

Make a list of any concerns you have about challenges you think you will face.

Who would you see as difficult participants in your work? What would make that group member challenging? How do you want to respond?

Take 10-15 minutes to write out and/or note what you want to put in place to mitigate against this, or how you will react if it does happen.

What resources (human or other) will help you with your concerns? Who do you have in your network that you can reach out to around tricky issues and other concerns?

Make note of any key action steps from this chapter in your Action Plan Tracker.

CHAPTER 9

# IN FOCUS: VIRTUAL MEETINGS OF ALL STRIPES

*"Meetings run best when there are clear rules or norms to follow. These are sometimes difficult to set at the start of the meeting. People may feel reluctant to speak up and suggest rules or there may be pressure to start discussing the agenda items."*[107]

*- Ingrid Bens, Facilitating with Ease! Core Skills for Facilitators, Team Leaders and Members, Managers, Consultants, and Trainers*

11 million meetings take place every day, with a third noted as being ineffective. $37 billion is wasted every year on ineffective meetings.[108]

This chapter will explore:

- Virtual meeting basics
- Setting people up for success with virtual meetings
- Keeping things on track
- Virtual meeting faux-pas

- Structuring calls – the start, middle, and end
- Four Tools for virtual meetings:
  - Preparing for a virtual meeting
  - Follow-up (checklists, pre and post)
  - The One-Page Plan
  - Virtual Meeting Agenda

There are many different types of virtual meetings including planning meetings, coaching meetings, creation meetings (sprints), and team meetings. In this chapter we are going to look at the most mainstream virtual meetings—the conference call, or planning meetings. We will also explore core essentials for planning meetings. It is important to note that many of the principles and practices we have been discussing throughout the book are applicable to meetings, as well as other learning events.

For a close look at virtual team development meetings, go to Chapter 11.

## VIRTUAL MEETING BASICS

Just as "setting everyone up for success" has been a key message throughout this book, there are some basics around facilitating a successful virtual meeting. These are my Eight Essential Questions to ask before even sending out a meeting invite:

1. What's the purpose?
2. What takeaways do we want?
3. Who needs to be on the call?
4. What preparation is needed for us to be most effective in the meeting?
5. What pace to do we want in order to keep it engaging?
6. What will help keep the focus?
7. What is absolutely essential (versus what will be nice to cover or where can people go for more information around topics)?
8. What follow-up might be required?

## CREATING THE FOUNDATION FOR A SUCCESSFUL MEETING – EIGHT ESSENTIALS

There are a couple of things that are different with virtual meetings. Before the meeting, it will be useful to consider:

1. **Do you have all the right people at the table?** It is much harder to bring people into virtual meetings than going down the hall to grab someone you need in an in-person meeting. Before you send out the final meeting invite, note if there is anyone else who should be added. That person may be able to provide information, and/or the authority and responsibility to get things done.

2. **What can be done pre-meeting vs post-meeting?** In many ways, well-structured virtual meetings can be more focused than in-person events. Consider what people can—and must—do before they come to the call. How clear is communication around pre-work and what participants need to bring to the call?

   Likewise, there may be some follow-up required at the end of the session. Sending out a quick email with specifics around the next steps and who is responsible is important. Watch for the trap created by spending days on extensive minutes. Asking, *What is the format which will capture notes, agreements and next steps?* may lead to a shift away from extensive written meeting minutes to a bulleted tabular format. One of this chapter's resources is a blank tabular chart to capture meeting minutes.

   Send follow-up—next steps, responsibilities, agreements—as close to the end of the meeting as possible, while things are still fresh. If feasible, have people note decisions and next steps during the meeting in their own calendars and systems *during* the meeting. This can flag any conflicts for dates and/or priorities.

3. **Avoid multitasking and Death by Conference Call.** We have

all been there! There's nothing worse that hearing someone having a conversation in the background. Where possible, use streaming to avoid the Death by Conference Call mentality and multitasking. Create agreements around focus and/or presence during the calls.

4. **Watch for, and expect, technology glitches.** Make sure technology is really working for everyone. How accessible is the technology to everyone? Would it be useful to reduce it to the lowest common denominator, so all can participate equally? Always have a backup and be asking yourself what technology is going to foster the most engagement, and ease, for group members. Consider how streaming might reduce a myriad of sins of virtual meetings.

5. **Get out of the rut with roles.** Having a job to do can boost engagement. Provide opportunities for equal participation by rotating roles. Roles include that of note-taker (or scribe) and time-keeper. If you are on a web-based platform set a timer. Assign times to each action or agenda item. Have a scribe/note-taker capture the minutes and circulate them.

6. **Be strong on process.** In the virtual realm, it is really important to have a strong focus on process. This includes:

   - Letting people know what they can expect from the process.
   - Is there an agenda you will be following? (A meeting template is included at the end of this chapter)
   - How will you be working with time?
   - What level of engagement do you expect?
   - Will you be going around the room?

Set a clear focus for the meeting. Have strict timeframes in mind. This also includes sending out agenda items and agreeing on and sticking to time frames. Given that it is likely that different group members will be in different time zones, going over time in virtual meetings is usually not likely. Have a game plan on what absolutely needs to be covered and what can wait.

7. **Create Ways of Working and shared agreements.** This is important if you are working together for multiple meetings. Organizations may also adopt a standard of practice around virtual meetings where everyone has bought into the way virtual meetings are run. Quickly review agreements at the start and end of the call.

8. **Consider multiple feedback loops.** One of the main challenges in the virtual space is not knowing where people are at. Create multiple touchpoints to get feedback on how the meeting is going and what changes may need to be made. In the virtual space, there is a dichotomy of *sticking to the agenda* if the agenda is not right to begin with.

---

### Practitioner's Tip:  Virtual Whiteboarding Process

In many instances, you may want to create real-time whiteboards during your virtual meetings to capture notes, discussions, and key learning. This is one way to keep the conversation going and track the outputs. In *Click*, Michael Wilkinson notes that there are three types of boards you may be wanting to capture information on throughout virtual calls (pp 58). These include:[109]

1. Issues

2. Decisions made

3. Actions

You may also have a fourth whiteboard—a *virtual Parking Lot*. The virtual Parking Lot is a valuable space where people can see items that need to be carried forward to other events or conversations. It is an important part of keeping track of loose ends and keeping conversations focused. Key to the successful use and adoption of the Parking Lot by everyone is to make sure issues noted there are being followed up on by the appropriate people. Be sure to address these issues or indicate how they will be addressed, or who they will be forwarded to. Otherwise, Parking Lots can erode trust.

In the virtual space, a Parking Lot could include a separate board where issues for follow-up are found. In platforms like Zoom, where chat is encoded in a separate file, noting Parking Lot issues there provides a quick way to find things after the call.

Being able to move back and forth between these areas/boards can be critical for virtual facilitation success. Boards can be created in several ways:

1. Using the whiteboard function in virtual meeting platforms, like WebEx, Zoom, or other. Note that this is not always a standard function in basic packages.

2. Using a blank PowerPoint slide, which you will annotate and save for platforms such as Zoom.

3. Physically using a whiteboard broken up into those areas during the call.

4. Using a MindMapping software that visually captures issues/decisions made and actions.

Regardless of the approach, make sure that there is agreement on what has been captured during the meeting and send it out immediately to group members.

## KEEPING THINGS ON TRACK – SEVEN KEYS FOR VIRTUAL MEETINGS

Used together, these seven quick items can be very effective in accelerating the impact and engagement of your next virtual event:

1. **Engagement is key.** Helping group members connect regularly with their WIIFM and engaging them in the dialogue is almost more important than it is in the in-person realm. Competition with emails and your desktop is often the reality. Keep the pace moving, encourage reflection and dialogue, and take the pulse regularly to see where people are at.

2. **Connection is the foundation.** While you might not be able to see each other in the virtual realm, feeling connected with others is an important foundation for virtual meeting success, particularly if these meetings will continue for some time. Refer to Chapter 7 for several activities to build connection during your calls. Without trust and connection, it is unlikely that people will engage fully. Spending a few minutes at the start of a call on building trust and connection with a group that is going to be working together for a while can go a long way in creating a sense of safety, trust, and connection.

3. **Trust is critical.** Just as in the in-person environment, trust is critical. Given that we don't have regular touchpoints where we can be "seen," building trust in the virtual environment can be even more pointed. Consider how you are building your reputation and ask what others think of you. Remember that in the virtual environment, trust is built through consistency, follow through, and clarity. Check in around where you see trust in your work with the worksheet for Chapter 1.

4. **Good design.** Good design is especially important in the virtual domain. Note the overall blocks of the meeting or event and how they fit together or are sequenced. More focus on process

rather than less is of benefit in the virtual domain. What are the design elements that will support the most effective virtual event? Consider breakouts, polls, use of a whiteboard, keeping it simple if technology is going to be a hindrance. Refer to the Start, Middle, and End Section in this chapter.

5. **Leverage technology.** Use the technology you have available and which is accessible to all. I often go to the "lowest common denominator" so we are not creating any new divisions based on technology available. If you can use more interactive supports such as breakouts to engage everyone, use them. Consider what support will help you. For example, have a co-facilitator who can set up breakouts while you are facilitating. Don't try to do it all alone!

6. **Visuals are an important boost.** Having a virtual anchor point, even on a phone call, is important in the virtual realm. Visuals can create a focus, and a grounding point. These can range from a handout, to slides, to the use of photo cards (refer to Chapter 7 for more on these). If you are only meeting by phone, consider sending out a one-pager prior to the call for meeting participants to download, print, and use. Make sure they are provided this well enough in advance of the call.

7. **Be nimble as a facilitator.** Being flexible as a facilitator in the virtual realm is essential. Expect technology glitches to happen because they will. Perhaps your recording will not start, or someone cannot get their audio to work. Have a contingency plan and several backups available that you can draw upon. Think through the various scenarios that may happen and how you will deal with them.

### Virtual Meeting Faux Pas

Five faux pas or mistakes to watch for as a virtual meeting host/facilitator include:[110]

1. **Not having an agenda and sticking to it.** Process is king in the virtual realm. It is important to have a plan which you share with others (so they can input into it before the meeting), and one that you refer to throughout the call so people know where you are and where you are going.

2. **Not starting and ending meetings on time**. This is critical in the realm of virtual meetings, particularly as it is common that people will be at different parts of their day.

3. **Not calling on people you haven't heard from.** Virtual meetings, particularly when you can't see each other, are a ripe opportunity to multitask and sign out. Let people know what's expected so when you do call on people, it's part of the norm and not seen as "being picked on."

4. **Not rotating meeting times.** When you lead a global team, it can be important to rotate meeting times so it's not always the same team members calling in at challenging hours. Be aware of time-of-day considerations when scheduling virtual meetings, and where it's feasible, change things up so everyone shares the burden of participating at odd hours.

5. **Not being clear on what's been agreed and who is accountable.** Make sure you remind people throughout a virtual meeting about agreements, key points and also where you are going next. It's easy to say a lot of "yes-es" and then forget or not be clear on what was agreed upon.

*What other virtual meeting faux pas/mistakes do you see?*

### Team Meetings in the Spotlight

Meetings can be an essential part of the communication needed for high-performing teams, and unfortunately have gotten a bad rap due to poorly planned and poorly executed meetings. We know teams that excel usually have shared team practices like meetings, which focus on building relationships and getting results.

With more than 35-50% of people's time being spent in meetings each week, the question of *What could we do to make team meetings more effective?* is a strategic one.

As a team, consider:

- What are the top three reasons we should be holding meetings?
- When is the best time to hold them?
- What's working with our meetings currently? What's not?
- What's the one thing we could let go of doing in our meetings without having too much of an impact?
- What is the one thing we wish we did more of?
- What is the best way to communicate information in different topic areas?
- What are the things we want to start doing as a team instead of meetings?

## SETTING EVERYONE UP FOR SUCCESS: FOUR TIPS FOR A SUCCESSFUL VIRTUAL MEETING[111]

Four key considerations in preparing for your virtual meeting are:

1. **Know your audience.** Who are you meeting with? What pace is going to work best for them? What strategies can you use to stay engaged and focused? What

key takeaways are they expecting from the meeting? Your audience should always be the "driver" and shaper of a virtual event. Helping them connect early on with their WIIFM makes it a win-win for all parties involved.

2. **Be comfortable with the tools at hand.** Knowing as much as you can about the platforms you are using is critical to success. Being comfortable in not really knowing is a key factor. Spending time on the platforms you are using prior to your session will help you gain confidence. Practice, even if you are the only person on the line. Consider how you will transition from section to section, engagement then content.

3. **Know when you will engage and how.** Having a plan around engagement strategies during virtual events is probably even more important than in the in-person realm, given the brevity of our attention span in the virtual domain. Consider the tools you have around engagement—polls, breakouts, annotation, chat etc. What is available to you within the platforms you are using? What are the engagement activities you are going to include?

4. **What is the end point or takeaway from the meeting/process**? Starting with the end in mind will help you with the overall arc or pace of the call, along with the questions you ask and engagement opportunities you choose. Make a note around the one or two things you want to make sure people leave with.

## THE START, MIDDLE, AND END OF MEETINGS – CORE COMPONENTS OF ANY VIRTUAL CALL:

As I have noted several times throughout this book, process is key in virtual calls. This section looks at how we can set everyone up for success with an eye to good virtual meeting design.

As with any presentation, there are three main segments of the program, the *Start,* the *Middle,* the *End.*

THE START:

Just like in the "real world," first impressions are key. If we don't connect with people or get their attention in the first few minutes, this may mean losing them to the world of multitasking and disengagement. However, there are several strategies we can use to get their attention such as:

1.  Helping them connect with their WIIFM (*What's in it for me?*). What is it that people want out of their experience? Ask questions such as:
    a.  What do you want to get out of your time spent here?
    b.  What's the takeaway you want to get out of our call today?
    c.  What's the one thing you want to leave this call with?
2.  Using an interesting fact or story to capture their attention.
3.  Using visuals or other media to get people's attention focused on the topic at hand.
4.  I like to keep things simple in the virtual realm. There is usually enough complexity between the group and the technology itself. Providing virtual attendees with a quick overview of the call is a best practice for keeping people focused and grounded in the call. Building trust, connection and safety amongst the group are also key considerations at the start.

Key elements at the start of any meeting include:

- **Welcome**
- **Rules of engagement/Ways of working** – How you as a group want to operate. Considerations might include: keeping to time, asking questions, staying focused or being present.
- **Preview of the process and where you are going** – What are the key items and how much time is available? What role is required in each—listening/updating, decision making?
- **What's brought you together** – any important context information.

- **Introductions**

The start usually comprises *10%* of the time in a presentation. So, if you have a one-hour presentation, the start is typically the first five minutes. It might be a little longer in a coaching space where you want to have people share or report back their actions or learning.

### Creating Powerful Starts

Creating connection and "safety" as well as providing an overview of what to expect from the call is key. Consider how you will open the session and welcome people as they arrive. Be clear about the expectations and guidelines for the call. Remind people how to use things like mute, annotation, chat etc. Don't assume!

Getting people to pin their location to a map is a great way of visually orienting people, or if you are together for a longer time period, get people to send out a quick intro/bio beforehand. Make this easy and consider creating a standard format for people to use.

Reinforce the importance of a clear connection that mobile phones often do not allow for!

THE MIDDLE:

The agreements that happen in the middle of virtual conversations often get lost, mimicking the way our brain remembers things. The latency and recency effect in neuroscience has shown that we tend to remember things at the start and end, while the middle is mucky.

The implication of this in virtual facilitation is that it's important to get very clear around process, and letting people know where they are. For example, in the middle of a one-hour call it may be useful to indicate where you've been (*So far, we've covered/explored...* or, *We've agreed to...*)

and alert people where you are going. Remind people of the key outcomes they mentioned at the start so you have time to cover the important items you came to the call for.

In the experiential process, the midpoint usually gets people moving beyond thinking about the *What?* and into the *So What?* What's important about what I am learning? So, what can I do now?

THE END:

Great learning events bring people full circle. During the end of a call you may be focusing more on the *Now What?* In the experiential learning process, the *Now What?* gets people to think about *What's Next?* and what they will do with the learning.

Key things to do at the close of a session include:

- Highlight or overview what you've covered, where you have been and/or some of the key themes.
- Specify the action steps agreed to and who is responsible for doing what.
- What next steps are needed? Give people the opportunity to share what their next steps are.
- Have people share what they've learned and/or what they are committed to doing next.

Check out the closure section of the activity list, as well as the appendix, to find several activities to close a virtual session. For more information, refer to Chapter 5, Designing for Powerful and Engaging Learning.

**Creating Powerful Ends**[112]

The end is just as important as the start. Providing a reflection point for people to consider what they have learned is key. As a facilitator, you may be very tired at this point of the process, so consider how you can create your own standard ways of bringing calls to a close. Some possibilities are asking:

What new learning or ideas are you leaving the call with?

What's the one action you are going to take in the next 24-76 hours to put this learning into action? (Note that the retention window after learning is very short, so the faster you can get people to apply their learning after the process, the better.)

*What other ideas do you have about creating powerful starts and ends to virtual learning?*

## FOUR TOOLS FOR VIRTUAL MEETINGS

To close out this chapter, I am including four tools or templates to support you in making your meetings more structured and flowing. These four tools include:

1. Pre-Meeting Checklist
2. Sample Agenda
3. The One-Page Plan
4. Post-Meeting Follow-up

You can download these tools at our website – www. EffectiveVirtualConversations.com.

## TOOL #1 – PRE-MEETING CHECKLIST

One of the themes of this book is setting everyone up for success—including yourself. Before you "step into the room" or send out the meeting request, look at these eight pre-meeting checklist areas:

| ITEM | DESCRIPTION |
|---|---|
| GET TO KNOW PARTICIPANTS | **What are their needs, learning agendas, where are they based?** The more you know about your group the better able you are to serve their needs. Do you want to schedule a quick 15-minute pre-call to meet each person? As I have written in the past, this is an essential part of building trust and connection with participants, and gives me a sense of who is going to be "in the room" (even if it's virtual!). |
| CREATE AN AGENDA | **What's the agenda?** Virtual facilitators play a key role in holding a strong focus on process. Creating an agenda that meets the needs and purpose of the call/session is critical. Consider what input meeting participants or learners want/need and how you will facilitate this. |
| BE CLEAR ON TIME CONSTRAINTS | **Be clear about how much time the meeting is really going to take.** Sloppy time-management can quickly derail a virtual meeting. Add time to your agenda and let group members know how much time there is for each section so they can prepare their input. Remember, accurately estimating time comes from experience, so know you will get better at it! |
| CONSIDER WHO SHOULD BE PRESENT | **Who needs to be at the table?** Who is needed to provide information, supply resources, make decisions or provide authority? |
| ENSURE YOU HAVE THE NECESSARY MATERIALS | **What will you need during the meeting?** Do these need to be sent out to others prior to the meeting? What will they need to have on hand to participate? |

| | |
|---|---|
| SEND OUT LINKS AND MATERIALS WELL IN ADVANCE | **Aim for the week before if possible**, or at least at the start of the week for a meeting later in the week. Keep in mind people's travel schedules and time zones. |
| CHECK YOUR TECHNOLOGY | **Double-check that you have sent out the right bridge line with access codes** and/or that your meeting links work and are set for the right time! |
| OTHER | |

## TOOL #2 – VIRTUAL MEETING AGENDA

Having a tight hand on process and flow is important and you may want to evolve the agenda format I typically use for meetings. Note the virtual table can be filled with participant names for phone-only programs where you may not have a list of who's who on the call.

# TEMPLATE: VIRTUAL CALL AGENDA

| | |
|---|---|
| Virtual Meeting Date: | |
| Time (Across Time Zones): | |
| Participants: | |
| Key Takeaways – List Top 3: | |

| Time | Agenda Item | Agreements | Who/When |
|---|---|---|---|
| | | | |
| | | | |
| | | | |
| | | | |
| | | | |

## TOOL #3 – THE ONE-PAGE PLAN

The One-Page Plan is one of my favorite planning tools that can be distributed to group members before a call. This will allow people to note for themselves their own action steps: what's required, what's going to help, and what will hinder. This format can be adapted for coaching conversations, as well as longer virtual events, where people may have a cumulative One-Page Plan tracker.

The One-Page Plan is a one page template used to capture actionable notes for group members about their next steps. You will note the template includes space for each person to note their key goals, a description of what each goal is, what resources they need, key timelines and things that will help and hinder them along the way.

This document can be useful in articulating simplifying next steps agreed to. Each person can have a One-Page Plan or a one-pager can be developed for the entire meeting.

## THE ONE-PAGE PLAN

| GOAL | DESCRIPTION | KEY TIMELINES | RESOURCES (WHO AND WHAT) | ENABLERS/ DERAILERS |
|------|-------------|---------------|--------------------------|---------------------|
|      |             |               |                          |                     |
|      |             |               |                          |                     |
|      |             |               |                          |                     |
|      |             |               |                          |                     |
|      |             |               |                          |                     |

## TOOL #4 – POST MEETING FOLLOW-UP

There are a number of key items you will want to follow up with after any virtual meeting including:

| ITEM | DESCRIPTION |
| --- | --- |
| AGREEMENTS | What agreements have been made? Make sure to summarize these and let people know how you will follow up on these agreements. |
| ACCOUNTABILITIES | Who is going to do what? By when? Create a plan for when you will check in on follow-up items. |
| PROCESS REFLECTION | Reflect on how the timing went. What adjustments need to be made for future meetings? Were there any technical issues faced? Accessibility issues? Challenges faced by different participants? |
| PARKING LOT | Identifying what needs to happen with Parking Lot items. Over time, if Parking Lot issues are left without being addressed, it can start to erode trust in the process of meetings and follow-up. Make sure you agree as a group what needs to happen with Parking Lot items. |
| SCHEDULING | Schedule your next call. |
| THANKS AND CLOSE-OUT | Thank people for their time, especially acknowledging those who might have had to dial in at difficult times of the day. |
| TECH CHECK | Note and address any technical issues that were present and make adjustments for next time. |
| OTHER | |

Remember to download these templates at our website – www.EffectiveVirtualConversations.com.

# CHECK IN WITH JANE – VIRTUAL MEETINGS

Jane is getting ready for a high-stakes virtual meeting and makes sure she has covered all the bases with her pre-meeting checklist. She takes note of:

1. Her pre-engagement with meeting participants. The agenda went out more than ten days ago and the feedback received on additional agenda items and participants was incorporated.

2. The 8 Essential Meeting Questions and how she will incorporate them.

3. Her set up for breakouts and the virtual whiteboards in the meeting, including a Parking Lot.

4. The five-faux pas to avoid in virtual meetings.

5. The roles which need to be filled at the start of the meeting—note taker and time keeper.

6. How she is going to address the Start, Middle and End.

## END OF CHAPTER QUESTIONS

What pre-preparation do you want to undertake for your upcoming meetings?

What will help you keep the meeting focused and moving?

How do you want to create a powerful start and end to the meeting?

What follow-up resources and/or process do you want to focus on?

Make note of any key action steps from this chapter in your Action Plan Tracker.

CHAPTER 10

# IN FOCUS: VIRTUAL TEAM LEADERSHIP DEVELOPMENT

*"The more complex society gets, the more sophisticated leadership must become."*[113]

*– Michael Fullan, Leading in a Culture of Change*

From leaders leading remote teams across large urban centers, to project managers supporting distributed teams, to global leaders leading across the world, virtual team leadership development continues to expand. This chapter explores the core foundations of virtual team leadership development, the nuances and differences with developing a cohort of virtual and distributed leaders, and essential elements for the first 90 days on the job. Virtual team leadership has been the central focus of my own work and support since the early 1990s. Having lead across countries, managed teams regionally, and supported team members globally, I continue to be active in coaching, mentoring, and training virtual team leaders today.

In this chapter we explore:

- Core skills for virtual team leaders
- Global business leader attributes
- Onboarding new virtual leaders
- Key characteristics of virtual team leaders
- A multi-dimensional approach for developing new virtual team leaders—coaching, mentoring, training

## WHAT THE RESEARCH SHOWS

*"Prior experience working in virtual teams, particularly with the technologies that support the virtual work, are the most significant factors that predict leadership behavior."*[114]

There has been a slew of research since the early 2000s around what makes for effective virtual team leadership. Of particular note is Kayworth and Leidner's research on Leadership Effectiveness in Global Virtual Teams, which found that "effective team leaders":

1. "...demonstrate the capability to deal with paradox and contradiction by performing multiple leadership roles simultaneously (behavioral complexity)."
2. "...act in a mentoring role and exhibit a high degree of understanding (empathy) toward other team members."
3. "...are able to assert their authority without being perceived as overbearing or inflexible."
4. "...are found to be extremely effective at providing regular, detailed, and prompt communication with their peers and in articulating role relationships (responsibilities) among the virtual team members."[115]

Regardless of how much the technology has changed, we can see that the principles of virtual team leadership remain the same. Research published in 2000 by Joyce Thompsen identified five core categories of effective leadership skills in virtual project team or distance-management situations:[116]

1. Communicating effectively and using technology that fits the situation
2. Building community, based on mutual trust, respect, fairness and affiliation, among project team members
3. Establishing clear and inspiring shared goals, expectations, purpose, and vision
4. Leading by example with a focus on visible, measurable results
5. Coordinating/collaborating across organizational boundaries

Throughout this chapter, we will be focusing on practical ways for team leaders to build their skills and confidence. As you may have noted, many of these skills are reflective of the skills we've been exploring throughout the book—creating shared expectations, building trust, clarifying goals, or fostering collaboration.

## LEADERSHIP DEVELOPMENT FOUNDATIONS

Just as the opening quote of this chapter illustrates, leadership needs to change as the context changes. The new norm for many virtual leaders is continued volatility, ongoing change, and complexity in different locations. While foundational skills for all leaders are essential, virtual and distributed leaders (and their team members!) can benefit from additional skills.

**First, let's take a look at best practices and core areas of leadership development for team leaders today:**

In my book, *From One to Many: Best Practices for Team and Group Coaching*,[117] I outline a dozen areas which are critical for a leader's evolution including:

1. **Emotional Intelligence:** Emotional Intelligence (EI) was originally touted as "the softer side of leadership," and as we know now, these skills are critical for a leader's success, particularly as they move up the leadership ladder. I would also assert that this is especially true when they work virtually. Our ability to work through others and be self-aware are critical skills for virtual team leaders. Most models of emotional intelligence comprise dozens of skills ranging along the skill areas of self-awareness (knowing yourself), social awareness (knowing others), self-management (managing your own emotions) and social management (managing your own networks). Looking at where virtual leaders excel across the twenty plus EI Competencies is a starting point for many coaching conversations I have with virtual leaders.

2. **Understanding Myself as a Leader**: Helping team leaders of all levels become more aware of their styles and strengths helps them be more proficient in knowing their natural approaches, which often get exaggerated when under stress, during ambiguity (every day for a virtual leader!), or under pressure.

3. **Influence:** Virtual team leaders work through others. In the virtual domain, it is likely that we are working with matrix managers, peers, as well as internal and external stakeholders. As such, influence becomes a core skill set as we do not manage these other people and need to work *through* them in order to get things done.

4. **Communication:** Under the umbrella of communication, virtual team leaders must bring exceptional communication skills—written, verbal, and sometimes multi-lingual skills. The ability to have difficult conversations, read between the lines and provide feedback are critical. A virtual team leader's efficiency in

communicating across different platforms—text, phone, email—and knowing when and which channel is most appropriate is key.

5. **Coaching Skills:** Coaching skills are critical for virtual team success, so leaders can support their team members to tap into the knowledge and wisdom they bring. Coaching skills such as asking powerful questions, listening, supporting goal clarification, and supporting accountability is part of the *Coaching Skills for Virtual Leaders* toolbox.

6. **Developing Trust and Respect:** Key to engagement in a virtual team is the sense of connection team members have with each other. As such, developing trust and respect with each team member and across the team is a critical issue for virtual team leader success. This topic is explored later in this chapter.

7. **Team Leadership Issues:** Great virtual team leaders are well versed in the foundations of group dynamics (refer to Tuckman's model early in the book), understand the elements of team effectiveness (see Chapter 11 for the Six Factors of High-Performing Teams), and understand other elements such as providing feedback, rewards and recognition, budgeting issues and other technical team issues.

8. **Relationship Management Issues:** The ability to build relationships across the team, the organization, with other matrix managers and external and internal stakeholders—all virtually—is key to success.

9. **Conflict Resolution:** Proficiency in supporting the resolution of conflict across the team, in addressing conflict as it emerges, and how different team members may approach conflict cross-culturally is another important team leadership skill.

10. **Managing Up and Managing Down:** As virtual team leaders we are usually managing up, down, *and* across. As such our ability to do this with diplomacy, as well as tact and grace, is critical.

11. **Leadership Styles and Strengths:** Whether it's an MBTI or

DiSC, virtual team leaders can benefit from understanding their strengths and styles. These topics have been addressed in other parts of this book.

12. **Navigating Change:** Change is the norm in the virtual domain. Being able to lead through uncertainty and not always having all the details or knowing the context is key to virtual team leadership. This is another area where open communication and empowering the team become critical for success.

You are encouraged to take a stock of where your skills are in the Self-Assessment around Virtual Team Leadership capabilities at **EffectiveVirtualConversations.com.**

## CORE ESSENTIALS IN VIRTUAL TEAM LEADERSHIP

Central issues which take on enhanced significance with virtual team leaders are:

- Building relationships – virtually as well as with other matrix managers
- Building trust
- Creating connection amongst the team that isn't always face-to-face
- Providing clarity—providing clear instructions and creating shared expectations, and being able to adjust these for the different team members
- Being intentional—given that touchpoints can feel magnified due to regular connection, be intentional in what you want to create

Additionally, four other skills, which have been addressed throughout the book, are also key to note:

- Working across differences—fostering diversity and inclusion
- Intercultural know-how

- Innovation
- Resilience/Agility

In virtual teams, it is also imperative that we build capability in the skills of our team members. Usually team members in distributed, virtual or remote teams are working more autonomously than those in the in-person domain. Traditionally these skills have been seen as the development realm of leaders. In the virtual realm, we also need to support team members in building better relationships, decision-making skills, prioritizing, understanding their own strengths and styles, communicating more effectively, managing up and down (and across the matrix), as well as working across differences. You are encouraged to take a look at the next chapter, which focuses more widely on virtual team development.

## CHARACTERISTICS OF GREAT VIRTUAL LEADERS:

Meet Jo. She is your typical virtual leader. Tech-savvy, Jo can keep up with the ongoing changes different platforms require. She's able to work on her feet, making adjustments as she goes. Like most virtual team leaders, she's well read, bringing a depth and breadth of experience in many different areas. She's good at working with others to identify and quickly solve problems—and hence is a good trouble shooter. Given that she's working remote, she's very comfortable in not knowing all the details or being able to see what's happening on the ground every moment. She's a *micro-monitor*, not a micro-manager, using intuition to pick up on issues and conversations that need to be had. Like other virtual leaders Jo is a gracious host, with a firm but gentle touch. She's confident in her team and their abilities, making sure they have the training and resources to do what they need to. She passes things over to the team more often than not, given their local level and technical expertise. She's good at mutli-tasking.

Like Jo, specific to the global, distributed, and virtual environments, exceptional leaders also demonstrate these characteristics:[118]

- **The ability to build connection and relationships** quickly, and to connect others with each other, especially if you are leading a multi-national team.
- **Flexibility and adaptability** – when working globally, everyone may be working on a different timeframe. Our A to Z list may become A cubed to C.
- **Openness to not knowing** – the comfort with ambiguity is something many global leaders embrace as the norm rather than the blip. Whether it's not exactly knowing how things are done, or how things operate, being okay with not knowing or getting it right is key to success.
- **Awareness of our own biases and strengths** and how this can serve you, and sometimes get in the way. We each bring our own sub-set of baggage built from the experiences and socialization we have had. For example, a big-picture thinker will need to be comfortable in thinking and communicating in a granular way.
- **Humility** and an appreciation of the multitude of layers of culture which can exist.
- **The ability to see connections and patterns** amongst what might seen disparate.
- **The ability to work and excel across differences** and help others

do the same.

- **The ability to work through people and influence**. As a former virtual team leader, I learned quickly how important it is to be able to support those on the ground. As a former colleague of mine always said, "It is important to micro-monitor, not micro-manage."

Given that we don't always see our staff face-to-face, or see their context, we need to trust in their abilities and empower them with resources, knowledge and information.

The role of the virtual team leader is often one of liaison and trouble shooter. In our valuable time with team members we want to make sure that we ask them questions along the lines of:

- What do you want and need support in from me?
- How can I support you best?
- What are the biggest challenges you are facing right now?
- What resources do you need to be successful?
- What should I know about your work and priorities right now?

These skills are critical for any team leader today. *What are the development opportunities for each virtual team leader in your organization?*

**Four areas in which there are some important nuances between virtual and in-person leadership**

The following are ingredients needed to create the foundation for virtual team success:

1. **Ensuring a clear understanding of roles and responsibilities:** As a virtual team, the need to clearly define roles and responsibilities becomes even more paramount than in face-to-face team environments. As a manager or even a team member, it is critical that everyone fully understand their roles and responsibilities, reporting relationships, as well as where roles and responsibilities

overlap. If you are part of a virtual team, are you clear on this?

2. **Negotiating matrix management relationships:** Matrix management is commonplace in the virtual team realm, where team members may be supported by you as the overall leader, and possibly other local technical managers.

A matrix management structure exists when a professional may be managed by two different managers, delineated often by projects they are involved with. Given the nature of virtual teams, individual members may often be part of a matrix management reporting process. Matrix management is an art form and skill-set in and of itself. Key to making matrix management work is:

- Clarifying roles, responsibilities and reporting structures. Who will be providing direction on what?
- Identifying overlap and gaps.
- Clarifying goals and priorities (especially if there are different perspectives on this).
- Identifying resources required.

It is often beneficial to have a three-way discussion between both managers and the staff member, ensuring that everyone has a common understanding regarding who manages what, what reporting relationships exist, and how work processes will be weighted and prioritized. The topic of matrix management has been a focus on the Teams365 Blog and is foundational to the training we offer in virtual team leadership.

Questions to consider: If you are a matrix manager, what's working well? What's not? What needs clarification?

A terrific resource for those new to matrix management is the Life in a Matrix blog, which provides ample ideas and tips for those stepping into matrix management. The blog comes to you from Kevan Hall of Global Integration.

3. **Working across cultural differences:** Given that virtual teams are often cross-continental or even global in nature, it is important that cultural differences are understood. Differences may exist along several continua, including prioritization, language, the concept of time and management. Explore individual cultural differences while creating a common ground and Ways of Working for the team. Refer to our earlier chapter on some of the differences across cultures.

4. **Creating opportunities for face-to-face interaction:** The effectiveness of virtual teams can be greatly enhanced by budgeting and planning for face-to-face interaction at least once a year. A multi-day retreat can serve as a forum for getting to know each other, creating a shared workplan, discussing strategic directions and creating a shared vision for the team and its work.

## WHAT MAKES A GLOBAL LEADER EXCEL?

As a former global leader throughout the 1990s and into the early 2000s, I was part of programming which evolved the competencies as we went. Today, there are several pieces of research that document what makes global leaders excel. Here is some of the range:

Michael Fullen writes, "True leadership has five components—moral purpose, understanding change, relationship building, knowledge creation and sharing, and coherence making."[119] Note these five areas. Where do you excel?

Paula Caliguiri has researched the attributes of global leadership. Five characteristics of global leaders include:[120]

1. Goal-oriented Tenacity
2. Managing Complexity
3. Cultural Sensitivity
4. Emotional Resilience
5. Ability to Form Relationships

What are you doing to boost these capacities?

Susan E. Kogler-Hill (2007) indicates that there are three important decisions any leader must make:[121]

1. Should I monitor the team or take action?
2. Should I intervene to meet task or relationship needs?
3. Should I intervene internally or externally?

Keeping these questions top of mind can be useful in leading from a distance as virtual leaders do. They can support a virtual team leader in deciding whether to take action or troubleshoot. These questions also get leaders thinking about what level they should be intervening at—internal or external, or to enhance results (tasks) or relationship.

## A MULTI-FACETED APPROACH TO LEADERSHIP DEVELOPMENT

With the advent of virtual work, we are now able to fully offer a range of leadership development supports beyond the traditional classroom learning experience. From mentoring, to peer coaching circles, to video-based courses, there is an opportunity to individualize training and development for virtual leaders. With the complexities and uniqueness of each role a virtual leader will hold, this is an exciting time to innovate and customize leadership development.

Having been involved in leadership development for almost three decades now, I am a firm believer in getting people into practice around leadership, and just like virtual facilitation, setting them up for success.

In addition to building skills in the dozen areas I've mentioned earlier in this chapter in Leadership Foundations, it is important to note areas which may be more important for certain roles. For example, a leader who is new to supporting team members from a certain geographic region might benefit from some support from a mentor who has worked in that area so that they can understand more quickly the cultural nuances and avoid the cultural faux-pas, which can make or break the relationships that are essential to inter-cultural work. Support to a team leader's self-awareness, particularly around biases and assumptions, is also key. Understanding different parts of the business is also a key component of virtual team leader success, and peer partnering or shadowing can provide an important development activity.

Regardless of approach, the development of new virtual leaders should be real-time, grounded in experience, customized for role and team dynamics, and multi-faceted. New leaders can benefit from a multi-faceted approach of training (real-time, on-demand), mentoring and coaching. There are several main support roles to the traditional leadership development training. Let's look at each one of these.

## TRADITIONAL LEADERSHIP DEVELOPMENT TRAINING

Whether delivered virtually or in person, there is benefit in offering training sessions for virtual leaders in core leadership areas (such as Emotional Intelligence and Conflict Resolution). As with other training, place emphasis on the need for customization, tailoring and adjustment to local realities. Provide supervisors with discussion guides which can provide an overview of the training their supervisee is taking, and some prompting questions to foster dialogue. Training can be enhanced and supplemented by additional modalities including mentoring, coaching, and best practice calls.

## PAIRING WITH A MENTOR

As described earlier, mentors are able to share their stories and experiences of what has worked and what hasn't. Mentors play a key role of being able to dip below the surface and get at the environmental (political, economic, social) factors at play in workplaces today. While many organizations are supporting individual mentoring conversations, some organizations

I have worked with have looked at the option of assigning more than one protégé to a mentor, especially when there are not enough mentors available. Similar to what's been shared about peer learning, paired or small-group mentoring can provide valuable learning and networking process. Be sure to provide some guidelines or a virtual training session to both mentors and mentees. My colleague, Susan Combs, and I developed the Mentor RoadMap as a resource to provide such a baseline of training.

## Five Keys for Mentoring Virtual Team Leaders

In his 2014 *HBR* article "Getting Virtual Teams Right"[122] Keith Ferrazzi mentions the case of an engineering firm which found that a significant factor in exceptional virtual team leadership was past experience. Given the complexities many team leaders face, those who have walked in our shoes before can provide valuable insights. While each one of our experiences as virtual team leaders will be different, the role of mentoring in virtual team leadership development is often under-leveraged.

Here are five things to consider if you are integrating a mentoring component within your virtual team leadership development initiatives:

1. Identify potential mentors who bring past experience and would like to share their learning/experience with others.

2. Consider how you want to pair people—is it on regional experience, programmatic experience, role similarity? You may also want to consider the value in matching people cross-functionally.

3. Provide a frame or broad structure. Formal mentoring programs usually have a start and end point. Will the support run over a six- month period, nine-month period, other? Consider what

will work best in your context.

4. What supports would be useful to provide mentors and their protégés/mentees (the people being mentored)? In the mentoring training and program development work I undertake, we can provide training and also a toolkit of resources.

5. What are common theme areas mentors and protégés may have as a backup? This could include discussion around work-life issues, virtual team support, virtual team development, addressing tricky issues, different platforms you use for connection etc. At the start of the mentoring engagement, make a list of the different focus areas to explore.

What is going to be important for you to note about mentoring and supporting your virtual team leaders? What best practices have you evolved in your organization?

## GROUP COACHING SUPPORT

Some organizations have been adding on group coaching conversations (virtually, of course!) after their leadership training. These calls are usually an hour to an hour and a half in length, and occur between the training modules. The conversations bring the cohort of learners together to share best practices, talk about what they are doing and focus on any other goals the group members may have. Some groups also use this as a time to bring current business challenges forward and receive coaching support around them. While there may be a tendency to put regional groups together, from experience I have seen the benefits created by a more varied group.

## ON-DEMAND PROGRAMMING

We have come a long way from the days of global leadership being delivered on CD. E-learning programs which are interactive, as opposed to solo, can be a wonderful supplement to new training required, for example, on safety or security issues. On-demand programming has the additional benefit of being available at any point of the 24/7 cycle. Two examples of on-demand programming we provide are:

- The **Teams365 Team Leader Foundations Program,** a video-based program which consists of a dozen micro-modules and takes two hours to complete.
- The **Teams365 Blog** is also an on-demand resource for many organizations, with easily searchable entries to topics ranging from feedback, to holding one-on-ones, to mentoring and team tools.

## SO, WHAT CAN THE DEVELOPMENT SUPPORT LOOK LIKE?

Given the range of different modalities, there is a range of possibilities for providing developmental support to your new and experienced virtual team leaders. Here are several different options for how you might support the development of your virtual leaders including:

| Option 1 | Option 2 | Option 3 | Option 4 |
|---|---|---|---|
| •Traditional Classroom Training <br> •Discussion Guides to supervisors who can provide support | •Classroom Training (quarterly modules) <br> •Mentor Support between each classroom training | •Virtual Webinars <br> •Group Coaching support monthly. Peer Dialogue around the questions: What are you using, doing and applying? | •Quarterly Virtual Sessions <br> •Mentor Support <br> •Supervisory Support and Discussion Guides <br> • Best Practice calls. |

*What are the optimum approaches for support for your leadership development?*

## AREAS OF FOCUS IN THE FIRST 90 DAYS FOR NEW VIRTUAL OR REMOTE TEAM LEADERS

The first 90 days of any leader's role is usually the most challenging. Here are some of the key activities new leaders will want to make sure they put some attention around:[123]

1. **Getting to know your team as a team** – What is their history? What have been their past successes? What accomplishments are they most proud of? What geographic span do they cover?

2. **Getting to know your global team as individuals** – Consider the following:

    a. *Meeting each individual team member:* Who are they, how long have they been on the team, what do they see as their contribution? How would they like to be supported? What should you know about their work style preferences? This might include working hours, best way to be contacted, type of support they prefer, communication channels.

    b. *Location:* Where are they located? What offices are they connected to? What are regional priorities? What are regional opportunities? What type of office are they connected to (large/small, rural/urban, other)?

    c. *Other supports team members leverage:* Many global teams have matrix management structures. Who are the other supervisors/leaders this person connects into? What are their priorities?

    d. *Team member individual roles:* What are their roles? How does their work connect with others on the team you are leading? How is it different? What history do they bring? What is unique about their role?

    e. *The cultural element:* Understanding the distinct cultures of each of the locations your team members operate, along with their cultural background, is a key area to learn more

341

about. Recognize that regional managers should be aware of the cultural differences that exist. Consider differences in doing business across the US or Canada, the East Coast vs. the West Coast, differences in business across Europe, etc.

*f.* ***Projects:*** What major projects are they involved with? Globally/nationally? How are they connected to team goals? What are the priorities for the next year? Quarter? What resources do they need in order to be successful?

What other areas do you see as being important during the first 90 days of post? What conversations are needed? Can all of these be done virtually?

## THREE CORE ESSENTIALS FOR VIRTUAL TEAM LEADERSHIP SUCCESS:[124]

In managing and supporting your virtual or remote team, it can be important to keep these in mind:

### KNOW YOUR PEOPLE

In the virtual teams I led over the years, I always found that the connection I had with each team member was critical. Given that our touchpoints are often not as frequent, it's critical to know the strengths, preferences, and nuances of each team member. Are they someone who is a big-picture thinker? Do they want to receive quick emails regularly, or would they prefer a bi-weekly, five-minute phone call?

As virtual team leaders, it is even more important for us to empower our team members. We are not there beside them, and we may only see each other once a year. Supporting our team members in knowing and utilizing their strengths can also be an important activity. Today, as a coach working with virtual and in-person teams, helping them explore their strengths is a key part of the work that I do. It provides tremendous insights for all team members in knowing who is who on the team, the support you may be seeking as a team leader, and the support they want and value.

As with any team environment, it is important for team members to get to know each other as well, not just you. How are you encouraging a *Get to Know You*—virtually or in-person—even if it's only once a year? The perceived connection people feel with their peers is also important in the virtual team domain.

Questions to consider:

- What are the unique needs of each team member?
- What do they need from you? What do you need from them? What do they need from each other?
- What activities (in-person or virtual) will facilitate getting to know each other, connection and understanding the business of the team?

## KNOW WHAT TYPE OF SUPPORT IS NEEDED

Knowing your people is one of the most important foundations for any team leader. Inherent in this is knowing each team member's preferences around support:

- Email, text, phone call, in-person when possible?
- Short and to the point, or long and conversational?
- Big-picture thinker, or small-details valued?
- What support needs do they have already from their local environment?
- What's unique to their context?
- What time of day is going to work best (especially if you are managing a global virtual team)?
- What support do they need from you? Others?

Undertaking styles work with team members using a tool such as the Everything DiSC is another way to explore various preferences and support needs. Contact us to learn more how the DiSC profile could support your virtual team. Team leaders can also benefit.

## KEEP IN TOUCH

As mentioned early in the chapter, research has shown that team leaders who communicate more frequently are more effective. Keeping in touch in a virtual environment may have a slightly different focus. Given that communication touch points may not be as frequent, it is very important to make sure that individual team members are getting what they need out of individual calls with you. In virtual teams, connection with other group members is also important.

As I mentioned earlier in this book, Richard Hackman's research found that it takes only 10 conversations for every person on a team of five to touch base with everyone else—but that number increases to 78 for a team of 13. Group size matters.

Consider keeping in touch and communicating with the entire group not only via phone, but email, shared message boards, and even a shared newsletter. On the individual level consider that each team member may have a different preference for how they like to communicate.

*What does "keeping in touch" mean for you and your team?*

There are many valuable tools for virtual and distributed teams to leverage for communication, meetings and planning including:

- Slack – Slack is being used by many virtual teams. One virtual team member recently shared that the most important tool they use is Slack, which allows them to share materials real-time, as well as messaging.
- Zoom – Zoom provides a large number of benefits for holding virtual meetings; including stability and ease of connection from many parts of the world that may experience challenges on other

platforms, screen sharing of different members, and breakout capability. Group members can stream and see each other, boosting trust and connection.

- Skype – Many organizations today use Skype as their main platform. It offers benefits including streaming and screen sharing.

As we wrap up this chapter, take a moment to consider what is working well in your organization with virtual team leadership.

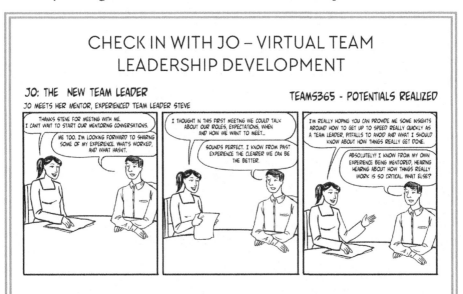

Jo has now been in post for several months and is being mentored by a more experienced leader named Steve. Together they have spent time designing their mentoring relationship making sure that Steve is clear on what Jo's mentoring goals are, and they have both ensured that they are clear on what their different roles are going to be.

As Jo knows, one of the best predictors of success for virtual team leaders is having past experience in a virtual team. Her mentor, Steve, has worked remotely for most of his career, as has she. She is hoping to make sure that they leverage this experience.

Key areas they have agreed upon as mentor and protégé are:

- Keep mentoring conversations regular—by phone or Skype.
- Jo will identify a key focus area for each mentoring conversation.
- Steve and Jo will continue to check in regarding the roles and responsibilities of mentors and protégés.

Three areas Jo will like to explore and learn more from Steve's experience are the areas of:

- Knowing your people
- Working in matrix management relationships
- The nuances of virtual team leadership

*If you are involved in mentoring, how can you make the conversations more effective?*

### END OF CHAPTER QUESTIONS

What strengths do the virtual leaders in your organization bring? What characteristics and skills do they exhibit? Are they like Jo?

What is most important for each virtual leader to develop skills and confidence in?

What development approaches will work best in your organization—training, coaching, mentoring? What is the optimum mix?

Make note of any key action steps from this chapter in your Action Plan Tracker.

## CHAPTER 11

# IN FOCUS: VIRTUAL TEAM DEVELOPMENT

*"You don't get harmony when everybody sings the same note."*[125]

*- Doug Floyd*

This chapter provides a focus on the virtual team development or team-building space. Virtual and remote teams continue to expand in reach. Research undertaken in late 2014 by Keith Ferrazzi[126] found that 79% of people surveyed were part of at least one "distributed" work experience. While we may not always be part of a full-time virtual team, it is likely that we might be part of a project team, committee or other part-time team.

This chapter explores:

- The context of virtual teams today
- What we know about high-performing teams and making teams excel

- Opportunities for virtual team development
- Activities you may want to use in virtual team development

## THE CONTEXT OF VIRTUAL TEAM DEVELOPMENT TODAY

High-performing teams—in both the virtual and in-person realm—don't just happen. They require work, focus, and support. Whether it's training, coaching, or mentoring, virtual team leaders and virtual team members benefit from focus.

Many employees today are hungry for training to help them to do their job more effectively. We also know that the appetite for team development and team training often outpaces the budget available. As we look to the realm of virtual teams, many teams do not have access to training to help them be the best team that they can. According to Charlene Solomon of R3 Culture Wizards in her Fourth Biannual Survey,[127]

- 22% of respondents have participated in virtual team training,
- 34% in formal global leadership training.

In the same survey, team members identified these challenges:

- 68% reported that cultural challenges were the biggest hurdle to global virtual team productivity.
- 18% of respondents reported that their companies have lost business opportunities because of cultural misunderstandings.

What training are you offering to virtual teams collectively, and individually, to help them be most effective?

We know that virtual teams are unique in that they are usually:

- Geographically and culturally diverse
- Operating across time zones
- Involving matrix relationships where team members may report to multiple leaders and be part of several teams

Training can be made more challenging given these factors, however, even with these differences, it can be useful to return to the foundations of what makes teams excel. I call these the *Six Factors*. Whether a team operates in-person or virtually, these six factors are part of the foundation of highly functioning teams.

## WHAT MAKES TEAMS EXCEL – THE SIX FACTORS

Increasingly we are focusing more on what makes teams excel. As we return to the foundational literature, as Wageman and Hackman found there is a core series of ingredients that make teams excel. I call these the *Six Factors of a High Performing Team*. They are actually a blend of some of the writing of Wageman and Hackman,[128] as well as Katzenbach and Smith.[129] Teams, which excel have a clear line of sight around:

1. Shared vision, purpose, or mission
2. Shared performance goals
3. Shared team practices
4. Shared behavioral norms
5. Clear roles
6. Shared commitment

Let us take a look at each one of these in turn, and as we do, consider where your team is at.

### FACTOR #1 – SHARED VISION, PURPOSE, OR MISSION

High-performing teams have a shared purpose or mission, as well as a shared vision. Another word for shared purpose and mission is the *why*. How clear is it for everyone on your team why you exist? Exceptional teams understand *why they exist, what is their purpose,* and *why are they here*. If you haven't had that conversation recently with your team, it can be really important to talk about your *Why*, and ensure that everyone is working towards a shared vision, which is another part of this first factor.

Where does the team see itself at the end of the year? Three years from now? Does everyone share the same vision?

If you are a team leader looking for resources around facilitating this dialogue around the *why*, your shared purpose and mission, a great resource is the work of Simon Sinek—his TED Talk and his book, *Start with Why*.

## FACTOR #2 – SHARED PERFORMANCE GOALS

The second factor, which is important for high performing teams is having shared performance goals—goals that are clear and understood by all. As we saw in Chapter 3, goals are often framed using the SMART-E methodology. As a virtual team who may not always see each other or interface regularly, it is important to have crystal clarity on what the key goals are, how goals are measured and what quality looks like. Perhaps you work in a KPI (Key Performance Indicator) framework, or maybe you work through Management by Results and have a very specific series of SMART goals. Team leaders and teams themselves are most effective when there are shared performance goals. As you look at your plans, your organizational goals, your KPIs, ask yourself:

- How do our team's and department goals fit into this?
- Do people understand how their individual effort impacts the organizational goals?
- Do individuals on the team understand how their work interfaces and supports others, feeding into other goals focused on by other team members?
- How do we measure these goals and results? Is there clarity around this?

There is often an opportunity for teams to have dialogue around shared performance goals.

## FACTOR # 3 – SHARED BEHAVIORAL NORMS

High-performing teams have created shared behavioral norms. Norms are related to values, and are often known as a *Team Charter*, or Ways of Working. We can usually identify our norms by asking a series of questions:

- What is acceptable here?
- What is important here?
- What does that look like?

Teams may also start with their values and specify what their values look like in action. For example, the value of respect may translate into behaviors such as placing issues on the table (rather than sweeping them under the rug); encouraging alternative points of view; and showing up prepared for team discussions. Norms make the values visible—they are things we can see the team does behaviorally. High-performing teams create agreements around the behaviors which are acceptable.

Throughout this book, I have discussed the importance of taking time to co-create Ways of Working or team/group agreements with those groups you are working with. Taking time to explicitly state how you are going to operate, and what is acceptable and unacceptable from a behavioral standpoint, is critical. Our norms extend from our values—what is important to us. They shape how we interrelate. They are also an important part of creating safety in a team.

In the virtual environment, shared behavioral norms are important, as there is the added advantage of making things explicit, rather than assuming we "all know it" or are "all practicing it."

Working with teams I find that putting attention around this factor as well as the next one—shared team practices—can really make a difference to the outcomes and relationships of the team.

## FACTOR #4 – SHARED TEAM PRACTICES

Shared team practices are the regular team activities teams undertake. It could be a monthly virtual lunch you host or a monthly design hack. Shared team practices boost both relationships and results, core elements of high performance. As you consider your team, questions to ask are:

- Do we hold a Monday morning huddle every week?
- Do we get together once a week to really share experiences, share priorities, share challenges, or are we a team who comes together every two weeks or once a month for a formalized meeting?

Exceptional teams do things together on an ongoing basis, even in the virtual space. Team practices have a purpose—usually involving communication, sharing of information, and bonding with others. A message I constantly reinforce around team meetings is that *they are important*. In today's busy business world, it is very common for teams to say they just don't have time to meet. As virtual teams, meetings are even easier to ignore, but ignoring them will likely weaken team connection, communication, and alignment. Seasonally, you may want to revisit what shared practices you have as a team and recommit to what you want to do with your workload and priorities.

If teams don't spend time together, it is very hard for them to be in alignment with each other. Keep in mind that spending time together is not just spending time, but it's spending time with a purpose. One practical thing you could do as the team leader is take these six factors and use each one as an anchoring theme for dialogue in one of your team meetings.

## FACTOR #5 – CLEAR ROLES

High-performing teams have clear roles. What are the functional roles in the team? How are you organized? Take a look at this with the team.

You might want to look at how your roles overlap, and how they may be creating some gaps. One thing we often see in dysfunctional teams is lack of role clarity. Annually, or when team composition changes, it can be really useful to really step back and take a look how those roles are fitting as your work evolves.

As a team ask yourselves:

- What are our roles?
- Where is there overlap?
- How do our roles leverage people's strengths?
- In our work, what do we need to do?
- How are our roles supporting the performance goals, supporting our practices and supporting our *Why?*
- What else is important for us to notice around our calls?

Going hand-in-hand with clarity of the roles, we want to make sure that team members are very clear with reporting about their responsibilities. Ultimately if you are asking people to do certain tasks, how are they given the authority to do them?

## FACTOR #6 – SHARED COMMITMENT

*"Commitment is a map with well-marked roads that you can travel to arrive at your destination, whereas follow through is more of a pirate's treasure map. You have to figure out for yourself how to get to the X between the palm trees…Follow through and commitment work in tandem. Commitment is the body of your idea, follow-through is its legs."*[130] – Gene C. Hayden

The final factor that allows teams to excel is shared commitment. How do we have each other's back? A question to be asking the team on a regular basis is, *What are you individually committing for your own work and for the team?* Facilitating these types of conversations can really start to shift the culture. This can be a risky conversation and trust is needed to be really honest with each other around this factor. Accountability has

353

very different connotations in different contexts. Questions to consider in this area are:

- What is the state of commitment within your team right now?
- How is that mirrored in the organization?
- How is commitment working for you?
- If there isn't a lot of commitment, what results are you seeing?

Once again what we know about high-performing teams is that they have shared commitment. *What are they going to commit to doing no matter what?* What are those things that they are definitely going to make sure they check off—regardless of what gets put on their plate? We know through research that the act of public declaration increases the possibility or probability that things will get done. Therefore, it can be really useful to have people publicly articulate in a team meeting what they are going to be focusing on. This has the reinforcing factor of also helping others know how they can support others, and what they can expect from each other.

In virtual teams, it is likely that you will have been exploring some of these areas on two levels - separately and as a team. As a team you may want to complete the checklist on the *Six Factors of High Performing Teams* and see how you would rate yourselves.

## WHAT MAKES VIRTUAL TEAMS AND THEIR DEVELOPMENT CHALLENGING?

There are several factors that can make virtual team development challenging. It is not only the time zone differences, but different priorities, the perceived lack of connection, feelings that team members don't understand your reality or the lack of everyday cues.

Sebastian Bailey's *Forbes* article, "The Five Killers of Virtual Learning,"[131] references the writing of Wayne Cascio in 2000 on *the Five Disadvantages of Virtual Teams*. Cascio had identified the following five areas as disadvantages:

1. Lack of everyday non-verbal face-to-face communication
2. Lack of social interaction
3. Lack of trust
4. Cultural clashes
5. Lack of team spirit

Let us take a look at what we can do to proactively address these areas:

## #1 – LACK OF EVERYDAY NON-VERBAL FACE-TO-FACE COMMUNICATION

A large shift has been occurring in recent years in the ability to have team members come together for face-to-face communication. Zoom is one such technology which allows team members to connect via the internet and see each other. For example, if you have eleven people on your team, Zoom would enable all 11 of you to actually see each other. Or those with slower connections could phone in. Conversations are transformed when we can see each other.

## #2 – LACK OF SOCIAL INTERACTION

In teams, it is not only about getting things done, it is also about *having fun* together. What are some opportunities for you to have fun? Virtual team-building events could include potlucks. Have a drop-in lunch a couple of times a quarter/year (if timeframes permit). This can be a chance for team members to get together and share what they are working on. Note that there may be some variance amongst group members in terms of what their "appetite" is for eating on camera!

Later in this chapter we will explore some other things you can do to build your team virtually.

## #3 – LACK OF TRUST

"Trust takes on a whole new meaning in virtual teams. When you meet your workmates by the water cooler or photocopier every day, you know instinctively who you can and cannot trust. In a geographically distributed team, trust is measured almost exclusively in terms of reliability."[132] – Erin Meyer via *Forbes*

In the virtual domain, trust-building is different, and as Erin Meyer said, reliability plays a key role in maintaining and building trust. How are you walking your talk? Are you following through with both the big things and small things? How are you providing opportunities for team members to get to know each other and build trust with each other?

A strong hand on process and roles and responsibilities (overlap, gaps, clarity as we discussed in the "matrix management" tip in our last post) also contribute to trust-building in virtual teams.

We know that trust is boosted when we have a focus on the following:

- **Connection**—We feel supported when we feel valued, known, and heard. Connection is a critical factor for high performing teams. Teams who feel connected with each other have often invested time in getting to know one another, and schedule time for regular connections. Perhaps a 2 p.m. daily meeting is the norm, or a Monday morning huddle kicks off your week. Consider what will boost connection amongst your team members.
- **Clarity**—Clarity is key in creating trust. When we know what is expected of us, it is easier to follow through and know how we are doing. Creating shared and clear expectations of each other is important, as is having clarity around roles.
- **Communication**—Communication is the foundation of connection and clarity. Consider how the team wants to communicate with each other, and what in fact is most effective.
- **Knowledge/Competence**—Many trust models talk about

the importance of skills and knowledge, or what they call competence, in building trust. If we know that others have the skills and knowledge to have our backs, we can rest easier that things will get done.

Take note of the Trust Self-Assessment from Chapter 1 for yourself. It can also be a good discussion tool for the entire team.

## BUILDING STRONGER RELATIONSHIPS IN THE VIRTUAL SPACE

*"The real basic structure of the workplace is the relationship. Each relationship is itself part of a larger network of relationships. These relationships can be measured along all kinds of dimensions–from political to professional expertise. The fact is that work gets done through these relationships."*[133]
– Michael Schrage

There are several things we can do to support our teams in building stronger relationships in the virtual space, including creating structured and prioritized focus on team relationships. It is important to take time during meetings to help everyone understand, *What do you do? What's a priority? What is important to your work right now?*

We also want to put a focus on the following:

1. Creating connection, getting to know each other
2. Focusing on team culture
3. Developing a team identity

Note that focusing on team culture, and developing a team identity help to mitigate against Bailey's #4 and #5 Killers of Virtual Learning.

## CREATING CONNECTION, GETTING TO KNOW EACH OTHER

In a virtual team, connection and building relationships is not always on the top of our list. We do know that virtual teams need the same ingredients to do their best work—clear and shared vision, clear roles, accountability, clear performance measures, and commitment. Virtual team members also need to feel a sense of connection with their other teammates. So what are some quick ways we can accomplish this?

Here are three quick activities that you might also find useful:

- **What's on my desk?** – Understanding what our team member's context and reality is can be very useful in building trust and connection. It also helps us to understand where we may have synergies and overlap, as well as competing pressures. This activity sparks the conversation around what each person has on their desk. Visually, it can be a snapshot of each person's desk shared as part of the team meeting. Think about collecting these before the call and putting them into a blank slide. Depending on your time available this might be a quick 30-second share from each team member, or it might be a longer presentation around *What's on your desk—projects, priorities, etc.?*

- **What's outside my window?** is a similar activity which can be scaled according to your time available. A picture of what's outside your window provides a bigger snapshot than what we see of you. It is bigger than the virtual screen permits and can facilitate useful sharing about different office contexts, location priorities, customs, and time of day when people are connecting. It provides another way for people to connect across the team.

- **What's in my lunch bag?** A final quick connector is having people share what they have in their lunch bag (which might also be breakfast or dinner for some team members!). Likewise, have people share what their meal of the day is.

These three short activities are one quick way to "widen the lens" on the context of each virtual team member. How might you incorporate this into your work?

## Size Matters

Team issues can become exponential as more people are added. OnPoint Consulting's research found that at the team level, the worst performing teams had 13 members or more. *Social loafing* is one cause. The social loafing effect occurs when we rely on others, and kicks in when there are more than four or five people on the team. In social loafing, I tend to not offer my best, and will usually offer less as the group size increases.

As team size grows it also takes more effort to cultivate good relationships. As previously referenced is Hackman's research on the number of conversations needed—10 conversations for every person on a team of five to touch base with everyone else, but the number increases to 78 for a team of 13.

The span of a virtual or remote team leader can be more than in traditional face-to-face teams. *How does size matter in your virtual team work?*

### #4 – CULTURAL CLASHES

*Culture: The visible and invisible values and beliefs that underlie behaviors and are unique to each society.*[134]

Culture clashes were identified by Bailey as killer mistake #4. Focusing on team culture is critical for virtual teams. It's always important to remember that culture is like an iceberg—there are things that are visible to us, such as how people dress, or their building, and art. There are also those things that are deep below the surface line such as our values, belief systems, assumptions, our mindsets, what we value and what we don't. Conflict in virtual teams is often due to the things below the waterline. In working virtually, it is important to make sure that you are not just making assumptions based on what you are seeing or believing.

As explored in Chapter 2, it is common to have cultural clashes in a virtual team, given the various layers of culture that exist—national, regional, even head office versus branch office. What are the clashes that exist? How do you navigate these?

In virtual teams, it is likely that you will be evolving your own culture. It is important that as a team you develop your own culture in terms of what is acceptable and not acceptable, and what comprises the team culture. As a team consider, *What are your values? What are your beliefs?*

In my former world of work, my last role involved supporting more than two dozen professionals from more than fifteen cultural backgrounds. What was important in our work as a virtual team was to create shared team practices and baselines. These were beyond each of our own cultures, and reflected the local cultures we were part of, while respecting our own cultures as well. This third virtual team culture became uniquely ours, and was evolved through dialogue and compromise.

#5 – LACK OF TEAM SPIRIT

Lack of team spirit is killer mistake #5, according to Bailey. An antidote to this is developing your team identity. Developing a team identity can take time, which is where the added advantage of face-to-face time comes in. Being able to spend time together physically, even once a year, starts to forge a team identity. Maybe there are some themes you are noticing over time. Maybe there are some adjectives that continue to surface in how others see your team.

For example, one of the virtual teams I led for many years had a *cook-up* of different cultures. In the Caribbean, cook-up is a term for a super-savory dish made with many different things. Given that our team was comprised of more than a dozen nationalities, we made a concerted effort to savor the unique elements of each one of our cultures. We were able to get together once a year for face-to-face meetings, and kept the conversation alive with a Yahoo Group and a monthly newsletter which spotlighted each member's work. This was in the days before Skype, and I often wonder how much closer we might have become with today's instant access.

*Question to Consider: What adjectives would you use to describe your team spirit? Have you had time to connect and create one?*

## CORE SKILLS FOR VIRTUAL TEAM MEMBERS

As mentioned in the last chapter, equipping your team members with enhanced leadership skills will benefit everyone. Enhanced autonomy and responsibility for each team member is often the norm on virtual and remote teams given that they are operating in their own location.

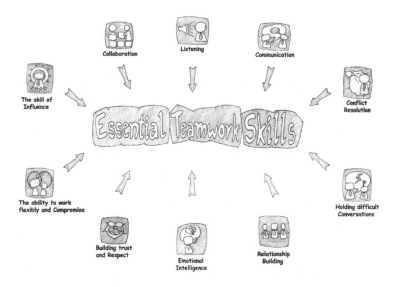

**Teams 365 Blog by Jennifer Britton**

©B.Dev Prakash.2014

Virtual teams can also benefit from a number of core teamwork skills including collaboration, listening, communication, conflict resolution, holding difficult conversations, relationship building, Emotional

Intelligence, building trust and respect, the ability to work flexibly and compromise, and the skill of influence or working through others.

*Candor* is also an essential skill set for virtual teams. Candor allows us to place issues on the table for discussion, respectfully. Candor is also about taking time to go above and beyond in working across differences. Differences are the norm in virtual teams, and candor allows us to more effectively, and respectfully, navigate these differences.

In her book, *Teaming*, Amy Edmonston also offers these behaviors, which support "Teaming" success:[135]

- Speaking Up
- Collaboration
- Experimentation
- Reflection

*Teaming* is a term she uses to describe how leaders need to focus on "actively building and developing teams even as a project is in process, while realizing that a team's composition may change at any given moment." This is a norm for most virtual teams. In her book, she explores the three pillars of Teaming, which include helping everyone on the team become more curious, passionate, and empathetic.[136]

Many of these skills are further explored in our blog posts at the Teams365 Blog at PotentialsRealized.com. You are invited to take a look. Take a moment to take stock of these skills with the downloadable worksheet to help the team identify their skills in these core areas.

At the Teams365 Blog I have explored the topic of additional skills required by virtual team members. Helping the team develop these skills helps everyone to be a more effective unit. In addition to the core skills listed for virtual facilitators, additional skills include:

1. Global mindset
2. Openness to learning and exploration of new ideas

3. Self-awareness and ability to work across differences
4. Autonomy and initiative
5. Flexibility, adaptability, and agility

## #1 – GLOBAL MINDSET

We want to make sure we support the team in creating a "global mindset." A 2010 *HBR* article explored this notion and found that a global mindset includes three elements:[137]

- *Intellectual Capital:* Global business savvy, cognitive complexity and a cosmopolitan outlook.
- *Psychological Capital:* Passion for diversity, thirst for adventure and self-assurance.
- *Social Capital:* Intercultural empathy, interpersonal impact and diplomacy.

*How does your team exhibit a global mindset? What type of capital can you leverage?*

## #2 – OPENNESS TO LEARNING AND EXPLORATION OF NEW IDEAS:

In recruiting members for virtual teams, it is important to look for people who are open to learning and exploring new ideas. Throughout every team conversation it is likely that virtual team members are learning something new about a different geography, culture, values, and set of priorities. Being open to learning and exploring these ideas, some which may contradict or be in opposition to your own, is an important ingredient for teams to align and/or work across differences.

*What do you notice about the team's openness to learning and exploration of ideas? What about each individual member?*

## #3 – SELF-AWARENESS AND ABILITY TO WORK ACROSS DIFFERENCES

While self-awareness is a characteristic I believe we want to foster in all employees, in a virtual team, self-awareness takes on a whole new meaning. Our understanding of ourselves, our styles, our strengths, triggers and defaults can be important in a context where we are often operating by ourselves. The need to build relationships across internal and external stakeholders, with a matrix series of relationships, requires a high degree of self-awareness. Strengths and styles may also become augmented in the virtual realm, given that touchpoints are not as frequent as in some in-person teams.

Team members can benefit from doing more work around styles and personality preferences, using tools such as the Everything DiSC or MBTI.

In undertaking this work, it is important for virtual team members to become more aware of the natural style, the styles of those around them, and also the changes they need to make to be more effective as team members and in working across differences.

*What opportunities do you have to support team members in learning more about their own styles? In learning to work across differences?*

## #4 – AUTONOMY AND INTERDEPENDENCE

There is an inherent tension in virtual teams today—we want them to be part of a bigger collective, while simultaneously being autonomous and independent. As a team, you will want to explore this dynamic together and what it means in terms of how you communicate. A starting set of questions for dialogue are: *What do you communicate to whom, when, and at what level?*

## #5 – FLEXIBILITY, ADAPTABILITY, AND RESILIENCE

As someone who recruited national and international staff for global teams for more than a decade I often found the most successful employees to be the ones that were naturally flexible and adaptable. These are skill sets which are hard to develop, but are essential in today's global and virtual space.

Flexibility is required as it is likely that things will not go as planned, and resources may not be available when each team member needs them. In a virtual team, there will be different needs that require different styles. Technology may not work to connect with other team members as it should.

The need for adaptability is seen in virtual teams on many levels—being able to adapt your style for the different contexts and styles you work with, adaptability to different business paces that exist cross-culturally, and adaptability in adjusting our style to meet the needs of others.

Part of flexibility and adaptability is also about being agile and resilient. Resilience is about continuing to move forward after a failure, persevering and also bending with the wind. From the field of Positive Psychology, we are seeing that there are different activities to boost resilience including:

- Undertaking the *Three Good Things* exercise has been found to lead to people being more optimistic and hopeful. In this daily activity, individuals reflect and write out on a daily basis three good things that have happened to them that day.
- The *Best Possible Self* exercise has been found to increase optimism and sense of purpose. In this activity, a person is coached on questions which get them to think about what is their best self. Ask them who can they be, or to simply describe a time when they were at their best.

## OPPORTUNITIES FOR VIRTUAL TEAM DEVELOPMENT

Samantha McDuffee indicates that 65% of employees say that they have never had a team-building event.[138]

Teams benefit from ongoing team development throughout the year, as well as when new team members join. Key focus areas could revolve around:

- **Working across differences** – This is a Top 5 topic for teams of all kinds, but is a need-to-have for virtual teams. Spending time helping the team develop shared approaches for working across differences (processes and steps) makes this an intentional and focused thing to do, rather than one that just happens.

- **Skill development** – Teams work better when they have shared frames of reference and skills. Take a look at the team skills mentioned in this chapter, or consider how you can use the worksheet in a team meeting. What skills would team members feel they could benefit from some training around? Conflict resolution, innovation, working across differences, and difficult conversations are often flagged as key areas virtual teams struggle with.

- **Checking assumptions across the team** – This is also an important area to explore as a virtual team, given the variety of contexts we operate within and possible different values we may hold in our work. Asking the team to name and unpack their assumptions can be an important part of the leadership role.

- **Regular dialogue and focus** – Having a question to discuss every week as a team can make a significant difference in the realm of team work. Several years ago, we started a series of Thursday posts dedicated to a team question to spark dialogue on team-related issues. Some of these questions were then combined to create the *Teams365 Sparker Deck*—a card deck of 52 weekly questions for teams to talk about. The cards (and questions) have been used as discussion questions in team meetings. Others have brought the questions into the team intranet or chat where they can post comments on the questions each week. Take a look at our Team-Building Tips at the Teams365 Blog.

**Activity:** Make a list of two questions you would like to pose to the team every month.

## WHAT'S DIFFERENT ABOUT VIRTUAL TEAM DEVELOPMENT

There are several things that make virtual team development a little more out of the ordinary, including:

1. **The need to make it a priority.** It is very easy to get caught up in the slog of ongoing daily work, without paying attention to what the team needs on a daily, quarterly, and annual basis.

2. **It is about the collective.** Given that virtual team members may be dispersed, and team leaders may be reaching out to individual members more common on virtual teams, it is important to remember that it is also about developing the collective, and fostering team spirit. Creating a sense of identity and finding the common ground helps virtual teams excel. Knowing where the overlap exists, and building connections across peers helps to lay the groundwork for good connections that may prove to be useful in future projects and work.

3. **Finding a budget and scheduling it in.** It is likely that there won't be any budget to bring people together unless you make a business case for it and schedule it in well in advance. From experience, being able to find resources to bring people together can make a "splashy" statement, attracting senior leaders to come and speak to the team. Virtual teams experience the value of a face-to-face meeting on a regular basis, even if it's only once a year. Key learning from years of organizing and scheduling these annual meetings are:
   - Be specific around what you want to accomplish.
   - Have an agenda—create it in advance and circulate it to the team to ensure their needs are included.
   - Consider how will people feed forward their learning and

367

action steps into the matrix.

- Invite a variety of stakeholders to participate in parts of the meeting, including matrix managers as appropriate.
- Provide a tangible takeaway for people to return home with (i.e., reports, core organizational documents, supports to help them do their work more effectively).

## ACTIVITIES FOR BUILDING A VIRTUAL TEAM

With the continued advent of virtual teams, it is likely that virtual team development will continue to come into its own in the next few years. While many virtual teams try to come together at least once a year, this may not always be feasible. Getting together on a more regular basis to focus on team work and team development can be an important focus area.

There may be a number of times when virtual team development is in order including:

- When new teams are forming
- When teams are merging
- Annual meetings
- Year-end activities
- Virtual retreats

The rest of this chapter explores several other activities you may want to bring into your virtual team, including:

- Fostering connection—getting to know each other
- Leveraging strengths
- Creating a sense of the collective
- Building relationships within your virtual team
- Creating a vision as a team
- Virtual meeting tune-ups
- Working across conflict with your virtual team
- Year-end activities for virtual teams

- Activities to use at any time

Any of these activities, as well as some of the earlier ones mentioned like The Six Factors or The Three Connection Activities, can support the team in enhancing relationships and results.

In selecting activities consider:

- **Activities matched to level of skill.** Lebron (2015)[139] notes:

  - Too low a challenge = boredom
  - Too high a challenge = anxiety
  - Challenge just right = flow

  We know that flow is that space where we can really capitalize our strengths.

- **Sequencing.** How do topics build on one another? Is the necessary level of trust and connection in place before we move into other areas?

- **Amount of time.** How much time will it take and how much time do you have?

- **Preparation.** Is there any pre-work needed to set people up for success?

- **Follow-up.** What follow on activities are needed to maximize this focus? What instructions do you want to provide for people to take back to the workplace?

## FOSTERING CONNECTION – GETTING TO KNOW EACH OTHER

Just as in in-person teams, getting to know each other is critical for team identity, as well as creating trust and connection. If team members don't know each other it is hard to create a shared sense of responsibility or identity.

Some "getting to know you" questions which you can bring into a virtual team meeting include:

- What do you enjoy most about your work?
- What's the one thing you wish you could do more of each day?
- What is the most important thing you do through your work?
- What impact does your work have?
- What is one interesting thing we should know about the context of your work?
- What's one significant thing that has happened in your life?

Other ways to foster connection can include:

- Using a question deck like the Teams365 deck to help team members have better dialogue.
- Having each team member do a presentation on their work during team meetings.
- Creating pairings across the team where team members meet together on a regular basis and share more about their work.

## LEVERAGING STRENGTHS

There is a growing case for strengths-based work. Gallup has found that when employees get to use their strengths every day they are:

- 6x more engaged
- 3x more likely to report having excellent quality of life
- 8.9% more profitable

Teams that focus on strengths have 12.5% greater productivity.[140]

For teams that are interested in learning more about strengths, I would encourage you to take a look at the rich strengths-based literature and assessments including StrengthsFinder2.0 and VIA Strengths.

In virtual facilitation, it is important to create a learning environment which is positive. Taking an appreciative or strengths-based approach can be important in creating a positive, growth-oriented learning environment.

Part of creating a growth-oriented environment means leading from strengths, rather than leading from detriment. It means holding the space for possibility and learning, rather than consistently looking backwards at what doesn't work.

Consider the impact of the statements *What's wrong?* versus *What's possible?*

Providing feedback from a strengths approach may sound like:

- I appreciated…
- I saw one of your strengths as…
- I'd like to see more of/differently next time…

While this is one of many tips in this book, you might be surprised at how much of a difference using these three questions makes in your conversations. Star these three questions now, and try them out this week!

## CREATING A SENSE OF THE COLLECTIVE

In virtual teams it can be natural to feel like you are an island, working by yourself. Fostering more dialogue around the *collective* nature of the team can be useful in creating team identity and connection with the bigger whole. Topics and questions for teams to consider in the context of team development can include:

- We are at our best when…
- Success for this team is…
- What gets in the way of our success is…
- We are driven by the beliefs of…
- What's taboo is…

- The written rules of this team are...
- We avoid talking about (or the elephant in the room is)...
- The one area which is important to focus on is...

# BUILDING RELATIONSHIPS WITHIN YOUR VIRTUAL TEAM

Since virtual and remote team leadership is a new entity for not only team leaders but also team members, there can be a number of questions about how to build an effective virtual team. At the heart of strong teams is strong relationships. Here we will explore several points to keep in mind when building relationships in your virtual team.

First, in the virtual realm, team members may feel very isolated from one another, not just the team leader. Therefore, it is important for team leaders to enable team members to connect with other team members, as this peer support may be as close as you are as a leader. Consider the different vehicles your team has to reach out to each other. This might include a shared workspace, an Intranet, IM capabilities or email.

Creating the sense that everyone is at the same table is a powerful metaphor for virtual connection. Creating a shared identity and shared norms is important in boosting a sense of team, and creating team identity. Our shared team practices (having a virtual potluck once a quarter, or bi-weekly team meetings) also foster relationships and team identity.

At the heart of virtual team development is providing proactive ways for team members to get to know each other and work together. Some ideas to do this include:

- Use platforms like Facetime, Skype video or Zoom to give people a visual connection with each other. Check with your IT and HR departments about what works within your IT and security settings.
- Provide an opportunity for the team to meet for shared team

development or planning once a year (even virtually!), so they operate from similar frameworks, have a shared vision and understand what the plan for the team is.

- Host regular team meetings virtually to get everyone on the same page. On a rotational basis, each team member might be responsible for leading part of the meeting or sharing something about the priorities and unique landscape of their portfolio and area.

- Use a team newsletter or other communique (social media page) to keep people connected and aware of what others are up to.

These approaches are very tactical and work. In fact, they are things I did with my teams as a virtual team leader. My last virtual team was spread across ten countries, and these regular activities strengthened connection, boosted engagement, and provided team members with a sense of team and being part of the organization, even though we sat thousands of miles apart.

## CREATING A VISION AS A TEAM

Creating a shared vision for where you are going as a team can be a useful exercise. This may be at a higher, more macro level than intact teams share, *and* what we know about the importance of having a shared vision is that it does support alignment, and an understanding of how our work fits into the whole. While individual members may have their own vision for their own work, co-creating a shared vision for the entire virtual team can be a great activity—as part of a virtual team session, or if you are coming together annually.

Some of the creative ways you can work with vision with your team include:

- Creating a vision board together using a blank screen/whiteboard. This could be done real-time by the team using annotation tools and asking people to bring pictures.

- Having each team member bring a photo or item and share it with the others on the call, creating a tapestry from that.
- If you are meeting face-to-face, give the team time to create their own vision board or storyline of what they want the team to look like in the next period (i.e., next year, two years, five years).
- Using visual cards—where team members are asked to select a photograph which represents their vision for the team. Download a collage of nine photos you can use to spark this discussion at **EffectiveVirtualConversations.com.**

## VIRTUAL MEETING TUNE-UPS

As stated earlier, inefficient team meetings can take up a lot of valuable time, and can be perceived as a waste of time. Given the importance of bringing virtual team members together on a regular basis, it is important that virtual team meetings are "tuned up" regularly.

With so much time being spent in meetings each week a great question to be asking regularly is, *What could we do to make our meetings more effective?*

Some things to consider might be:

- How do we hold them?
- When do we hold them?
- Is a meeting the right way to address this topic or share this information?
- What's the one thing we could let go of doing in our meetings without having too much of an impact?
- What is the one thing we wish we did more of?
- What are the things we want to start doing as a team instead of meetings?

## WORKING AROUND CONFLICT IN YOUR VIRTUAL TEAM

*"In great teams, conflict becomes productive. The free flow of conflicting ideas is critical for creative thinking, for discovering new solutions no one individual would have come to on his own."[141] – Peter Senge*

Conflict can be enhanced in a virtual team given the differences in values, priorities, and approaches. What is important in virtual teams is not to have "harmony all the time," but to have strategies to work across the differences which exist. The elephant in the room of unsurfaced conflict can become very large within a virtual team, and while it may not have the same visceral impact it might in in-person teams, it can lead to disengagement and lower productivity. Just as in the in-person domain, addressing conflict early on is usually better than letting things fester.

Questions and ideas to consider as a team or individuals when facing conflict:

- Find the similarities that exist. What is the common ground?
- When you feel you are polar opposites, consider the 2% that is similar or in common.
- Get to know each other—strengths, roles, preferences, etc. This can take additional time and building relationships together are very important for virtual team success.
- Approach each other as individuals and as unique. Watch for, and avoid, stereotypes.
- Check in around your assumptions—are they correct? What different assumptions are being held by different team members? How clear are expectations?
- Try to create opportunities to be together, even if it only happens once a year.
- Use face-to-face time as much as you can, even if it is via Skype.[142]

For more on working with conflict, refer to Chapter 8.

## More Questions for Teams to Consider

I continue to be inspired by the work of many others in the field of team development. About a year ago, I attended a wonderful webinar hosted by Peter Block, author of **Flawless Consulting**. He shared the following questions for teams to consider:

- What do you want from each other?

- What are you doing to contribute to the problem?

- What do you want to say *No* to?

- What is working for us?

He also posed these trust-building questions for teams to consider and be in dialogue around:

- Why was it important to be here today? What would it take for you to be present?

- What crossroad are we at?

- What are we up against as a group?

- Are we getting what we came for?

*Consider how you might incorporate these questions into your next team discussion.*

## Year-end Activities for Virtual Teams

The end of the year can be a great opportunity to bring virtual teams together. It is an opportunity to take stock of what the year was like, and also look at what lies ahead for the upcoming year. What do you have planned for your virtual team? Bringing people together could be as simple as hosting a one-hour year-end call, or as elaborate as bringing in an external facilitator to facilitate a full-day virtual (or in person) team-building session.

In a year-end activity you may want to:

- Provide acknowledgement for what everyone has done.

- Provide a summary of the different activities/milestones people have achieved.

- Explore and set goals for the upcoming year.

- Create your vision for the upcoming year.

- Identify a theme for the upcoming year.

- Schedule in key dates (the old adage being what doesn't get scheduled doesn't get done). As a team, talk about the different activities you want to participate in in the new year. When will they happen?

Potential sections of the program could include:

1. Welcome and overview

2. Questions to explore:

    - What's been your biggest success this year?

    - What have you learned about yourself?

    - What's important for you to do more of next year? What's important for you to do less of next year?

    - What do you need to stop doing?

    - Who do we need to build better relationships with?

    - What activities need to be refined?

    - How do we keep things on our radar screen?

    - What can we do to mitigate the downfalls we experienced this year?

    - What can we do to augment or maximize our successes?

- Where are we with the Six Factors:
    - Shared vision, purpose, or mission?
    - Shared performance goals?
    - Shared team practices?
    - Shared behavioral norms?
    - Clear roles?
    - Shared commitment?
3. Action planning for the next year—key activities each quarter
4. Accountability loops

## FUN ACTIVITIES TO USE AT ANY TIME:

- **Take a photo.** Every month, each person in the group can share a different photo of their own space with each other. This might include a photo of your desk, meal, restaurant, drive to work, or vacation spot.

It provides a way for people to feel more connected and have a window into their world.

- **What's the connection?** This activity gets people to find the synergy amongst themselves. Time is of the essence! Give team members a limited amount of time for people to learn three things they have in common with each other.

- **Solving the puzzle—*What would you do?*** Going back to the "stranded on a desert island" scenario, this game brings people together. Provide the team with a scenario and possible solutions on how they might approach it. The goal is to get the groups or the entire team to discuss their possible approaches. This is a great activity in creating connection, problem-solving and decision-making. It also can shed light on different roles and strengths within the team.

# VIRTUAL TEAM DEVELOPMENT EXERCISES IN SUMMARY

Here's a quick table to refer to as you are thinking about selecting activities for the different focus areas of virtual team development:

| FOCUS AREA | ACTIVITY |
|---|---|
| FOSTERING CONNECTION – GETTING TO KNOW EACH OTHER | What's on your desk? What's in your lunch bag? |
| CREATING A SENSE OF THE COLLECTIVE | Mapping the team (on a map). Finding the connection—what's common across all of our work, how does my work connect to yours? |
| BUILDING RELATIONSHIPS WITHIN YOUR VIRTUAL TEAM | Peer partners—Quarterly pairing of partners from across the team so they can learn more about each other. Special committees—We had a number of special committees in some of the teams I led, including ones that would pull together a team newsletter (quarterly), and those that would plan for our annual event. Virtual shadowing of different roles. Mapping connection points. Undertaking strengths work—StrengthsFinder or VIAStrengths. |
| CREATING A VISION AS A TEAM | Vision cards (Conversation Sparker™ Cards, Visual Explorer, etc.). Collaborative story board on your screen. |
| VIRTUAL MEETING TUNE-UPS | Bring a question to spark dialogue or use a Conversation Sparker™. Revisit your shared vision—where are you on the journey? Do a checkpoint around your skills and how you rate on each of the Six Factors. |

| WORKING ACROSS CONFLICT WITH YOUR VIRTUAL TEAM | Styles work. |
| --- | --- |
| | TKI Assessment. |
| | Creating shared expectations and identifying a shared framework to approach conflict. |
| | Difficult conversations. |
| | Trust work. |
| YEAR-END ACTIVITIES FOR VIRTUAL TEAMS | Year-end retreat questions. |
| | Strategic issues planning. |
| ACTIVITIES TO USE AT ANY TIME | Take a photo of—what's at your desk, what's outside your window, etc. |
| | What's the connection? |
| | Solving the puzzle. |

## RESOURCES FOR YOU TO CHECK OUT

The following are resource-rich websites which can further enhance your knowledge:

Virtualicebreakers.com

www.PotentialsRealized.com/Teams-365-blog.html (Check out the different team development activities spotlighted)

Wrapping up our focus on virtual team development, consider:

1. What are the most pressing issues facing your virtual team right now?
2. If you were to put attention around one area to have the greatest impact, what would that be?
3. What does the team need from you as a leader? From the team themselves?

As we complete this chapter, what is important for you to note about team development on your team right now?

*What areas require attention? What areas are you doing well in?*

## CHECK IN WITH JANE AND JO – VIRTUAL TEAM DEVELOPMENT

Jo has decided that her virtual team needs time to put attention around getting clear on their results (vision, values, workplace) and boosting their relationships (building trust, boosting connection, and looking at strengths and connections). She reaches out to Jane and has a brainstorming session around possible ideas for what the team might be able to focus on.

While it is not possible to bring the team together physically this year, they have agreed that a regular focus on team development could include:

1.  A bi-weekly team question to spark a conversation.
2.  A quarterly, two-hour virtual session designed as a booster shot around different areas of the Six Factors. For example, they have earmarked four key areas for this year as:
    a.  Developing a shared vision across the team.
    b.  Planning and goal-setting—creating a shared understanding of key goals and how those goals are measured and contributed to by each team member.
    c.  Clarifying roles needed.
    d.  Discussing shared commitment to each other, or answering the question, *How will we have each other's backs, no matter what?*

They have also decided to complete both the Everything DiSC assessment to learn more about each person's natural styles, and also to undertake work using the StrengthsFinder2.0 assessment.

## END OF CHAPTER QUESTIONS

What are the key areas the team could use some attention on? Refer to the Six Factors.

What skills does the team bring? What skills could use some attention?

Make a list of the activities/exercises you would like to incorporate into team-building/team development this year.

Make note of any action steps from this chapter in your Action Plan Tracker.

CHAPTER 12

# PARTNERING, CO-FACILITATION AND CREATING A CULTURE OF EFFECTIVE VIRTUAL CONVERSATION

*"The lightning spark of thought generated in the solitary mind awakens its likeness in another mind."*[143]

*– Thomas Carlyle*

As we get to the end of this book, it is time to turn our attention on one critical element. We don't do this work alone. Our clients, fellow facilitators, and the next generation of virtual conversationalists are always a click away.

We look at three important aspects of partnering in this chapter:

- Partnering with your group members
- Collaborating with co-facilitators

- Building a culture of virtual facilitators

Virtual work is grounded in collaboration. In designing powerful programs, we want to ensure that we are creating the richest collaborative spaces. As virtual facilitators, we are partnering on a multitude of levels:

- The first layer of partnering—collaboration and/or co-creation—is with our clients.
- The next layer of partnering, which adds benefit is with other professionals as a co-facilitator.
- The third layer is expanding the impact of collaboration through the development of new virtual workers, and creating a culture of virtual conversations.

## FOUNDATIONAL PRINCIPLES OF PARTNERSHIP

The book *Yes, And* goes into the characteristics of ensembles, which represent one of the highest levels of teamwork. The book's authors note that three factors help ensembles really work:[144]

1. Be in the moment.
2. Give and take.
3. Surrender the need to be right.

*Consider how you are integrating these three factors into your approach to team work and partnership.*

## CORE INGREDIENTS FOR COLLABORATION

In developing partnerships certain ingredients need to be in place. Whether it's developing a team, or enhancing the way you work with a producer or other co-facilitator, these seven ingredients usually need to be in place before the work flows.

| Trust | Candor | Connection | Flexibility/ Adaptability |
|---|---|---|---|
| Self-Awareness | Working Across Differences | Relationship Development | Other |

Take a few minutes to download the worksheet and consider how you are working to boost trust, candor, connection, flexibility/adaptability, self-awareness, working across differences and relationship development in your team.

## EXPLORING THE DIFFERENT LAYERS OF PARTNERSHIP

We are now going to explore the different layers of partnership. You may be working at one, or all, of these levels.

## THE FIRST LAYER – CREATING A PARTNERSHIP WITH YOUR VIRTUAL GROUPS

Collaboration and co-creation is at the heart of partnership. In any virtual event, the notion of partnership is critical as we are always creating a partnership with our virtual groups, in helping them connect with their WIIFM and in order to avoid assumptions which are rife in the virtual space. *Co-creating* your space (another phrase for "designing your space together") is essential in the virtual realm for boosting trust, connection, and learning.

In recent years, we have become more specific in demarking collaboration from co-creation. Co-creation usually involves more risk, ownership, and time. The term co-creation signifies a partnership, one that is deeper than in collaboration.

385

In the virtual space, we have many opportunities to co-create. We can shape the conversation by asking our group members questions such as:

- What is the purpose of the call?
- What are you bringing to the call?
- What do you want out of the call?
- What do you need out of the call?
- What will success look like?
- What do you need?
- How do you want to be supported?
- What is important to emphasize? What is important to expose? What is important to avoid?

The benefits of collaboration and co-creation are multi-fold, including:

- When programs are co-created, they are jointly owned. Participants are not just bought in, they own it, which naturally boosts engagement.
- Enhanced trust is formed when we create something together.
- When participants get to shape their learning experience, there is greater impact and connection with their everyday work.

The downside to collaboration and co-creation is:

- It takes more time.
- It might not always be realistic—for example, when a leadership decision needs to be made or has been made.
- It might not always be needed—for example, do you need to always ask the group whether they want to go to A or B?
- It is likely that the level of co-facilitation and partnering will be dependent on the type of conversation you are undertaking. For example, a coaching conversation, which is based on deep partnership between the coach and client, is going to be different than a conversation with a trainer who is there as expert to impart knowledge to the group.

*Take note of how the benefits and downsides weigh against each other in the
different partnering opportunities you have.*

## FUNDAMENTALS FOR COLLABORATION IN THE VIRTUAL SPACE

Knowing when to collaborate and when not to is an art form. There is
often a fallacy that collaboration is always the best approach. In fact,
collaboration is not always the best route to go. While it will vary, some
things to consider are:

When to collaborate:

- When a group decision is important.
- Where groups are homogenous.
- When you are working with a team.
- When buy in, and engagement, is important—for example,
  having everyone back from break ready to go may benefit from
  asking the group how much time they really need.

When to not collaborate:

- When the group is very diverse and the focus is more on the
  individual level.
- When time is limited.
- When the issue is straightforward.
- When there is no shared purpose or end result.

## CREATING A PARTNERSHIP WITH YOUR VIRTUAL GROUP MEMBERS

One of the stakes I have as a leader and facilitator is that I am working in
partnership with the virtual group members I am bringing together. In
doing this, there are several key focus areas to note:

## RECOGNIZE THAT RELATIONSHIPS START BEFORE THE PROGRAM BEGINS AND END AFTER THE PROGRAM ENDS

One of the changes we are seeing with virtual programming is that we are moving away from single learning events to longer-term learning processes. In the virtual space, things do take time and you may not be able to cover all of the same things you could in the in-person realm. Therefore, it is important to recognize that virtual events require an ongoing dialogue with group members that start before the official program and often end after. Setting people up for success often means that we create contact points before the start of the first group call, and we may meet after to check in with the group and/or individual members.

## REALLY GET TO KNOW PEOPLE

Really getting to know people—their needs, styles and preferences— is integral to moving to an environment of co-creation. It is about empowering them and handing the reins over to them to create the format with you.

## FOCUS ON SKILL DEVELOPMENT OF PEERS

As mentioned in Chapter 4, leveraging peer processes can benefit from skill development, particularly in the areas of listening, questioning, helping peers shift from advisor (*telling you what to do*) to explorer (*helping you discover what you want to do*). Consider how you can support skill development with your team members.

## CO-CREATE AGREEMENTS

This step is very easy to overlook, especially when there is great excitement to get going with a virtual event. Spend time creating shared agreements/

Ways of Working or guiding principles on how you want to operate. These shared agreements provide the foundation for exceptional collaboration.

## PROVIDE FEEDBACK REGULARLY

It is critical to get feedback regularly throughout a virtual call. Whether it is stopping to check for understanding by asking questions such as *Tell me, what did you connect with?* or, *Who would like to share how they will be applying what we are learning right now?* These questions invite more engagement than *Does that make sense?* In other instances, it might be appropriate to get a "thumbs up" or "thumbs down" to ideas.

# THE SECOND LAYER – COLLABORATION AS CO-FACILITATORS

*"Successful solo acts are rarely, in fact solo."*– Yes, And

Whether we are co-coaching, or have a co-facilitator, there is a second layer of collaboration as co-facilitators. Once again, intentionally designing your relationship can be a great benefit. The next section explores the co-facilitation arc, and questions you will want to use to intentionally design your relationship together.

## THE CO-FACILITATION ARC

In my book, *From One to Many: Best Practices for Team and Group Coaching,* I write about the Co-Facilitation Arc, recognizing that there are several stages of the co-facilitation journey. There are conversations which are useful to have at the start when we come together, conversations during design, during implementation (the actual program itself), and conversations we have after the program.

Take a look at key activities and conversations for each of these four stages:

**At the Start**

- What are our strengths?
- How are we complimentary?
- Where do gaps exist?
- What blindspots do we have?
- What is important in our work? What values drive our work?
- What business philosophies are important to us?
- Share samples of work

**During Design**

- Who will take a lead on what? - Design and Facilitation
- Accordion points - what can be expanded and needs to be contracted if needed?
- What is our common stake for this program?
- What do we want to ensure happens, no matter what?

**During Implementation**

- Review leads for each section
- Observations with Group - energy, impact, engagement
- Add additional questions
- Accordion
- Touch Base throughout regarding changes needed

**Post Program**

- Review of program - What worked well? What didn't?
- Successes
- Roles, flow and fit
- Lessons learned
- Changes for next co-facilitation

(Adapted from page 270, Britton,
*From One to Many: Best Practices for Team and Group Coaching*, 2013)

Successful partnerships don't usually just happen, they evolve through dialogue, planning, and adaptation. Part of making co-facilitation work is to have regular discussion regarding how you want to work together. Over the years, I have evolved the following list of questions to ask before, during and after our work as co-facilitators. These questions help with intentionally planning your work together. Consider how you can have dialogue around these.

QUESTIONS TO CONSIDER AS PARTNERS:

| BEFORE | DURING | AFTER |
|---|---|---|
| • Who are we as individuals? As a pair? As a team? <br><br> • What are our values individually? As a partnership? <br><br> • What are our goals for this partnership? What do we hope to achieve? <br><br> • What is our stake? <br><br> • What unique skills, abilities or characteristics do we bring? <br><br> • What are our expectations of each other? Of ourselves? | • What is working well? What's not? <br><br> • What is aligned? <br><br> • What are our blindspots? <br><br> • What are we missing? <br><br> • Where are we overcompensating? <br><br> • How do we have each other's back? <br><br> • What is different about our values? <br><br> • What do we want to keep on doing? <br><br> • What do we want to change? | • Review – What worked well? What didn't? What would you do next time? <br><br> • Lessons learned <br><br> • Successes to note for future experience <br><br> • Roles, flow, and fit |

(Adapted from pages 272 - 273, Britton,
*From One to Many: Best Practices for Team and Group Coaching*, 2013)

A couple of additional notes to making co-facilitation work are:

- **Check your ego.** Leaning into the "one plus one is greater than two" principle means that we need to be open to doing things differently and creating things differently in service to our partnership. Remember you are in service to the group. What do you need to do to check your ego at the door?

- **Consider roles.** What are your strengths? What do each one of you naturally bring? What do you intuitively focus on (i.e., big picture or little details)?

- **Consider how you complement each other**. Some of the best co-facilitation work occurs when you are different from each other. How can you complement each other's styles? How can you feed off each other?

- **What can you rely on each other for?** How do you have each other's backs? What will you do if things go off the rails? If you have challenges in working with each other, how do you address that off line? Co-facilitators' first responsibilities are towards the group, and not picking at each other.
- **Walk through the program together.** Taking time to walk through the program together—from before you start to what happens after—is an essential activity. Co-facilitation usually does not allow for the same level of "winging it" some facilitators leverage.
- **Take time at the end of the program to note what worked and what didn't.** What did you learn? What did you notice about strengths? What didn't work? What's important for you to note going forward?

As you do a walk through, notice:

- Who is doing what? When?
- Walk through the schedule together. Identify when breakouts are needed and who needs to be in each group. When are breakouts going to happen? For how long? Will groups stay the same or move through different combinations?
- Who is taking a lead on different sections?
- What will the other person be doing during the different sections?
- Who will deal with technical issues that arise?
- How will you transition from section to section?
- What handoffs are needed?
- What set up is needed?
- What areas do you want to elongate if things are moving quickly and what could you do to shorten things if they are moving slowly?

In doing a walkthrough it can be useful to be regularly asking the question *What if…?* This may surface issues that could potentially arise along with strategies and solutions you can jointly use if they do.

## CONSIDER WHAT YOUR STAKE IS IN THIS WORK

Whether you are co-facilitating or working alone, what is your stake in this work? To have fun, to make it easy, create safety, create a wow, or help the team and group move through challenging and important waters?

### Making Co-Facilitation Work: 12 Questions to Ask

These twelve questions are useful as a frame for dialogue as you and your co-facilitator start your new partnership:

1. What do we each bring to the partnership?
2. What are the strengths of each person?
3. What are our weaknesses?
4. How are we complimentary?
5. What blindspots might our strengths create?
6. How do we compensate?
7. What can we create together that we can't do alone?
8. How do we provide contrast for each other (good guy/bad guy or big picture thinker/granular perspective)?
9. What is our stake in this work?
10. What will success look like?
11. What do I need to do to really be present, and bring my best to this work?
12. What am I committed to, no matter what? What are we committed to, no matter what?

## PRACTICAL THINGS TO TALK ABOUT IN YOUR CO-FACILITATION

Making co-facilitation work has a very tactical element as well. Areas you will want to discuss together as part of your pre-program meetings are:

- What is your stake in the work, i.e., what is extremely important for you?
- What will you do if things "go south" or aren't working?
- What roles are you best suited for? Being a foil for each other? How can you leverage your skills and capabilities?
- How will you provide feedback to each other before and during the program?
- What can you count on each other for?

## THE FACILITATOR AND THE PRODUCER – AN ESSENTIAL PARTNERSHIP

It is likely that you will be working with producers as part of the program roll-out, especially for larger groups (20 plus) and in organizations. Key to making this work successful is clearly defining the roles and responsibilities of each person. In general, the role of the producer is to:

- Open up the line.
- Ensure line quality.
- Start the recording.
- Monitor and respond to technical challenges.
- Track questions and issues that come into the chat.
- Set up breakouts for future use.

The producer frees up the facilitator to facilitate and not have to worry about a lot of the granular technical details, which may not be in their wheelhouse.

Not every call will have a producer, so it is important to consider these additional areas if you are facilitating alone.

While the role can be distinct, really working in partnership is key to a successful virtual event. Knowing what is upcoming is critical. A best practice for making sure you are both on the same page is to do a walk-through, particularly for longer programs or those with higher visibility. Walk through from the time that the two of you will log in (30 minutes before) to what happens as you hang up, in terms of what needs to be done, by who, and noting any tricky issues you might encounter along the way.

Questions to be asking yourself as producer and facilitator:

- What are your separate roles?
- Who is doing what? When?
- Where are those areas that intersect?
- What are the things you want to do together?
- What support do you need from each other?
- What signals do you have for each other?
- Who is going to follow up on what?

## OTHER PARTNERS

It's also likely that you will be working with a variety of other program resource people who will make your work come to life. This could include Instructional Designers who can help roll out your program, or Graphic Designers who can help to make it look pretty!

Who are the people you want to bring onto your team who can help you expand the work? This might include:

- Other co-facilitators
- Producers
- Other program supports—instructional designers, graphic designers

# THE THIRD LAYER – BRINGING IT FULL CIRCLE: CREATING A TEAM OF VIRTUAL LEADERS, FACILITATORS AND CONVERSATIONALISTS

In developing a team of virtual leaders, facilitators, and conversationalists, there is often a natural progression of skills people evolve through. There are a number of different paths virtual facilitators take—from virtual team member, to someone working on special virtual project teams, to leading a team, to mentoring others, to possibly training others in doing this work.

As with any skill set, there are introductory skills people need in the work, as well as skills that we develop as we move to mastery. There are a number of paths virtual facilitators can take during their evolution.

If you are responsible for developing other virtual facilitators, the following chart includes a progression of skills we will develop from introductory to mastery levels. Consider what opportunities and pathways virtual professionals have in your organization to grow.

| INTRODUCTORY SKILLS | INTERMEDIATE | MASTERY |
|---|---|---|
| Confidence in leading the room. | Reading the room (group dynamics, energy, patterns, what's aligned, what's not). | Mastery with the technology. |
| Understanding the technology. | Managing energy. | Ability to work with multiple groups at one time. |
| Asking powerful questions. | Confidence around a range of skills. | Confidence around most virtual facilitation skills. |
| Listening. | Managing technologies. | Evaluation. |
| Delivering created content for different audiences. | Creating basic virtual programming. | Innovation in design. |

| Opening and closing calls. | Working with conflict. | Training/mentoring with other facilitators. |
|---|---|---|
| Troubleshooting technical issues with support. | | |

Having been involved in the training and development of virtual team leaders for almost two decades, and virtual facilitators/coaches since 2004, I know there are several things to keep in mind:

1. **Practice makes better.** Ongoing practice with the various technologies we use is critical. In training new virtual facilitators we need to have them practice and lead. It's through this hands-on experience and feedback that virtual facilitators really grow.

2. **Modelling of best practices.** As a trainer, be mindful of modelling different approaches and getting people into the practice of this work. Do it, don't just think about it.

3. **Experimentation is key.** Every situation is different and adopting a mindset of experimentation can lead to more innovation and less stress on the part of the facilitator.

4. **Regular review/debrief of how it is going.** This may be to review recordings, consider after each delivery what further changes could be made to both content and facilitation strategies.

5. **Encouragement to get creative.** We often are the ones who create our own boundaries. In virtual learning, conversation and teams the sky is the limit! Experimentation is the norm. Spend time fostering creativity and innovation.

Just as we saw in Chapter 10 on Leadership Development, supporting new virtual facilitators in a variety of modalities can be important. Consider how you can support people through coaching, mentoring, and other ongoing supports. What will you do to supervise? How will you measure development? What feedback loops are there going to be? Who can help you with this?

## CREATING A CULTURE OF VIRTUAL LEARNING

As budgets are scaled back, consider how you will create a culture of virtual learning. Just because you opt to lead with virtual doesn't mean that you don't come together as a group. If it is feasible, do some in-person events annually to further deepen relationships and strengthen learning. Blended opportunities can leverage the best of both worlds—in-person and virtual.

In creating a culture of virtual learning or *The Way We Do Things*, it is important to:

1.  Create ownership of learning by all staff. Not just HR or learning, and not just leaders, but everyone.
2.  Notice who would be well suited to champion, lead, and sponsor the work. Some staff members may have more enthusiasm for leading this work.
3.  See what works best and spread best practices. A virtual session does not always mean a learning session with PowerPoint. With today's laptops and tablets, we can make things highly interactive. Daylong sessions spent on planning can be effective, as can short, 45-minute sprints with people who are working on their own plans.
4.  Equip people with skills and practice in this. It is important to create the space for people to work virtually and see how others work.
5.  Be open to experimentation. Unless you try it, you may not know it works.
6.  Consider the best settings for establishing and embedding virtual learning. There may be some parts of the business that are earlier adopters than others. There may also be some programs that are easier to translate to the virtual domain as well.

In creating a culture of virtual learning, a lot of different elements will go in—including building a team of people who are keen and eager to get things moving, along with skills to collaborate more effectively.

# CHECK IN WITH JANE AND JO – PARTNERING AND CO-FACILITATION

Finally the day has come for Jane, the virtual facilitator, and Jo, the virtual leader, to partner together. They have been tasked with creating a new virtual and in-person training program for leaders across their organization. As they move through discussions they use the questions found in the Co-Facilitation Arc, and are in dialogue around how they can build opportunities for new virtual facilitators and virtual leaders across the organization. They have set up a weekly meeting schedule for the next few months, given the launch of the program in less than six months. They are utilizing the One-Page Action Plan to keep each other posted on progress in their respective worlds, and are making sure to incorporate the best practices of meetings (Chapter 9), as well as building onto the list of core skills needed for virtual leaders (Chapter 10) and virtual facilitators (Chapter 12).

## END OF CHAPTER QUESTIONS

Consider what you want to create in terms of partners and collaborators.

What are you looking for in terms of characteristics with a virtual co-facilitator?

Make a list of possible partners you can work with.

If you are in the process of designing a virtual train-the-trainer, what are the elements you want to include pre-program, post program?

Make a note of any action steps in your Action Plan Tracker.

# WHERE TO NEXT? EMERGING PRACTICES AND RETURN TO THE BASICS

*"Science and technology revolutionize our lives, but memory, tradition and myth frame our response."*[145]

*- Arthur Schlesinger*

In most of my books, I like to take a brief look at where we are going. At the time of this writing, there are many influences that are shaping our virtual conversation space, namely:

- Agile and Lean Methodologies
- Design Thinking
- Virtual Reality
- Augmented Reality (AR)

While the post-Brexit world may be turning people's attention inward nationally, we know that we continue to operate in a globally connected world. Virtual teams are continuing to flourish—across cities, regions, countries, and borders. Virtual approaches may become more appealing given the tightening of movement for some globally.

As we have progressed throughout the book we have touched on several key themes, namely:

- The importance of trust and connection in the virtual space as a foundation for effective and engaging digital dialogue.
- Setting people up for success.
- Leveraging skills, talents, strengths, and styles with the diverse groups you are working with.
- Expecting the unexpected.
- Keeping things simple given the complexities that exist in this work.

These themes are all foundations of leading and working in today's ever-changing work environments. Whether you work remote, or in-person, many of the principles and practices we explored throughout this book can be incorporated into your work.

No doubt the context of the virtual realm will continue to change rapidly and exponentially. While the platforms may change, it is likely that we can continue to return to the basics around these principles for leading engaging—and interactive—virtual conversations.

What are you inspired to have dialogue around? How do you want to add your voice?

Thank you for joining me on this journey!

# APPENDIX A
# PLATFORM CHOICES

Download a table copy of this appendix at
www.EffectiveVirtualConversations.

At the time of writing, the following were some of the different platform choices available. Given the rapid change in technology, refer to the individual platform choices for more information on what is currently available.

## NAME: FREECONFERENCING.COM

**Major Uses**
- Bridgeline.
- Benefit of a VOIP Dial in for international Callers
- Free bridgelines allow a large number of callers

**Group Size**
- Up to 1000 callers

**Additional Features**
- Also an iPhone App to connect.
- You can record calls – listening on line or url. Also can choose to download or not.

**Interactivity**
- Very good

**Breakout**
- YES – and easy to use

**Webinar/Screensharing**
- Yes if you add this on

**Chat Function**
- No

**Other/Instructions (current as of April 2017)**

- www.freeconferencing.com
- Phone dialers will have to pay long distance charges to access the bridgeline.
- To get started:
  1. Visit website
  2. Establish an account
  3. Explore how to start a call, record, and where to access recordings

## NAME: FREECONFERENCECALLING.COM

**Major Uses**

- Bridgeline

**Group Size**

- Up to 1000 callers

**Additional Features**

- Recordings are archived.
- You can share these via Facebook and Twitter
- Up to six hours of call length

**Interactivity**

- Good

**Breakout**

- No breakout feature at present

**Webinar/Screensharing**

- No

**Chat Function**

- No

**Other/Instructions (current as of April 2017)**

- www.freeconferencecalling.com
- Free recording, web portal so you can see who is on the call, mute, get participants to raise hands.

- Recordings can be listened to online, downloaded, and now Tweeted and placed on Facebook.

## NAME: FREECONFERENCECALL.COM

**Major Uses**
- Bridgeline

**Group Size**
- Up to 1000 callers

**Interactivity**
- Good

**Breakout**

**Webinar/Screensharing**
- Video and Screen sharing

**Chat Function**
- No

**Other/Instructions (current as of April 2017)**
- www.freeconferencecall.com
- Recording services are by phone only so people have to dial back to listen.
- Local dial-in numbers in 61 countries

## NAME: SKYPE

**Major Uses**
- Video and/or voice only
- Limit in terms of numbers

**Group Size**
- Limit based on format

**Additional Features**
- Video group calls really help to connect.

**Interactivity**

- Very good especially if video

**Breakout**

- No

**Webinar/Screensharing**

- Screen sharing

**Chat Function**

- Yes – speech bubble

**Other/Instructions (current as of April 2017)**

- Harder to record – there is an app you can synch.
- Refer to this blog post: www.real.com/resources/how-to-record-skype-video/

## NAME: MAESTRO CONFERENCING

**Major Uses**

- Paid service
- Bridgeline

**Group Size**

- Depends on account

**Additional Features**

- Breakouts
- Easy recording

**Interactivity**

- Excellent

**Breakout**

- YES - very good portal for facilitator to use to manage breakouts

**Webinar/Screensharing**

- Yes

**Chat Function**

- Hands Raise

**Other/Instructions (current as of April 2017)**

- www.maestroconference.com

- Call facilitator has a web dashboard to see who is on the call, who has raised hands etc.
- Also able to section group members into virtual breakout rooms with the click of a button (i.e., if you have a group of 8, you can put people into 2 groups of 4, and as facilitator you can drop in and have discussion).
- At time of writing only drawback is if you are the only caller there is background music.

NAME: WEBEX

**Major Uses**
- Webinar

**Group Size**
- Dependent on account

**Additional Features**
- Recording is easy

**Interactivity**
- As per facilitation style.
- Many facilitators rely only on screen sharing

**Breakout**
- Yes – Facilitator uses portal to set these

**Webinar/Screensharing**
- As a foundation

**Chat Function**
- Yes

**Other/Instructions (current as of April 2017)**
- www.webex.com
- Web Ex is widely used across organizations.
- Callers have option to view online and call in to bridgeline.
- Note that high speed is often needed to download WebEx platform.

- Considerations:
    - bandwidth and location issues
    - if you bring on another person to moderate and look after technology consider making them a co-facilitator

## NAME: GOTOMEETING

**Major Uses**
- Yes

**Group Size**
- Free version currently allows you to connect with up to 3 clients.

**Additional Features**
- Yes

**Interactivity**
- Yes

**Breakout**
- Yes

**Webinar/Screensharing**
- Yes

**Chat Function**
- Yes

**Other/Instructions (current as of April 2017)**
- www.gotomeeting.com
- There is also GoToTraining which provides a training module so you can "test" learning.
- Considerations:
    - Bandwidth and location issues
    - If you bring another person to moderate and look after technology, assign the role.
    - Consider confidentiality agreements as needed.
    - GoToConferencing is now available as a kit so you have the equipment to be able to live stream as a team.

NAME: HANGOUTS – GOOGLE

**Major Uses**
- Instant Messaging, SMS, VOIP and Chat
- Has video streaming capabilities – up to 25 persons through Meetings.

**Group Size**
- Conversations can have up to 150 people.
- 25 in meetings

**Additional Features**
- Can use emojis and chat function

**Interactivity**
- Yes

**Breakout**
- Not at present time

**Webinar/Screensharing**
- No

**Chat Function**
- Yes

**Other/Instructions (current as of April 2017)**
- Historically, bandwidth issues have been an issue for some callers.
- Ease of use has been problematic for some to join.
- No way to secure the line so confidentiality may be an issue, and people can drop in.
- Able to use as a tool to collaborate on documents.
- Google has indicated that Hangouts may evolve into other products.

NAME: ADOBE CONNECT

**Major Uses**
- Web portal for meetings, training session

**Group Size**

- Dependent on account

**Additional Features**

- VOIP, notes, chats, whiteboards, recording.

**Interactivity**

- Chat. Annotation may need to be activated or permission given.

**Breakout**

- Yes, up to 20 breakout rooms available

**Webinar/Screensharing**

- Yes – screen sharing and webinar host can stream

**Chat Function**

- Yes

**Other/Instructions (current as of April 2017)**

- www.adobeconnect.com

NAME: ZOOM

**Major Uses**

- Paid accounts or free calls (up to 35 minutes)

**Group Size**

- Dependent on account

**Additional Features**

- Yes – primarily a video streaming service.
- Callers can also phone in.

**Interactivity**

- Dependent on facilitation

**Breakout**

- No

**Webinar/Screensharing**

- Yes – as foundation. Paid accounts have up to 50 breakouts

**Chat Function**

- Yes

**Other/Instructions (current as of April 2017)**

- www.zoom.us

- Recording function allows you to save to your computer or store it in the cloud.
- The mobile app function allows you to also join from your phone.
- Screen sharing is available for the presenter and group members.

NAME: JOIN.ME

**Major Uses**
- Paid and free

**Group Size**

**Additional Features**
- Screen sharing and phone

**Interactivity**
- Dependent on facilitation

**Breakout**
- No

**Webinar/Screen sharing**
- Primarily Screen sharing

**Chat Function**
- Yes

**Other/Instructions (current as of April 2017)**
- www.join.me
- Provides audio conferencing, video conferencing, white boarding.
- There is also a mobile app to join from your phone.
- Screen sharing and white boarding (iOs only).
- Free accounts can host up to 10 people.

**Effective Virtual Conversations**

## Chapter 1 - Introduction

|  |  |
|---|---|
|  |  |
|  |  |
|  |  |
|  |  |
|  |  |

## Chapter 2 - Foundations

|  |  |
|---|---|
|  |  |
|  |  |
|  |  |
|  |  |
|  |  |

## Chapter 3 – Essential Elements and Core Skills

|  |  |
|---|---|
|  |  |
|  |  |
|  |  |
|  |  |
|  |  |

## Chapter 4 - Ecosystem

|  |  |
|---|---|
|  |  |
|  |  |
|  |  |
|  |  |
|  |  |

## Chapter 5 - Design

| | |
|---|---|
| | |
| | |
| | |
| | |
| | |

## Chapter 6 – Preparing For Blast Off

| | |
|---|---|
| | |
| | |
| | |
| | |
| | |

## Chapter 7 – Activities and Engagement

| | |
|---|---|
| | |
| | |
| | |
| | |
| | |
| | |

## Chapter 8 – Tricky Issues

| | |
|---|---|
| | |
| | |
| | |
| | |
| | |

## Chapter 9 - Meetings

| | |
|---|---|
| | |
| | |
| | |
| | |

## Chapter 10 – Virtual Team Leadership Development

| | |
|---|---|
| | |
| | |
| | |
| | |

## Chapter 11 – Virtual Team Development

| | |
|---|---|
| | |
| | |
| | |
| | |

## Chapter 12 – Partnering/Co-Facilitation

| | |
|---|---|
| | |
| | |
| | |
| | |

## Next Steps

| | |
|---|---|
| | |
| | |
| | |
| | |
| | |

## My Resources

| | |
|---|---|
| | |
| | |
| | |
| | |
| | |

## Conversations To Have....

| | |
|---|---|
| | |
| | |
| | |
| | |
| | |

# END NOTES

1. Elizabeth Kraus. "Changing the Game: 12 Quotes About Disruption, Creativity and Winning in Business." *DB Squared*. September 18, 2015. Accessed June 12, 2017. https://www.dbsquaredinc.com/make-change-12-inspiring-quotes-about-disruption-and-winning-in-business/.

2. Jennifer Britton. "Teams365 #741: Four Core Skills in Virtual Facilitation." *Potentials Realized*. January 11, 2016. Accessed June 13, 2017. http://www.potentialsrealized.com/teams-365-blog/teams365-741-four-core-skills-in-virtual-facilitation.

3. Matthew Sparkes. "WhatsApp Overtakes Text Messages." *The Telegraph*. July 22, 2016. Accessed November 16, 2016. http://www.telegraph.co.uk/technology/news/11340321/WhatsApp-overtakes-text-messages.html.

4. Annamarie Mann and Jim Harter. "The Worldwide Employee Engagement Crisis." *Gallup*. January 07, 2016. Accessed June 13, 2017. http://www.gallup.com/businessjournal/188033/worldwide-employee-engagement-crisis.aspx?g_source=Business%2BJournal&g_medium=CardRelatedItems&g_campaign=tiles.

5. Sam Pudwell. "The Rise of Telecommuting: 45 Percent of US Employees Work from Home." *BetaNews*. February 04, 2016. Accessed June 13, 2017. http://betanews.com/2015/09/11/the-rise-of-telecommuting-45-percent-of-us-employees-work-from-home/.

6. Laura Shin. "At These 125 Companies, All or Most Employees Work Remotely." *Forbes*. February 08, 2017. Accessed June 13, 2017. https://www.forbes.com/sites/laurashin/2016/03/31/at-these-125-companies-all-or-most-employees-work-remotely/#67b1ff7e6530.

7. Lindsay Kolowich. "How to Stop the Most Common Productivity Prohibitors [Infographic]." *HubSpot*, August 11, 2015. Accessed June 19, 2017. https://blog.hubspot.com/marketing/productivity-prohibitors?utm_campaign=blog-rss-emails&utm_source=hs_email&utm_medium=email&utm_content=21245584#sm.000003vx6itvx4f97z6nwaqyn9dmv.

8. Jeffrey M. Jones. "In U.S., Telecommuting for Work Climbs to 37%."

*Gallup.* August 19, 2015. Accessed February 26, 2017. http://www.gallup.com/poll/184649/telecommuting-work-climbs.aspx.

9. Ibid., 5.

10. Keith Ferrazzi. "Getting Virtual Teams Right." *Harvard Business Review.* March 10, 2015. Accessed June 13, 2017. https://hbr.org/2014/12/getting-virtual-teams-right.

11. Matthew Guyan. "5 Ways to Reduce Cognitive Load In eLearning." *ELearning Industry.* July 08, 2015. Accessed June 16, 2017. https://elearningindustry.com/5-ways-to-reduce-cognitive-load-in-elearning.

12. Christoforos Pappas. "Top 10 e-Learning Statistics for 2014 You Need to Know." *ELearning Industry.* January 25, 2015. Accessed March 25, 2017. https://elearningindustry.com/top-10-e-learning-statistics-for-2014-you-need-to-know.

13. Helen A.S. Popkin. "How Much Time Did We Spend on Social Media in One Month?" *CNBC.* December 04, 2012. Accessed January 17, 2017. http://www.cnbc.com/id/100275798.

14. Ibid., 12.

15. Drake Baer. "These 12 Meeting Mistakes Cost Companies $37 Billion a Year in Lost Productivity." *Business Insider.* November 20, 2014. Accessed June 16, 2017. http://www.businessinsider.com/common-meeting-mistakes-2014-11.

16. Kate Lister and Tom Harnish. *The State of Telework in the U.S. How Individuals, Business, and Government Benefit.* (PDF. Telework Research Network, 2011).

17. William Isaacs. *Dialogue and the Art of Thinking Together.* (New York, Currency, 1999), 148.

18. Press Release. "Apple Launches iPad." *Apple Newsroom.* January 27, 2010. Accessed November 7, 2016. http://www.apple.com/pr/library/2010/01/27Apple-Launches-iPad.html.

19. William Isaacs. *Dialogue.* 44.

20. Ibid., 11.

21. Ibid., 45.

22. Ibid., 48.

23. *Trends in Global Virtual Teams.* (PDF. New York, NY: CRW Culture Wizard, April 17, 2016). http://cdn.culturewizard.com/PDF/Trends_in_VT_Report_4-17-2016.pdf.

24. Geert Hofstede. "Dimensions of National Culture." *The Hofstede Centre.* 2010. Accessed June 16, 2017. https://geert-hofstede.com/national-culture. html.

25. Sarah Kessler. "IBM, Remote-work Pioneer, is Calling Thousands of Employees Back to the Office." *Quartz.* March 21, 2017. Accessed June 16, 2017. https://qz.com/924167/ibm-remote-work-pioneer-is-calling-thousands-of-employees-back-to-the-office/.

26. Ibid., 17 (262).

27. Charles Duhigg. "What Google Learned from Its Quest to Build the Perfect Team." *The New York Times.* February 25, 2016. Accessed June 19, 2017. https://www.nytimes.com/2016/02/28/magazine/what-google-learned-from-its-quest-to-build-the-perfect-team.html?_r=0.

28. Amy Edmondson. "Psychological Safety and Learning Behavior in Work Teams." *Administrative Science Quarterly* 44, no. 2 (1999): 350. url: http://www.jstor.org/stable/2666999.

29. Jennifer Britton. "Creating Connection Amongst Group Members." *Group Coaching Ins and Outs* (web log), January 01, 1970. Accessed November 1, 2016. http://groupcoaching.blogspot.ca/2014/02/creating-connection-amongst-group.html.

30. Stephen M. R. Covey and Douglas R. Conant. "The Connection Between Employee Trust and Financial Performance." *Harvard Business Review.* July 18, 2016. Accessed June 19, 2017. https://hbr.org/2016/07/the-connection-between-employee-trust-and-financial-performance.

31. Jim Asplund and Nikki Blacksmith. "How Strengths Boost Engagement." *Gallup.* April 07, 2011. Accessed June 19, 2017. http://www.gallup.com/businessjournal/146972/strengths-boost-engagement.aspx.

32. Jennifer Britton. "Teams365 #983: Virtual Facilitation Enablers." *Potentials Realized.* September 9, 2016. Accessed November 2, 2016. http://www.potentialsrealized.com/teams-365-blog/teams365-983-virtual-facilitation-enablers.

33. Jennifer Britton. "Teams365 #986: Derailers in Virtual Facilitation." *Potentials Realized.* September 12, 2016. Accessed November 2, 2016. http://www.potentialsrealized.com/teams-365-blog/teams365-986-derailers-in-virtual-facilitation.

34. Alan M. Webber. "What's So New About the New Economy?" *Harvard Business Review.* January-February 1993. Accessed June 19, 2017. https://hbr.org/1993/01/whats-so-new-about-the-new-economy.

35. Sam Kaner. *Facilitators Guide to Participatory Decision-making.* 3rd ed. (San Francisco (CA): Jossey-Bass, 2014).

36. Ibid., 15.

37. Ingrid Bens. *Facilitating with Ease! A Step-by-Step Guidebook with Customizable Worksheets on CD-ROM.* (San Francisco: Jossey-Bass, 2002), 9.

38. Britton, Jennifer J. *From One to Many: Best Practices for Team and Group Coaching.* Josey-Bass, 2013.

39. Simon Metcalfe. "International Listening Association." In *Building a Speech.* 8th ed. (Nelson Education), 65.

40. Wikipedia contributors. "Albert Mehrabian." *Wikipedia, The Free Encyclopedia.* Accessed June 19, 2017. https://en.wikipedia.org/w/index.php?title=Albert_Mehrabian&oldid=758997080.

41. Henry Kimsey-House, Karen Kimsey-House, and Phil Sandahl. *Co-active Coaching: Changing Business, Transforming Lives.* 3rd ed. (Boston, MA: Nicholas Brealey Pub., 2011).

42. Peter M. Senge. *The Fifth Discipline Fieldbook: Strategies and Tools for Building a Learning Organization.* (New York: Crown Business, 1994).

43. Jennifer Britton. "Teams365 #1035: Virtual Facilitation Tip #17." *Potentials Realized.* October 31, 2016. Accessed June 19, 2017. http://www.potentialsrealized.com/teams-365-blog/teams365-1035-virtual-facilitation-tip-17.

44. Ibid., 17 (159).

45. Ibid., 17 (135).

46. John C. Maxwell. *Good Leaders Ask Great Questions: Your foundation for successful leadership.* (New York: Center Street, 2014), 55.

47. Ibid., 17. (149).

48. Edgar Schein. "Dialogue and Culture." *Organizational Dynamics.* Autumn 1993. Mentioned in: Isaacs, *Dialogue and the Art of Thinking Together.* 327.

49. John Whitmore. *Coaching for Performance: GROWing Human Potential and Purpose.* (Boston: Nicholas Brealey, 2009).

50. Christine Keene and Peter Scott. "Appreciative Inquiry: Business Planning Using SOAR." *Design Research Techniques.* Accessed June 19, 2017. http://designresearchtechniques.com/casestudies/appreciative-inquiry-business-planning-using-soar/.

51. Ibid., 23 (21).

52. Amy Cuddy and Joy Casselberry. *Presence: Bringing Your Boldest Self to Your Biggest Challenges.* (New York, NY: Little, Brown and Co., 2015).

53. Richard Koch. *The 80/20 Manager: The Secret to Working Less and Achieving More.* (New York: Little, Brown, 2013), 239.

54. Rick Warren, *The Purpose Driven Life: What on Earth am I here for?* Quoted in Maxwell. *Good Leaders Ask Great Questions.*

55. Linda Kaplan Thaler and Ron Koval, *Power of Small: Why Little Things Make All the Difference* (Broadway Books, 2009), 71.

56. Timothy Clark and Conrad Gottfredson. "Agile Learning: Thriving in the New Normal." *Nxtbook Media.* CLO Magazine, December 2009. Accessed June 19, 2017. http://www.nxtbook.com/nxtbooks/mediatec/clo1209/index.php?startid=18.

57. Ibid., 12.

58. Jake Huhn. "How Microlearning Enables Micro Moments." *ELearning Learning.* July 14, 2016. Accessed June 19, 2017. http://www.

elearninglearning.com/2016/statistics/?open-article-id=5328209&article-title=how-microlearning-enablesmicro-moments-&blog-domain=bottomlineperformance.com&blog-title=bottom-line-performance.

59. *Evaluation of Evidence-Based Practices in Online Learning: A Meta-analysis of online learning studies*, PDF, pp xiv-xv. Quoted in "Benefits of Blended Learning." *Blended Learning Toolkit*. April 24, 2014. Accessed June 19, 2017. https://blended.online.ucf.edu/about/benefits-of-blended-learning/.

60. "The 70:20:10 Model for Learning and Development." *Wiki: Training Industry*. Accessed November 15, 2016. https://www.trainingindustry.com/wiki/entries/the-702010-model-for-learning-and-development.aspx.

61. Karl M. Kapp. "Is eLearning Dead? Is Instructional Design Dying with It?" *ELearning Learning*. January 31, 2017. Accessed June 19, 2017. http://www.elearninglearning.com/edition/weekly-learning-technologies-learner-2017-01-28?open-article-id=6145629&article-title=is-elearning-deadis-instructional-design-dying-with-it-&blog-domain=karlkapp.com&blog-title=kapp-notes.

62. Jennifer Britton. "Teleclasses and Teleseminars 5 Tips." *Group Coaching: Ins and Outs* (web log), March 1, 2011. Accessed November 13, 2016. http://groupcoaching.blogspot.ca/2011/03/teleclasses-and-teleseminars-5-tips.html.

63. Modulates. "According to Cisco, 84% of Internet Traffic Will Be from Video by 2018." *MarketWired Newsroom*. News release, June 25, 2014. Accessed September 21, 2016. http://www.marketwired.com/press-release/according-to-cisco-84-of-internet-traffic-will-be-from-video-by-2018-1924156.htm.

64. Danny Donchev. "Youtube Statistics - 2017." *Digital Marketing Education*. March 23, 2017. Accessed September 21, 2016. https://fortunelords.com/youtube-statistics/.

65. Jennifer Britton. "Teams365 #133: Five Keys for Successful Conference Calls." *Potentials Realized*. May 13, 2014. Accessed November 4, 2016. http://www.potentialsrealized.com/teams-365-blog/teams365-133-five-keys-for-successful-conference-calls.

66. Roger Connors, Tom Smith, and Craig R. Hickman. *The Oz Principle: Getting Results Through Individual and Organizational Accountability*. (New York: Portfolio, 2010). https://www.partnersinleadership.com/.

67. Sherpa Coaching. *Info 2017 Executive Coaching Survey: Public Report.* (PDF. Cincinnati, Ohio: Sasha Corporation, 2017). Accessed March 27, 2017. http:// www.sherpacoaching.com/pdf%20files/2017_Executive_Coaching_Survey_ PUBLIC.pdf.

68. Jennifer J. Britton. *Effective Group Coaching: Tried and Tested Tools and Resources for Optimum Group Coaching Skills.* (Mississauga, Ont: Wiley, 2009).

69. Jennifer J. Britton. *From One to Many: Best Practices for Team and Group Coaching.* (Jossey-Bass, 2013), 146-147.

70. Jennifer Britton. "Teams365 #196: Coaching Questions: A Baker's Dozen." *Potentials Realized.* July 15, 2014. Accessed November 20, 2016. http://www. potentialsrealized.com/teams-365-blog/teams365-196-coaching-questions-a-bakers-dozen.

71. "Walt Disney Quotes." *BrainyQuote.* Accessed June 19, 2017. https://www. brainyquote.com/quotes/quotes/w/waltdisney131631.html.

72. Gert-Jan Pepping and Erik J. Timmermans. "Oxytocin and the Biopsychology of Performance in Team Sports." *The Scientific World Journal* (September 2012): 1-10. doi:10.1100/2012/567363. Abstract online: https://www.researchgate.net/publication/230895865_Oxytocin_and_the_ Biopsychology_of_Performance_in_Team_Sports.

73. Jennifer Britton. "Four Neuroscience and Learning Considerations for Group and Team Coaching." *Group Coaching: Ins and Outs* (web log), July 31, 2014. Accessed June 19, 2017. http://groupcoaching.blogspot.ca/2014/07/ four-neuroscience-and-learning.html.

74. Ashoka. "The Neuroscience at The Heart of Learning and Leading." *Forbes.* May 08, 2013. Accessed June 19, 2017. https://www.forbes.com/ sites/ashoka/2013/05/08/the-neuroscience-at-the-heart-of-learning-and-leading/#3b3329ac67df.

75. Dr. Richard E. Boyatzis. *Inspiring Leadership Through Emotional Intelligence.* (Case Western University, Coursera), 24.

76. Ibid

77. Barbara Frederickson. "Micro Moments of Love." *Awakin.* June 17, 2013.

Accessed June 19, 2017. http://www.awakin.org/read/view.php?tid=949.

78. Barbara Frederickson. "Positive Psychology." Module, week 5. *Coursera*. Accessed June 19, 2017. https://fr.coursera.org/learn/positive-psychology?authMode=login#.

79. Marcial Losada and Emily Heaphy. "The Role of Positivity and Connectivity in the Performance of Business Teams: A Nonlinear Dynamics Model." *American Behavioral Scientist* 47, no. 6 (2004): 740-65. Accessed June 19, 2017. doi:10.1177/0002764203260208.

80. "Debunking 4 Myths of Social Learning." *Blackboard*. Accessed June 19, 2017. http://www.blackboard.com/sites/social/thought-leadership/myths.html.

81. Matthew D. Lieberman. *Social: Why Our Brains are Wired to Connect*. (Crown Publishers, 2013).

82. Judith E. Glaser. "The Chemistry Behind Your Conversational Intelligence." *Vistage Executive Street Blog*. April 17, 2017. Accessed June 19, 2017. http://www.vistage.com/blog/beyond-business/20170104-the-chemistry-behind-your-conversational-intelligence/.

83. Richard J. Hackman. *A Normative Model of Work Team Effectiveness*. (PDF. Yale School of Organization and Management, December 28, 1983). http://www.dtic.mil/dtic/tr/fulltext/u2/a136398.pdf.

84. Wendy Suzuki and Billie Fitzpatrick. *Healthy Brain, Happy Life: A Personal Program to Activate Your Brain and Do Everything Better*. (New York, NY: Dey St., an imprint of William Morrow Publishers, 2015), 18.

85. Ibid., 146.

86. Nick Morrison. "The Myth of Multitasking and What It Means for Learning." *Forbes*. November 26, 2014. Accessed November 16, 2014. https://www.forbes.com/sites/nickmorrison/2014/11/26/the-myth-of-multitasking-and-what-it-means-for-learning/3/#70d1170b28e4.

87. "Humans Process Visual Data Better." *Thermopylae Sciences Technology*. September 16, 2014. Accessed Nov 5, 2016. http://www.t-sciences.com/news/humans-process-visual-data-better.

88. "Google Search Statistics." Google Search Statistics - Internet Live Stats.

Accessed June 19, 2017. http://www.internetlivestats.com/google-search-statistics/.

89. Douglas R. Vogel, Gary W. Dickson, and John A. Lehman. *Persuasion and the Role of Visual Presentation Support: The UM/3M Study*. (PDF. Minneapolis, Minnesota: Management Information Systems Research Center School of Management, June 1986). http://misrc.umn.edu/workingpapers/fullpapers/1986/8611.pdf.

90. George A. Miller. "*The Magical Number Seven, Plus or Minus Two: Some Limits on our Capacity For Processing Information.*" *Psychological Review* 63, no. 2 (1956): 81-97. doi:10.1037/h0043158.

91. Jennifer Britton. "Teams365 #987: *When Different Team Members are on Different Virtual Platforms.*" *Potentials Realized.* September 13, 2016. Accessed November 12, 2016. http://www.potentialsrealized.com/teams-365-blog/teams365-987-when-different-team-members-join-virtually-with-different-platforms.

92. Jennifer Britton. "Teams365 #976: Four Killer Mistakes Virtual Facilitators Can Make." *Potentials Realized.* September 2, 2016. Accessed November 12, 2016. http://www.potentialsrealized.com/teams-365-blog/teams365-976-four-killer-mistakes-for-virtual-facilitators.

93. "Andre Gide Quotes." *BrainyQuote.* Accessed June 19, 2017. https://www.brainyquote.com/quotes/quotes/a/andregide120088.html.

94. Ibid., 43.

95. Malcolm Gladwell. "The 10,000 Hour Rule." *Gladwell.com.* Accessed April 23, 2017. http://gladwell.com/outliers/the-10000-hour-rule/.

96. Geoffrey Colvin. *Talent is Overrated: What Really Separates World-class Performers from Everybody Else.* (New York: Portfolio, 2008).

97. Amy C. Edmondson. *Teaming: How Organizations Learn, Innovate, and Compete in the Knowledge Economy.* (Jossey-Bass, 2012), 121.

98. Jennifer Britton. "Teams365 #797: 4 Ways to Minimize Distractions with Remote Work." *Potentials Realized.* March 7, 2016. Accessed November 10, 2016. http://www.potentialsrealized.com/teams-365-blog/teams365-797-four-

ways-to-minimize-distractions-with-remote-work.

99. Brene Brown. *Daring Greatly.* (Avery Publishing Group, 2015), 184.

100. Jan Hills. "Five Ways Neuroscience Can Improve Your Engagement Results." *HRZone.* November 12, 2013. Accessed June 19, 2017. http://www. hrzone.com/engage/employees/five-ways-neuroscience-can-improve-your-engagement-results.

101. J. M. Stavros and G. Hinrichs. *The Thin Book of SOAR: Building Strengths-Based Strategy.* (Thin Book Pub. CO, 2009).

102. *Scenario Based Learning.* (PFD. University of New Zealand: Massey University). Accessed November 15, 2016. https://www.massey.ac.nz/massey/fms/NCTL/LMS%20News/NCTL%20Website/Scenario-based-learning.pdf?107931B283F439CFB77114AF3B9DCE03.

103. Jennifer Britton. "Teams365 #512: Four Keys to Conflict." *Potentials Realized.* May 26, 2015. Accessed June 19, 2017. http://www.potentialsrealized.com/teams-365-blog/teams365-511-four-keys-to-navigating-conflict.

104. Jennifer Britton. "Difficult Conversations Group and Team Coaches Need to Have." *Group Coaching: Ins and Outs* (web log), November 7, 2016. Accessed June 19, 2017. http://groupcoaching.blogspot.ca/2016/11/difficult-conversations-group-and-team.html.

105. Jennifer Britton. "Teams365 #512: Four Keys to Conflict." *Potentials Realized.* May 26, 2015. Accessed June 19, 2017. http://www.potentialsrealized.com/teams-365-blog/teams365-511-four-keys-to-navigating-conflict.

106. Jennifer Britton. "12 Types of Difficult Participants in Group and Team Coaching & How to Deal with Them." *The Coaching Tools Company.* January 02, 2015. Accessed June 19, 2017. https://www.thecoachingtoolscompany.com/12-types-difficult-participants-in-group-team-coaching-workshops/.

107. Ingrid Bens. *Facilitating with Ease! Core Skills for Facilitators, Team Leaders and Members, Mangers, Consultants, and Trainers.* 3rd ed. (John Wiley & Sons, 2012).

108. Baer. "These 12 Meeting Mistakes." and Christian Jarrett. "The Scourge of Meeting Late-comers." *BPS Research Digest.* March 20, 2013. Accessed June

19, 2017. http://bps-research-digest.blogspot.com/2013/03/the-scourge-of-meeting-late-comers.html.

109. Michael Wilkinson and Richard Smith. *Click: The Virtual Meetings Book*. (Atlanta, GA: Leadership Strategies Publishing, 2013), 56.

110. Jennifer Britton. "Teams365 #742: Virtual Facilitation Faux-Pas: Five Things to Avoid." *Potentials Realized*. January 12, 2016. Accessed November 4, 2016. http://www.potentialsrealized.com/teams-365-blog/teams365-742-virtual-facilitation-faux-pas.

111. Jennifer Britton. "Teams365 #969: Four Tips for Prepping for a Successful Virtual Event." *Potentials Realized*. August 26, 2016. Accessed June 19, 2017. http://www.potentialsrealized.com/teams-365-blog/teams365-969-4-tips-for-prepping-for-a-successful-virtual-event.

112. Jennifer Britton. "Teams365 #560: Virtual Facilitation - Creating Powerful Starts and Ends." *Potentials Realized*. July 14, 2015. Accessed June 19, 2017. http://www.potentialsrealized.com/teams-365-blog/teams365-560-virtual-facilitation-creating-powerful-starts-and-ends.

113. Michael Fullan. *Leading in a Culture of Change*. (Wiley, 2014), 136.

114. Josh Iorio and John Taylor. *Identifying Potential Leaders for Virtual Teams*. (Proceedings of 47th Hawaii International Conference on Systems Sciences. 2014), 340-49.

115. Timothy R. Kayworth and Dorothy E. Leidner. "Leadership Effectiveness in Global Virtual Teams." *Journal of Management Information Systems* 18, no. 3 (Winter 2002): 7-40. https://www.jstor.org/stable/40398552?seq=1#page_scan_tab_contents.

116, Joyce A. Thompsen, Phd. "Leading Virtual Teams: Five Essential Skills Will Help You Lead Any Project—No Matter How Distant." *Quality Digest*. September 1, 2001. Accessed June 19, 2017. https://www.qualitydigest.com/magazine/2000/sep/article/leading-virtual-teams.html#.

117. Jennifer J. Britton. *From One to Many: Best Practices for Team and Group Coaching*. (John Wiley & Sons, 2013), 258.

118. Jennifer Britton. "Teams365 #587: Key Competencies for Global Team

Leadership." *Potentials Realized.* August 10, 2015. Accessed June 19, 2017. http://www.potentialsrealized.com/teams-365-blog/teams365-587-key-competencies-for-global-team-leadership.

119. Michael Fullan. *The Role of Leadership in the Promotion of Knowledge Management in Schools.* (PDF. Toronto: Ontario Institute for Studies in Education University of Toronto.) Accessed April 22, 2017. http://www.oecd.org/edu/school/2074954.pdf.

120. Paula Caligiuri. "Developing Global Leaders." *Human Resource Management Review* 16, no. 2 (2006): 219-28. doi:10.1016/j.hrmr.2006.03.009.

121. Susan Kogler Hill. "Team Leadership." In *Leadership: Theory and Practice.* (Sage, 2007). https://online.ist.psu.edu/sites/ist875/files/t3_leadershipchap12.pdf.

122. Ibid., 10.

123. Jennifer Britton. "Teams365 #589: The First 90 Days for Global Team Leaders - Additional Considerations." *Potentials Realized.* August 12, 2015. Accessed June 19, 2017. http://www.potentialsrealized.com/teams-365-blog/teams365-589-first-90-days-for-global-team-leaders-additional-considerations.

124. Jennifer Britton. "4 Tips about Virtual Team Leadership You Can't Afford to Miss." *LinkedIn* (web log), September 20, 2016. Accessed June 19, 2017. https://www.linkedin.com/pulse/4-tips-virtual-team-leadership-you-cant-afford-miss-jennifer?trk=mp-reader-card.

125. "Doug Floyd quotes." *ThinkExist.com.* Accessed June 19, 2017. http://thinkexist.com/quotation/you_don-t_get_harmony_when_everybody_sings_the/202532.html.

126. Ibid., 10.

127. Ibid., 23.

128. J. R. Hackman and R. Wageman. "A Theory of Team Coaching." *Academy of Management Review* 30, no. 2 (2005): 269-87. doi:10.5465/amr.2005.16387885.

129. D. K. Smith and J. R. Katzenbach. *The Wisdom of Teams: Creating the High-performance Organization.* (Boston: Harvard Business School Press, 1993).

130. Gene C. Hayden. *The Follow-through Factor: Getting from Doubt to Done.* (Toronto: McClelland & Stewart, 2011), 15.

131. Sebastian Bailey. "How to Beat the Five Killers of Virtual Working." *Forbes.* March 05, 2013. Accessed November 11, 2016. https://www.forbes.com/sites/sebastianbailey/2013/03/05/how-to-overcome-the-five-major-disadvantages-of-virtual-working/#7666f0927346.

132. Erin Meyer. "The Four Keys to Success with Virtual Teams." *Forbes.* August 19, 2010. Accessed June 19, 2017. https://www.forbes.com/2010/08/19/virtual-teams-meetings-leadership-managing-cooperation.html.

133. Michael Schrage. *No More Teams: Mastering the Dynamics of Creative Collaboration.* (Crown Business, 1995), 163.

134. Charlene M. Solomon and Michael S. Schell. *Managing Across Cultures: The Seven Keys to Doing Business with a Global Mindset.* (New York: McGraw-Hill, 2009), 37.

135. Ibid., 97.

136. Amy C. Edmondson "The Three Pillars of a Teaming Culture." Harvard Business Review. August 07, 2014. Accessed February 28, 2017. https://hbr.org/2013/12/the-three-pillars-of-a-teaming-culture.

137. Quoted in Limited, Communicaid Group. "The Importance of a Global Mindset for Success Overseas." *Communicaid.* August 12, 2010. Accessed June 19, 2017. https://www.communicaid.com/cross-cultural-training/blog/the-importance-of-a-global-mindset-for-success-overseas/.

138. Samantha McDuffee. "Out of Sight, Out of Mind? 5 Virtual Team Bonding Tips for Remote Employees." *TeamBonding.* March 03, 2017. Accessed June 19, 2017. https://www.teambonding.com/5-team-bondingtips-for-remote-employees/.

139. Tim LeBon. *Achieve Your Potential Through Positive Psychology.* (London: Hodder & Stoughton, 2015), 120.

140. Ibid., 31.

141. Peter M. Senge. *The Fifth Discipline: The Art and Practice of the Learning Organization.* (New York: Crown Publishing, 2006), 232.

142. Jennifer Britton. "Teams365 #524: Working Across Differences with Your Virtual Team." *Potentials Realized*. June 15, 2015. Accessed June 19, 2017. http://www.potentialsrealized.com/teams-365-blog/teams365-524-working-across-differences-with-your-virtual-team.

143. "Thomas Carlyle Quotes." *Search Quotes*. Accessed June 19, 2017. http://www.searchquotes.com/quotation/The_lightning_spark_of_thought_generated_in_the_solitary_mind_awakens_its_likeness_in_another_mind./414168/.

144. Kelly Leonard and Tom Yorton. *Yes, And: How Improvisation Reverses "No, But" Thinking and Improves Creativity and Collaboration—Lessons from the Second City*. (New York, NY: Harper Collins Press, 2015).

145. "A quote by Arthur M. Schlesinger Jr." *Goodreads*. Accessed June 19, 2017. https://www.goodreads.com/quotes/1199803-science-and-technology-revolutionize-our-lives-but-memory-tradition-and.

# INDEX

shared goals, 327, 350
shared team practices, 352, 360
Sherpa Coaching Survey, 133
silence, 77–78, 241–42
simplification, 98–99
Sinek, Simon, 350
SkillShare, 114
Skype, 3, 20, 45, 47, 227, 241, 345,
    405–06
Slack, 344
*Smarter, Faster, Better* (Duhigg), 49, 284
smartphones, 107
SOAR, 93, 262–65
*Social: Why our Brains are Wired to
    Connect* (Lieberman), 168
social brains, 168
social learning, 106, 108
social media, usage of, 6–7
Solomon, Charlene, 348
speaking, tips for, 230–31
spotlights, mentoring experiences,
    129–33
sprints, 221–23, 398
*Start With Why* (Sinek), 350
statistics
    on coaching, 133
    eLearning, 113
    meetings, 303
    on motivation, 240
    smartphones, 107
    on virtual learning, 105–06
    virtual teams, 5–6, 347–48
    YouTube, 117
status meetings, 128
stereotypes, 43
    danagers of, 39
storyboarding, 250
strategic planning activities, 271
strengths
    building on, 54
    taking advantage of, 370–71
subject matter experts, 46
success
    defining, 85–86
    setting up for, 56–57, 172, 207,
        232–33, 242, 282

supervisors, roles for, 170–71
SWOT, 93, 262–63
symbiotic relationships, 21
synchronous connections, 33
synchronous learning, 112–13
synergies, 253–55, 378

T
taboos, 288
taxi drivers, and brain size, 184–85
Teachable, 4, 118
team agreements, 50
    *See also* ways of working
team cultures, 359–60
    *See also* intercultural understanding
team goals, 89, 350
team leadership, 326–27, 335–36
    compared with virtual team
        leadership, 333–35
    emotional intelligence, 328
    self-understanding, 328
    styles, 329
    traditional development, 337
    *See also* virtual team leadership
team spirit, 360–61, 367
*Teaming* (Edmonston), 362
teammates, characteristics of, 96
teams
    coaching, 140–43
    conflict-avoidant, 289
    developing, 138–42, 331, 357, 365–
        67, 371–72
    life cycle of, 31–32
    meetings for, 139, 312
    new leaders and, 340–45
    six factors of, 349–54, 378
    social interaction, 355
    virtual retreats, 139–40
    vs. groups, 69–70
Teams365 blog, 2, 334, 340, 362–63,
    366
    cartoons, 5, 331, 361
Teams365 Team Leader Foundations
    Program, 340
technological changes, 20
technology, using, 310

# ABOUT THE AUTHOR

Jennifer Britton, MES, CHRL, CPT, PCC is the author of *Effective Group Coaching* (Wiley, 2010) and *From One to Many: Best Practices for Team and Group Coaching* (Jossey-Bass, 2013). An expert in the area of group coaching and team development and a performance improvement specialist, she founded her company, Potentials Realized, in 2004. Since early 2006, her Group Coaching Essentials teleseminar program has supported hundreds of coaches in the creation and implementation of their own group coaching practice.

An award-winning program designer, Jennifer is dedicated to supporting groups, teams and organizations in the areas of leadership, teamwork and performance. She draws on more than two decades of experience as an experiential educator and former manager with the United Nations and other humanitarian organizations, with a global client list that spans government, corporate and nonprofit sectors, from financial services to education and healthcare.

Jennifer is considered a thought leader in the field of coaching groups and teams. Her first book, *Effective Group Coaching*, was the first to be published on the topic globally, and has been well received by coaches all over the world and is used as a text and/or recommended resource for many coach training programs. She also speaks internationally to groups on topics related to coaching, leadership, teamwork, emotional intelligence and capacity building.

Credentialed by the International Coaching Federation, Britton was originally trained and certified by the Coaches Training Institute. She has also completed advanced coaching training in the areas of ORSC and Shadow Coaching. A Certified Performance Technologist (CPT), Britton holds a Masters of Environmental Studies (York University) and a Bachelor of Science in Psychology (McGill).

Jennifer divides her time between just north of Toronto in East Gwillimbury, Ontario, and beautiful Muskoka, where she enjoys her next passion—nature—with her family.

EMAIL:

info@PotentialsRealized.com

WEBSITES:

www.EffectiveVirtualConversations.com
www.PotentialsRealized.com
www.GroupCoachingEssentials.com

SOCIAL MEDIA:

**f** Facebook: www.facebook.com/potentialsrealized
**t** Twitter: www.twitter.com/jennbritton
**in** LinkedIn: www.linkedin.com/in/jenniferjbritton
**P** Pinterest: www.pinterest.com/jennjbritton
**You Tube:** www.youtube.com/user/effectivegroupcoach

Made in the USA
Monee, IL
10 April 2020

25075069R00252